Psychology of the Image

Michael Forrester

London and Philadelphia

First published 2000
by Routledge
11 New Fetter Lane, London EC4P 4EE

Simultaneously published in the USA and Canada
by Taylor & Francis Inc
325 Chestnut Street, Philadelphia, PA 19106

Routledge is a part of the Taylor & Francis Group

© 2000 Michael Forrester

Typeset in Garamond by
M Rules, London
Printed and bound in Great Britain by TJ International Ltd, Padstow,
Cornwall

British Library Cataloguing in Publication Data
A catalogue record for this book is available from the British Library

Library of Congress Cataloging in Publication Data
Forrester, Michael A.
  Psychology of the image / Michael Forrester.
      p. cm.
    Includes bibliographical references and index.
    ISBN 0-415-16515-6
      1. Imagery (Psychology) I. Title.

    BF367 .F675 2000
    153.3′2—dc21
                                    99-059599

ISBN 0-415-16515-6

Contents

Illustrations

Figures

Tables

Acknowledgements

This book is the product of many discussions which friends, colleagues and former students who supported my efforts when developing a course of the same name taught at the University of Kent (Canterbury, England). I am indebted to them all, but in particular I would like to thank Silvia Sbaraini for her insightful comments on numerous chapters as well as her encouragement and support throughout. I am also grateful to David Reason for the contribution to Chapter nine (easily recognisable for his erudite observations of post-photographic image technologies), and for our frequent conversations on the nature of images.

I would also like to thank the following for permission to reproduce quotes, photographs, figures and tables throughout the text: Manchester University Press (Figure 8.1); Open University Press; Scott Lipscomb (Figure 3.2); Werner Pawlok (Figure 7.1); Commerce Graphics, New Jersey (Figures 10.2 and 10.3); Churchill Livingstone for reproducing Figures 5.1 and 5.2 from *Gray's Anatomy*; Sage Publications for quotations from several authors and for sections of Chapter 5 (published by the author as 'Reflections and projections of the developing self' in the journal *Theory & Psychology* vol. 9 pp. 29–46); Harcourt Inc. for Table 3.1; the Designers and Artists Copyright Society (Figure 10.3); Macmillan Press; Minnesota University Press; William Horton Consulting (Figure 9.3); the Royal Society of Medicine (Figure 10.1); Karnac Books and Proctor & Gamble (Figure 7.3). The author and publisher apologise for any errors or omissions in this list and would be grateful to be notified of any corrections that should be incorporated in any future edition or reprint of this book.

1 Outlining a psychology of the image

INTRODUCTION

In contemporary culture images play a significant role in influencing our understanding of ourselves, those around us, and the environment we live in. Our everyday experiences ranging from the banal to the enriching are replete with images. Before leaving our homes in the morning we find ourselves checking to see whether we look right (i.e. displaying a good or at least an appropriate 'self-image'). We decorate our houses with pictures, photographs and other images both for the pleasure they bring us and for what they 'say' about our lifestyle. When we hear a piece of music that captures our attention, we might talk of an image coming into our minds, and often when we are buying something we suspect that the decisions we make have been influenced by the images we have seen promoting that product. Hardly a day goes by without politicians, theologians and social commentators warning us of the dangers of image 'over-exposure', while all the time making sure their own images are presented in line with the appropriate conventions.

On the one hand we experience a considerable range of diverse images from the external world, and on the other our mental life is saturated with, and constituted by, internal images, impressions, ideas and associated representations. Richard Kearney (1988) suggests that we are seduced by the implicit ideologies of the latest media cult or craze, and seem to have entered an age where reality is inseparable from the image, and where

> our understanding of the world is preconditioned by the electronically reproducible media of television, cinema, video and radio . . . where fantasy is more real than reality, where the image has more dignity than the original.
> (Kearney 1988: 252)

What we mean by understanding is itself conceived of as mental representation, one of a number of 'image related' metaphors of conceptual knowledge. When psychologists talk of cognitive representations and mental imagery they implicitly invoke constructs of the mental image, occasionally 'picture-like' and often presupposed on the image or model of the proposition (image as idea; idea as image). This ubiquitous and polysemous term (image) serves many functions in quite diverse contexts: it means many different things to different people and remains a rather elusive term in psychology. Nonetheless, the word 'image' provides an orienting concept for one aim of this book, namely to consider a range of theoretical perspectives which may bring us to a better understanding of the role of images in contemporary life.

In this book I aim to examine relationships between external images – for example what we are presented with on billboards, television, cinema or on computer screens – and internal images or imaging processes which make it possible for us to recognise, understand, reflect on or otherwise comprehend images. The desire to do so arose initially out of recognising the conceptual distance between theories in media and communication studies which focus upon image production and audience reception, and ideas in psychology where the aim has been to understand the relationship between mental life and behaviour. At first glance, there appears little connection between theories about images we have in our heads and corresponding ideas on the production or effectiveness of images encountered in everyday life. Our understanding of the social world is surely impoverished without addressing, or at least questioning, the relationships between external images, broadly conceived, and internal cognitions (at least those described as image based).

Given the wide range of topics which concern images, developing or at least outlining a psychology of the image may strike the reader as a rather grandiose enterprise. The aims of this book are, however, more direct and hopefully realisable. The first is simply to consider a number of research areas which contribute in significant ways to our understanding or conceptions of images. A second aim is to critically consider theories within the social sciences which inform our understanding of image production and recognition. A third aim is to reflect upon identifiable tensions between internal and external image domains, thereby highlighting future directions that a distinct psychology of the image might take. The topics in the book are organised into three general themes. The first focuses upon internal images including perception, mental imagery, sound imagery and dreams. The second theme addresses the interdependent nature of internal and external images over three chapters, with topics including images of the developing self, social identity, image-reputation and the gendered image. This last topic, the portrayal of gender through images, acts as a particularly useful link into the third theme of the book, external images. Here, two chapters focus upon the role of mass-media images (covering film, television and electronic contexts), one on the photographic image. Essentially, the final theme of the book focuses on topics where the processes of image production and recognition seem to be quite separate from internal image processes. The remainder of this introductory chapter considers whether it is possible to conceive of an orienting theoretical framework for a psychology of the image, given the very diverse nature of image study. We can begin with some comment on the definition or rather definitions of image employed throughout the text.

A linguist might easily describe the word image as a polysemous expression, (i.e. a word or phrase possessing multiple meanings) and one with many richly related connotations and derivatives: the imaginary, imago, imagination, imagery, imaginable and so on. The *Oxford English Dictionary* (1989) provides at least a dozen definitions of the word image ranging from the commonplace to the obscure and the highly technical. For example we have image defined as 'an artificial representation of the external form of any object, especially a person', or again as 'a mental representation of something'. We can contrast these with 'a visible figure, an appearance, an apparition' or 'an undesired signal frequency heard as interference [a radio term]'. We can also find definitions which distinguish the term on the 'internal/external' dichotomy outlined earlier with image described as:

1   a mental representation of something (e.g. a visible object), not by direct perception but by memory or imagination; a mental picture or impression; and
2   a concept or representation created in the mind of the public of a particular person, institution or product – public-image.

Possibly it is the terminological diversity of the word image (and its associated derivations) which underlies the conceptual distance found across disciplines with interest in the topic (from whatever angle). At the same time, the polysemous nature of the term image provides an opportunity for articulating a conceptually coherent theory of the image: an integrative construct reflecting a psychologically informed theoretical approach to the study of the image (or images).

At the risk of pre-empting elements of the framework outlined below, three particular definitions of the word image will be clarified and elaborated on. These reflect the focus on internal mental imagery, external culturally produced images and self-constructed images which span the 'internal–external' dichotomy. This classification is used in the first instance only as a starting point – a position which reflects some of the definitions and concepts associated with the word image in the current literature.

Each distinct domain of the word image takes two forms, a static or object-like aspect and a process or dynamic element. In the first domain, where the study of internal images is paramount, the static or object form can be defined as a mental representation of any object or event. The process counterpart, defined as the imagination, will be restricted to those actions of imagining or forming a mental concept of something that is not actually present. This encompasses both 'rationalist' forms such as scheming, hypothesis testing and impression formation and also 'non-rational' or less conscious activities such as dreaming.

The second meaning of image would emphasise external attributes and representations. Specifically, image here is defined as a representation of something to the mind by speech, writing or graphic description broadly defined. Note the significance of the phrase 'to the mind'; i.e. images are external entities which might be understood as intentional 'utterances' by some known or unknown generalised 'other'. In order to fulfil the criteria of being an image, in a sense they have to 'project' something or other. They say something to us, we can recognise what they are 'saying' and we respond to their 'signification' in appropriate ways. Correspondingly, where we come to consider process elements of this domain, the dynamic nature of television, film, music and radio operate in distinctly different ways to more static objects such as bill-posters, photographs, pictures, sculptures and postage stamps.

A third conception of the image will be developed with reference to domains where the 'internal' meets the 'external'. Here we focus on how the private finds expression in the public, as well as how the public underpins, reproduces and constrains, the private. Examples of the former would include the numerous ways we use fashion to display different versions of ourselves (or self-images); instances of the latter might be where members of the royal household take care in promoting an appropriate public image. In this third broad definition of the term image, although there are obvious examples of the 'static' versus 'dynamic' distinction (personal ads columns versus image as movement and 'style' on the fashion catwalk) the theoretical outline described below may help elaborate and extend this initial terminology. For now, these three definitions or broad domains of the image serve only to situate different academic, technical and everyday uses of the term.

FRAMING A PSYCHOLOGY OF THE IMAGE: PEIRCEAN SEMIOTICS

Outlining a psychology of the image which encompasses diverse domains can be realised through a reading of semiotics, particularly the work of the American semiotician C. S. Peirce. Semiotics, as the science of signs and sign-systems, provides a way of describing and explaining the structures and procedures of communication systems (in their broadest sense). A semiotician is just as likely to be interested in the symbol-system used by non-human primates as in the codes, rules and algorithms of machine-generated 'artificial intelligence'. Semiotics is

> concerned with the formulation and encoding of messages by sources, the transmission of these messages through channels, the decoding and interpretation of these messages by destinations, and their signification. The entire transaction, or semiosis, takes place within a context to which the system is highly sensitive and which the system, in turn, affects.
>
> (Saussure 1974: 69)

Historically, semiotics emerged as part of the structuralist movement in the early twentieth century which in part explains the debate over whether semiotics is part of the study of language or language (and linguistics) subsumed within semiotics. As semiotics is critically concerned with the production, recognition and transmission of signs, those who study images have often adopted a semiotic perspective. As will become clear, we find semiotic theories of the sign employed in photography, film and television, art and aesthetics, advertising and computer interface design.

At the risk of oversimplification, the relationship between semiotics and symbols, signs, emblems, images or any such related representation can be summarised as the process of signification: the study of how signs come to represent or 'stand for' anything at all. Saussure (often described as the originator of semiotics) pointed out that the signs and elements of any language acquire meaning not because there is some 'real' connection between words and things in the world, but as part of a system of relations. The sign for the word 'donkey' only means what it does with reference to all those signs in the language that do not mean 'donkey'. Likewise, the use of the colour red in traffic lights only means 'stop' with reference to the system of elements and relations within which it acquired meaning.

An important aspect of Saussure's conception of the sign was the indissoluble relationship between the components which made up any given sign and the nature of meaning (as in Figure 1.1).

A number of points are worth emphasising, particularly as this form of Saussurian semiotics has often been misunderstood or glossed over in psychology. First, there are two senses of the word meaning as it refers to the sign in Figure 1.1. There is the global sense of meaning (Meaning in the figure) which is addressing the question of how it is possible that any given sign has the potential for being read or understood at all (i.e. analysis of the sign such that the possibility and potential for a given meaning can be recognised). The other sense of meaning is that which is conventionally associated with the sign in question (e.g. 'donkey' is a sign that is made up of a number of letter characters (its surface form d-o-n-k-e-y) while its meaning is the horse-like four-legged creature we might find in the countryside.

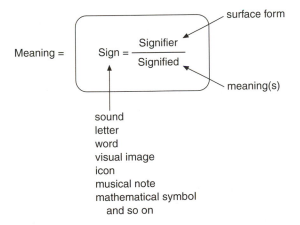

Figure 1.1 Semiotics and meaning

Second, semiotics is concerned with any sign-system. Although the semiotic approach is often associated with structural linguistics, the reason why it has much broader applicability is that any element which forms part of a meaningful system of communicative exchange can be analysed as a sign. If semiotics is defined as the discipline that studies all meaningful exchange, following Frawley (1992), this encompasses text, visual media, literature, art as conventionalised aesthetic meaning, cultural rules and codes of behaviour, dream interpretation and non-verbal communicative gestures. Arguably, semiotics can be used as a conceptual instrument in the three domains of the image described in this book. In fact, for radical semioticians there are few areas of social-cultural practice which do not lend themselves to sign-system analysis (e.g. see Sebeok (1994) on this point).

This brief résumé of structuralist semiotics reflects the European approach outlined by Saussure and others during the early to mid-twentieth century (see Hodge and Kress (1988) for an insightful critique of traditional semiotics). Slightly earlier, the American philosopher C.S. Peirce outlined an approach to semiotics as a response to a number of mid-nineteenth-century problems in logic and epistemology. In particular, Peirce was concerned with understanding the nature of knowledge and mind, i.e. under what conditions can we distinguish between what is 'real' from phenomena and things 'out of the mind', and whether (and how) natural science, specifically logic, can provide fundamental tools for a philosophical analysis of meaning. Hookway (1985) notes that in Peirce we encounter the 'mind-numbing claim that the elements of experience and reality may be classified into firstness, secondness and thirdness' (p. 2) with all other complexities and conceptions reducible to this tripartite essentialism. While post-structuralism might find such a 'metaphysics of categories' misplaced, Peirce's analysis may have considerable significance for a psychology of the image, a point we will return to in the final chapter.

Consider for now his ideas on the nature of signs. Rather than simply claiming there was an indissoluble relationship between signifier and signified for any given sign, Peirce introduced the idea of the interpretant: an additional element of sign comprehension determined by the sign itself. The sign is not simply a relationship between the signifier (surface form) and signified (its meaning), but also includes a third element, highlighting the observation that every sign determines an interpretant (Figure 1.2). To paraphrase Sebeok's (1994) analysis of this development, with the sign for the English noun 'horse', interpretants could include gee-gee, pony, stallion, and even the word heroin. There are no limits to the number and form of interpretants, 'signs and discourses on and of, signs which overlay another sign'. As Peirce notes, a sign is anything 'which determines something else (its interpretant) to refer to an object to which itself refers (its object) in the same way, the sign becoming a sign, and so on ad infinitum' (1966: 272). And any paraphrase or extended discourse on any sign 'will enrich comprehension of the object it represents, as will also its interlingual translations and intersemiotic transmutations' (Sebeok 1994: 13).

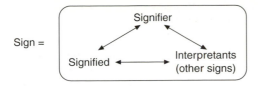

Figure 1.2 Peirce's conception of the sign

How the concept of the 'interpretant' fits into the signifier–signified relationship of a sign can be understood if we pay close attention to what Peirce termed 'scientific intelligence'. Peirce went to great pains to emphasise that the idea of an interpretant does not presuppose some kind of subjective cognitive state or mind (i.e. the interpretant is not necessarily a person). Consider a sign such as the marked and exposed bark of a tree signifying the presence of deer in the forest. First, the act of recognising the stripped bark as a sign at all highlights the idea of one thing signifying another, the notion that the first thing (the bark) is understood or interpreted as a sign of a second (deer). The link between the sign and what it signifies is mediated through subsequent thoughts which serve as interpretants for the sign. These thoughts are themselves made up of other signs (our thoughts, associations, reflections are made up of words, images, signs). Second, it is only because we know how deer behave in the woods when feeding that we see the marks on the tree as a sign of the presence of deer. The point, as Hookway (1985) stresses, is that signs contribute to our learning from experience by mediating between reality and our cognitions.

Any entity which has the capacity to learn from experience, for example to learn that the stripped bark of the tree can be interpreted as a sign of deer, warrants the status of a scientific intelligence. For anything to be recognised as a sign at all presupposes the existence of an intelligent entity (human, animal or artificial) capable of utilising their background knowledge of social practices and processes; 'thus physics, biology, psychology, and sociology each embodies its own peculiar level of semiosis' (Sebeok 1994: 7). Peirce's sign-interpretant theory is a non-cognitive theory of semiotics in the sense that there is no requirement to assume an essentialist 'cogito' or 'logocentric' self underpinning our cognitions and motivating our thoughts, a self somehow independent of semiotic systems. The condition which makes sign recognition possible is the exposure to particular cultural practices which establish the significance of learned associations. In other words, mental or cognitive life is itself a semiotic domain. There is no power of thinking without signs and the notion that all thoughts are signs indicates how the Peircean framework 'introduced to account for the working of ordinary, conventional and linguistic signs can be used to describe and explain mental phenomena' (Hookway 1985: 23).

Another important element of Peirce's analysis was his tripartite distinction between iconic, indexical and symbolic signs. Notwithstanding the observation that all signs are symbolic (in a general sense) this sub-division rested upon a 'grounding' of signification, one that corresponded to Peirce's category logic, firstness, secondness and thirdness. Primarily iconic signs (such as the road sign for 'falling rocks') are signs that share properties with whatever they represent, in this case the sign's similarity with how real rocks would look falling down the side of the hill. Indexical signs are those that exploit the dyadic relation between sign and object. Thus in the example of the stripped bark, recognising the mark on the tree as a sign of deer rests on the potential the marks have to produce an 'interpretant', i.e. the host of associations presupposed in the act of recognition. An indexical sign is sometimes described as a sign which refers to the object that it denotes by virtue of being affected by that object. Barometers, weathercocks and symptoms of diseases are all indexical signs.

The third category is symbolic signs, completely arbitrary signs which depend on conventions, codes, rules and cultural practices for their recognition. A symbolic message is one whose relationship to the 'state of affairs' that it claims to represent is arbitrary, that is, understandable only because of a pre-existing social convention which specifies that the message will stand for whatever it is said to represent. One symbolic sign, a flag flying at half-mast, is an icon of many other flags embedded in a triadic relation, a signifying relation to the death of a respected person: the flag-at-half-mast, conventions for flag flying and the event of the person dying. There is a language of signification appropriate to showing respect for the dead, the flag being one symbolic sign within the 'grammar'. We might note that all those signs which make up the written alphabet are symbolic signs: they only signify what they do with respect to conventions and rules for what constitutes a recognisable letter.

This tripartite classification does not mean that all signs fall uniquely into one or other of the categories. Any complex sign will probably contain iconic, indexical and symbolic elements. And many signs will show a predominance of one form over another (i.e. iconic over indexical). Nonetheless, this categorisation scheme provides a way of identifying the primary function of many signs which can prove very useful where analysis of image structure is concerned, and one aim of this book is to consider what elements of Peircean semiotics might serve as building blocks for a psychology of the image. One advantage of this semiotic theory is that it informs our understanding of images within and across many domains and contexts. As others have noted, there is the potential in Peirce's framework for an integrated theory of culture. It may also have some potential for revealing structures common to the images we have of the real and the illusory. For now it may be enough to understand that Peircean semiotics places considerable emphasis on the fact that it is our knowledge of social conventions and cultural rules which creates the possibilities of understanding and interpreting images at all.

AN ORIENTING FRAMEWORK FOR A PSYCHOLOGY OF THE IMAGE

Having summarised certain key ideas within semiotics, the next task is to provide a set of orienting ideas or constructs loosely conceptualised as a 'psycho-semiotic' theory of the image. Essentially, when we turn to consider the many different research areas where the study of images is paramount, it is very difficult to recognise how one topic might relate to another. For example, the study of dream images seems very distant from research into how people respond to photographic images. Likewise the study of sound imagery appears to have little or no relation to the study of images in computer design. In outlining a framework the aim is simply to provide an outline of perspectives which situate different discourses on the image. What follows is based around the elements highlighted in Figure 1.3.

This framework has two interdependent components: one concerned with the nature of agency and image theory (the upper half of the figure), a second with understanding images with reference to production and selection (lower half). The notion of agency provides us with a conceptual theme for considering relationships between whatever we understand as 'internal' images and associated processes, and 'external' image production and recognition. It can be argued, for example, that Goffman's analysis of display behaviour and associated conventions or 'folklore' of signs rests upon an image of the subject as an agent: whatever we consider the self to be, it is an enduring entity which has learned the skills of masquerade and deception and is motivated to displaying different 'self-images' depending on context. In contrast for the psychoanalyst-semiotician Lacan, the subject self-image is formulated in the imaginary. The

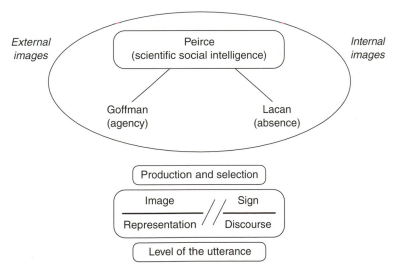

Figure 1.3 A framework for a psychology of the image

idea of a self is always and forever based on notions of absence and lack, a project 'doomed to failure' at one level. Within semiotics, communication theory and social psychology these theoretical positions have had a considerable influence within and beyond image studies. At the same time, elements of each approach may be better understood with regard to Peircean semiotics. Peirce offers an account of agency emphasising the self as an explanatory notion, while remaining essentially a non-cognitive theory of semiotics. There is no thinking without signs and a corresponding scientific intelligence with the capacity to learn. Throughout our discussion we will consider whether conceptualising different image studies on an agency dimension can help articulate a distinct psychology of the image.

The second part of the framework (lower half of Figure 1.3) aims at clarifying the nature of the definition 'image' with reference to contemporary ideas surrounding utterance production and interpretation. In what sense can we consider images as 'signs', and in doing so, can they be understood in terms of selection and production? As a designer of computer interfaces I might select or produce a 'wastebasket' or 'filing-cabinet' image to represent deleting or storing items, thereby invoking metaphors of the office desktop (Hron 1998). Arguably, the construction of any image brings into play the conditions within which sign recognition attains or signifies some meaning. Sign recognition is not possible outside of those social-cultural practices and discourses presupposed by the specifics of the context surrounding the sign. In this way the equation Image/Representation is akin to Sign/Discourse, where 'Image' and 'Sign' are best understood in terms of domains of selection and production by interested parties (whether media producers, authors, painters or architects), and 'Representation' and 'Discourse' as aspects of the utterance, communicative act, dialogue or speech. Critical theory, media studies, cultural criticism and discourse analysis focus on the relationship between sign and discourse (e.g. Hodge and Kress 1988). If we think of words as signs then we need to understand that they only attain meaning with reference to the texts within which they are embedded, and the social processes whereby these texts or discourses have any significance at all, i.e. their communicative function, and that in a sense an image is a 'disguised' sign and, like any sign, only understood against the background discourse which frames its recognition and interpretation. We can move at this point to firming out the theoretical contributions which Goffman and Lacan bring to a psychology of the image.

GOFFMAN AND THE DOCTRINE OF NATURAL EXPRESSION

The first thing to recognise is that Goffman's psychology was one concerning the relations between an individual and 'ritual' interaction. Goffman (1979) argued that as a matter of course in our everyday interaction we seek out information, about each other and the world about us, which appears consistent and enduring. We want to read such information as naturally 'basic', information about the characteristic or 'essential nature' of people and things. The central thesis of Goffman's theory is that this kind of information exists in the form of 'signs'. Essentialist characteristics, such as gender, ability/disability, ethnicity and so on, are displayed as signs in our everyday interaction. In an essay on the recognition and display of gender, Goffman points out that this most cherished distinction is taken as *the* prototype of expression, as 'something that can be conveyed fleetingly in any social situation and yet something that strikes at the most basic characterisation of the individual' (p. 7).

Within our framework, understanding gendered images will rest in part on articulating how the recognition of gender is realised. Through excavating the implicit rules, codes, social practices and procedures which provide the basis for the link between image (sign), object and representation (discourse) we might be able to understand the significance gendered images have for us. We should always keep in mind that the production or selection of any image presupposes an enunciator. Somebody is always trying to say something to someone else, even though what is being said is rarely made explicit. We might say that the image is always a sign trying to pretend it isn't a sign.

LACAN AND THE IMAGINARY SUBJECT

The concept of image and its relation to agency is radically different in the semiology of Lacan (1977). Lacan formulates the originating condition of the self (self-image) as one based on an existential problem. The child is born into an experience of 'lack', the forever irreconcilable condition of existence as disunity, incompleteness and loss. To be born is to be outside, cut off, excluded: in other words what was once united is now forever split. At one level our desire to understand the 'self' is a wish that can never be fulfilled, irrespective of whatever strategies we invoke to overcome the emerging recognition of disunity and precarious identity. Lacanian individuation (self-image construction) is coterminous with social-semiosis and entry into the symbolic order, i.e. the acquisition of, or entry into, language.

On the question of subjectivity and agency, for Lacan the development of the self only emerges with the child's recognition that its image is mirrored back in the desire of another. Lacan's[1] mirror is a metaphor for the imaginary, 'that which can be identified with me'. In this theory it is the idea of the image which brings the self into being, yet at the same time irretrievably splits the subject-being from itself (image vs. real). To understand this, we should note that for Lacan the self goes through two major self–other divisions. The first division comes about through looking in the mirror (or through experiencing what is reflected back to the child from the mother), and the recognition by the child that 'she/he is another'. Staying with the metaphor of the mirror, notice on the one hand that the child is phenomenally located in his/her body as she looks at the reflection, yet at the same time can see there is 'another' in the mirror, and another whose image moves in correspondence with her/his own movement. In this first acquisition of the sense of self, the imaginary self takes shape: only in the Gestalt of the image in the mirror is the fantasy of completeness presented and perceived as a possibility. The self of being and the 'other' in the mirror mark the initial division.

In acquiring language a second division becomes superimposed on the first. For Lacan, the significance of emergence into the symbolic order was coterminous with the notion of the self embedded in language. The ontology of one's being is constituted by language. We only have to think of the pronominal system (I, you, he/she) to recognise that we are positioned as 'subjects' by those around us before we can even speak: we are placed, located and constructed in the language of our culture. In Lacanian semio-psychoanalysis suture names the relation of the individual as subject to the chain of its discourse, 'the subject is an effect of the signifier in which it is represented' (Heath 1981: 54). The symbolic *Other* of language assigns the child a position and identity before it is even born.

For Lacan, the semiotician Saussure had over-emphasised the 'signified' at the expense of the 'signifier'. Sturrock (1986) notes that Lacan was intent on removing the illusion that the signifier (expression) answers to the function of representing the signified (meaning or content). Ultimately there may only be signifiers (the 'meanings' that signifiers point to turn out themselves to be other signifiers), and yet more signifiers, and thus a permanent slippage of meaning and an infinite possibility of interpretation. Meaning is not at all the stable relationship between signifier and signified presumed by Saussure. And what stops the continuous slide, and momentarily fixes meaning, is the punctuation of the signifying chain by the action of the subject. We can see why such a theory has had an influence in the study of images where we consider the positioning of the subject/viewer in film theory.

Film critics and analysts have theorised extensively about the nature of the spectator's experience when watching films, noting the difficulties in understanding how a coherent perception of the narrative is possible. When watching a film the spectator is involved in a sequence of successive interpretations as the images unfold. These interpretations presuppose a whole host of cultural beliefs, the absence of which would make the experience incomprehensible. In making film the producer is engaged in situating and constructing a viewing 'subject' as a technical accomplishment. Lapsley and Westlake (1988) make the point that when watching a film, meaning is produced by the subject in a process of punctuation (akin to constructing an ongoing interpretation); but equally, the subject is produced by the meanings available in the signifying chain (in the narrative construction of the film images). Lacan's theorising of subject identity, agency and language has provided a rich framework for film theory and critical studies as will be seen in Chapter 8. Lacan's theorising of the subject image-self also addresses questions relevant to understanding images of the developing self (Chapter 5). For now, we note simply that the dimension of agency (present/absent) provides a conceptual link for articulating a psychology of the image (external/internal) and does so with due regard to the significant contribution from semiotics.

CONCLUDING COMMENTS

The aim of this book is to explore external and internal images, and their inter-dependence and significance for our understanding of ourselves, other people and the environment. The topics to be considered are thematically outlined along the 'internal–external' image dichotomy proposed. This provides an important navigational aid for placing the different interests, issues and topics and also emphasises the themes of 'agency' and semiosis within the framework. The three immediately following chapters focus on the domains of the internal image, specifically mental imagery, sound imagery and dream images. The middle section of the book turns to an examination of images which span the 'internal–external' dichotomy. Chapter 5 begins by examining the diverse images of the 'developing self' including those from Lacan and other contemporary models found within developmental psychology. The next chapter focuses upon images of the self spanning the private and public domains, and in Chapter 7 the question of gendered images becomes paramount. Of particular interest in this section is the peculiar way images of masculinity and femininity rest upon important 'internal' images (e.g. gender schema theory) while predicated upon the accountability of the external and 'public'.

The final theme of the text concentrates on external image(s) and begins with an analysis of film and television. Each of these topics has been considered separately within psychology, with television research focusing primarily on 'effects', rarely considering the nature of image production or audience engagement. In contrast film theory has theorised rather more extensively on the relationship between image and the construction of the 'absent' viewing subject. Chapter 9 considers an emerging area of imaging studies which appears to extend the domain of a psychology of the image quite extensively. We will see that within multi-media and internet-based communication technologies there is an increasing dependence of 'image-theory' occasionally explicit but for the most part underdeveloped and implicit. The concluding chapter considers the idea of the photograph as a sign and examines psychological studies which have looked at people's perception of photographic images and the relationship between self-portraiture and identity. Throughout, care will be taken to articulate the many different functions that the photograph fulfils (both public and private) as well as describing contemporary theories of photography.

NOTE

1 Lacan's initial discussion of the comparative responses of monkeys and infants when confronted by a reflection from a mirror inaugurated certain speculations regarding the child's experience:

(the act of looking) rebounds in the case of the child in a series of gestures in which he experiences in play the relation between the movements assumed in the image and reflected environment, and between the virtual complex and the reality it reduplicates – the child's own body, and the persons and things, around him.   (Lacan 1977: 1)

What was critical was the difference between an animal mistaking the reflection for another monkey altogether (in or though the glass), while the human infant begins to joyfully play, experiment and manipulate the image by body movements, grimaces, smiling and so on. The child of course does not have to see him/herself in an actual mirror. Just as important is the reflected idealised image emanating from the mother back to the child. The mother's desire for the child to attain a true individuality and being: an idealised self.

Theme I

Images of what is 'inside' or internal

PREFACE

When we acquire a language we don't simply learn how to use the correct words, grammar and conventions for speaking appropriately in context, we also acquire a 'world view': an implicit set of assumptions and presuppositions regarding how to understand the world, who and what we are within it, and everything else that is entailed in categorising our experience. One of the earliest categorical distinctions we acquire is that of the 'mental world', i.e. learning to talk about our internal world as distinct from the external. We are tutored in discourses about imagery, dreaming, thinking for ourselves, thinking about what other people might be thinking and a whole host of associated ideas, metaphors, images and constructs regarding mental life. It is often difficult to recognise that presupposed in such discourses is the view that there is indeed a clear-cut distinction between an 'inside' and an 'outside'. So entrenched are we in this way of thinking that it is very difficult to recognise that our assumptions are culturally determined and rest in part on a particular way of conceiving agency and 'subjecthood'. It has been suggested that psychology has yet to move away from this essentially modernist and individualist perspective and resists engaging with late twentieth-century post-modernist thought (Kvale 1992). What follows could be viewed as an essay outlining how psychology could broaden its outlook and begin to incorporate a number of ideas, theories and conceptual frameworks traditionally viewed as outside the discipline's boundaries. The theme of the image serves as an orienting thread around which contemporary topics can be woven. It is also a concept which allows us to question the traditional distinctions made regarding thought, the imagination, the self, social relations and the texts or representations we encounter in our daily lives.

In the first theme of this book we consider a number of topics which in one way or another focus on the nature of imagery. We begin with the theme of mental imagery, a central topic within cognitive psychology and whose theoretical development is closely, and possibly somewhat restrictively, linked to the study of visual perception. A second, and rarely discussed, aspect of imagery, sound, is the central topic of Chapter 3. The study of sound in psychology has for the most part adopted a psycho-acoustic perspective, and a consideration of this work raises a number of questions about our understanding of sound and how we conceive of imagery more generally. The concluding chapter in our 'internal' theme considers psychological approaches to dreams. For many of us the experience of dreaming is one realm where the 'image' is paramount. Amongst other things we will consider why it has long been believed that it is impossible to have a 'sound-only' dream, again a question which allows us to critically reflect on the many ideas which surround the internal image(s).

2 Seeing, visualising and mental imagery

INTRODUCTION

When we talk of seeing an image, either in front of us or visualised with closed eyes, we invoke a range of metaphors and ideas which highlight the relationship between perception and imagery. For those of us with unimpaired vision, to see with 'the mind's eye' conjures up a picture of perception where there is not a great deal of difference between an external or internal image. What we *see* inside is an image of what we have already seen outside. Likewise, to consider perception as 'image stimulation' or 'inscription' on a retinal tableau evokes ideas of non-conscious automatic perceptual processing, where 'brain–mind' cognitive transformations make possible the phenomenon of perception. There are at least two meanings to the word perception: one being the reception of information through the senses, the other as 'mental insight', which would include processes dependent on memories and expectations (Rodaway 1995). The psychology of visual perception has concentrated on the former and avoided asking the question, 'under what conditions can it be claimed that one *sees* anything at all?', leaving such issues to philosophy and phenomenology. The aim in this chapter is to cast a critical eye over contemporary views of perception in order to understand why, among other things, perceptual psychology continues to provide the framework within which theories of mental imagery are formulated and understood.

PERCEPTION AS SENSATION AND AS COGNITION

The dominant position of perception research within psychology rests on the aims of cognitive science. The interdisciplinary synthesis that constitutes cognitive science is both 'anti-reductionist' and mentalistic, in that, 'The fundamental premise of cognitive science is that human behaviour is rule governed and generative. That is to say, algorithmic rules intervene between different stages in coding processes in order to permit goal-directed problem solving' (Sinha 1988: 115). Visual processing is taken to be a 'coding process' par excellence, given the traditional way of differentiating between perception as sensation and as cognition. As sensation, perception is grounded on stimuli activating the senses and their neural correlates: seeing, smelling, touching, hearing, tasting and kinaesthesis. However, as cognition, perception involves remembering, recognising, associating and other related cognitive processes. Gombrich (1957) points out that all perceiving relates to expectations and therefore to comparisons, i.e. what is in front of you with what you expect to see. Phenomenal size, like physical size, is relative and has no meaning except as a relation between objects. For psychology, sensation is somehow considered as inferior, and simply primary raw data, while perception as cognition is superior, presupposing knowledge and interpretation. To quote Roth and Frisby (1986):

> In order to recognise an object such as a chair from the information contained in the retinal image, we also need some knowledge about chairs . . . which is stored or represented in our memories.
>
> (p. 86)

Essentially the explanatory frameworks for understanding precisely how the level of sensation interrelates with the level of knowing rest upon theories of mental representation (symbolic, connectionist, propositional or whatever). The enduring metaphor or image is of 'picture-like' cellular excitation on our retina of objects and events giving rise to their recognition because of the related conceptual/categorical knowledge of such objects stored in our memories. When we try and imagine what memory might be or look like, the cultural images available to use speak of retrieval mechanisms, stores, data-banks and so on.

This kind of differentiation between image/sensation and image/knowledge creates a number of problems normally glossed over within introductory psychology textbooks. First, there is a certain conceptual incoherence in emphasising the importance of cognising the world, yet at the same time being somehow separate from it. Knowledge (cognition) of the world is conceptually abstracted from our actual presence and embodiment in the world. The 'information' in the light exciting our retinal receptor cells is conceived of as 'coming-in' from the *outside* to the *inside*. Second, the discourses about mental life, both in everyday and technical language, are infused with metaphors of the visual, i.e. second sight, insight, casting an eye, iconic store, visual buffer, visio-spatial scratch-pad, and so on. There is a kind of interdependence between the metaphors about 'knowing as seeing' and 'seeing by knowing'. In the discourse of visual representation, sense-stimuli are truly objective phenomena realised and measured by appropriate instruments, and knowing is forever separate, internal, private, and again somehow less real or at least more amorphous than that which is 'outside'. You cannot touch knowledge. Finally, in this prevailing view there seems little space for incorporating a corporeal dimension. As the phenomenologist Merleau-Ponty (1962) pointed out, perception is corporeal, mediated by our bodies and whatever extensions we might use (glasses, binoculars, microscopes and so on). Our bodies are surely a constitutive part of the perceptual process yet somehow they seem invisible in the psychology of perception; perception is an 'eye–brain' phenomenon and little else.

CONSTRUCTIVIST THEORIES OF PERCEPTION

The philosopher Bishop Berkeley is often considered as the founder of the empiricist view of perception. Among other things, this view asserts that because the image projected onto our retina does not contain enough information for us to perceive, there has to be some sort of constructivist processes mediating sensation and perception. To paraphrase Gombrich (1957), representation is not only the central problem for psychology (i.e. cognitive representation), it is quite obviously the basis upon which all interpretations of art and the aesthetic rest. Consider, though, how the problem of representation or the constructivist approach to perception is conceived. Theoretical discussion begins with the observation that light enters the eye and excites or activates nerve cells on the surface of our retinas – a two-dimensional surface at the back of our eyes. Yet the world we see is a three-dimensional one. It is in this way that the constructivist problem of perception is posed: perception as a puzzle of transformation between 2-D and 3-D information. Our perceptual system must somehow 'construct' the additional necessary information which makes it possible for us to see in three dimensions.

Ideas and assumptions about what constitutes the nature of three-dimensional reality provide the basis for an account of perception which emphasises the significance of the mind, a place where the problems and questions of constructivist representation will be answered. We should note that while the retinal image takes precedence in this perspective, it is not a 'copy-like' image. It is a dynamic, fluctuating, series of 'light points' inscribed on a cellular canvas. At the same time, reality consists of stable objects unproblematically perceived in three dimensions. The very absence of a direct correspondence between these outside objects and the fluctuating dynamic retinal 'image-series', leads to the insistence that there must be other complex (knowledge) processes which transform that which is outside into the inside. Our 'brain–eye' is forever busy constructing the phenomenally real world that we 'truly see'. Post-structuralist critics note that this account of perception is overstated, and somewhat open to question. As Sharrock and Coulter (1998) put it:

> The information processing account [of perception] actually revived a classical dogma – that the retinal image is itself a component facet of the causal conditions for vision. However, what actually mattered in the explanation of vision which had been developed by sensory neurophysiology was not the retinal image or picture at all, but, rather, the patterns of light

irradiation on the photoreceptor cells of the retina and the transduction of such energy quanta into electrochemical (ionic) impulses through the optic nerve. In a recent consideration of this issue, Hyman (1989) remarked:

> My retinal images are (natural) pictures which are invisible to me, and visible to another only with a suitable apparatus. They are not analogous to the neural activity in my optic nerve for they are not, as the irradiations of my retina are, causal conditions for seeing.
>
> (p. 50)

Thus, retinal images/pictures are epiphenomenal with respect to the explanation of how vision is possible. Since retinal images as such do not enter into the causal chain at all (rather, it is the photon-photoreceptor interaction which is placed at the beginning of the account), there is no 'problem' of inversion, and so on, to be explained.

(Sharrock and Coulter 1998: 152–153)

Notwithstanding such comments which question underlying assumptions of contemporary visual theory, within psychology the 'perception as cognition' account of vision remains the dominant theoretical position. Considerable research effort focuses on mapping out the numerous ways in which the visual system 'fills in' the third dimension, ranging from accommodation cues, Gestalt laws of continuation, similarity and proximity, cues of surroundness and symmetery (Eysenk and Keane 1995), and a whole host of representational/cognitive mechanisms which we are said to employ when constructing a veridical representation of that which is 'out there'. In a sense, it is as if the mind is intentionally projecting outwards and onto the world of sensory information. Such a view of perception owes its historical allegiance to Kantian categorisation-over-sensation philosophy.

Constructivist theories in perception fall into two camps, symbolic and connectionist. Those who favour a symbol manipulation processing metaphor, argue that the elements which make up any given recognisable object are stored in abstract representational form, separate from details of particular instances (Biederman 1987; Marr 1982). Here we find ideas of 'iconic' memory and short-term 'visual buffers' and associated storage mechanisms. Visual perception is understood as involving the construction and manipulation of abstract symbolic descriptions of any viewed scene (Bruce and Green 1990). In contrast, within the parallel distributed processing approaches the enduring image is of 'brain as representation'. Formulating a neuro-psychophysiological metaphor, connectionist accounts of perception are developed as images of 'neural-style' processing. Perception involves the 'emergence' of constructivist representations on the basis of interconnected neural activity. The metaphor of parallel distributed processing involves a conception of memory (and cognition generally) which is a kind of dynamic 'neuronal–mind' event. Cognitive processes are to be found in the particular pattern of neuronal excitations taking place at any given instance of 'brain-time' processing. Needless to say, theoretical debates over the merits or otherwise of the symbolic and connectionist accounts continue and provide the motivation for many present-day studies (Fodor 1997). However, although these accounts of perception continue to dominate visual perception and mental imagery research, since the mid-1960s an alternative account of perception has lived alongside mainstream psychology, the work of Gibson and what is sometimes referred to as the realist approach to psychology and action. Some consideration of this somewhat different perspective is warranted given the emphasis it places on an individual's history of learning for the emergence of perceptual 'affordances', a term which sits rather uneasily in traditional psychological approaches to perception.

ECOLOGICAL APPROACHES TO PERCEPTION

The first thing to note about the ecological approach is that in contrast to information processing constructivist accounts of perception, Gibson (1966, 1979) argued for an ecological perspective which emphasised the 'couplings' of organism and environment. In this account the focus is upon the symbiotic relationship between animal and environment, and to consider one without due regard for the other is both misguided and ecologically invalid. It is not the case that humans have to construct a picture of the world based upon impoverished perceptual information; rather the visual system and the structured information available in the visual field of a moving person, specify the perceptual world in a much more direct fashion. The environment, perception of it and action within it, are all directly tied up with, in fact coupled to, an organism. One resonates with the environment, and the environment 'affords' the sets of actions and events which a moving perceiver will engage in. Through the detection of the 'style of change' in a stimulus, one is provided with a specification of the characteristics of events. Learning to see, and perception itself, involve detecting the 'invariant' and 'transformational' aspects of events (and perception of them).

One important aspect of this perspective, which is often misunderstood, is the relationship between the perception or recognition of objects and events, and what such objects 'afford' in terms of activities or sets of actions. Aspects or attributes of situations, events or objects, permit or sustain certain forms of activities for a perceiving organism. So, a square solid object of sufficient strength and durability will afford sitting on, trees afford climbing, and so on. However, square solid objects will only afford sitting on for an adult if they happen to be about knee high; otherwise (if smaller) they might afford being stood on, used as a ladder, or whatever. The point here is that 'affordances' (a noun coined by Gibson) *offer*, or have the *potential* for, sets of actions; they do not cause or require them. In other words this is not a stimulus–response kind of approach, cloaked in the language of the 'ecological niche' and animal–environment synchrony; rather it is a framework which allows or, more importantly, stresses, the dynamic qualities of organism–environment contexts.

Gibson's (1966) early work in perception emerged out of his concerns as a trainer of air force pilots during the 1950s in the USA, and over time the orienting constructs of his research changed from stimulus–response psychophysics into what he termed an 'ecological approach' to perception and action. This is based on a reformulation of Euclidean geometry, which he termed ecological optics. This work has existed since the mid-1970s as a parallel contrastive theme to the dominant paradigm in visual perception research, i.e. information processing accounts. Numerous papers chart the various controversies (Johannson 1973; Neisser 1976; Ullman 1980) regarding these divergent perspectives, and there have been partially successful attempts at introducing the ecological approach into other areas of psychology, e.g. environmental psychology (Landwehr 1988); developmental psychology (Pick 1987) and social psychology (McArthur and Baron 1983).

One of the oft-cited advantages of this approach is that dynamic aspects of organism–environment interactions can be considered, while still maintaining a commitment to the requisite degree of formalism demanded by psychology (Michaels and Carello 1981). Adopting an ecological approach to social perception McArthur and Baron (1983) go as far as to make the claim that:

> research within the ecological perspective will reveal the meaning that is communicated by social events. More specifically, such research will reveal what it is in a person's movements, gestures, voice and facial appearance that communicates to us that person's momentary intentions, emotional state . . . and what it is in the interactions between two people that communicates to us the nature of their relationship even when we cannot hear the words.
>
> (McArthur and Baron 1983: 217)

Gibson (1979) asserts that, 'The affordances of the environment are what it offers animals, what it provides or furnishes, either for good or ill' (p. 153). There is an intrinsic relation between perception of an environment and action within it. It is the affordance that is perceived – defined, that is, as those behaviours which can be entered into with respect to the environment. To detect affordances is to detect meaning, based here upon a concept of information that is interlinked with both perception and action (by an organism). Information is 'revealed' in objective physical events; that is, it is dynamic, changing, multi-modal stimulus information. The ecological approach holds not only to a metaphor of 'dynamic revelation' accompanying movement in and through an environment, but also to 'electro-computational' notions of 'resonance' and 'modulation' and the 'tuning-in' of perception. Michaels and Carello (1981) maintain:

whether an organism does X or Y 'determines' the affordance it can detect. Because information specifies behaviours that are afforded and because different animals have different sets of effectivities, affordances belong to animal–environment systems and nothing else. The theory of affordances claims that perceptions are written in the language of action.

(p. 42)

It should not escape our attention, however, that the place of Gibson's work in perceptual psychology obscures the fact that his was a theory of agency. As Costall and Leudar (1998) put it:

Gibson was remarkably unimpressed by neurophysiology. In place of the mechanised corpse of traditional physiology, he appealed to something remarkably close to the phenomenological notion of embodiment. For Gibson, it was not a virtue but a fatal indictment of mechanistic physiology that it has absolutely nothing to say concretely about how we experience or act upon the world.

(pp. 168–169)

When we come to consider what the ecological approach implies for research into mental imagery and the imagination, a number of things become clear. First, Gibson's rejection of the classical dualism of perceptual psychology (biological entity/psychological subject) encourages a shift from the 'inside' to the 'outside'. There is an inherent suspicion of the mentalism or cognitivist constructionism endemic within contemporary psychology. Second, perceptual cognition is knowledge *of* the world, and this knowledge is intrinsically tied up with action, sensation and what Gibson called stimulus information. But knowledge *about* the world or symbolic cognition comes from other people, i.e. through language and social practices. Whatever we conceive the internal or mental to be, it remains knowledge about the world. The world of the imaginary comes to us through the language, conventions, codes and semiotic communicative systems we employ and which we are embedded within. Only through acquiring language do we even learn to differentiate the external from the internal in the first place. The one thing that Gibson's perspective highlighted, in ways not dissimilar to Freud and Marx, was the significance of the material conditions which underscore any individual's personal history (the historicity of phenomenal experience). Perception, action, learning and individual history are interdependent elements of our experience of the perceptual world.

VISUAL IMAGERY IN PSYCHOLOGY

We might begin by observing that the language of knowing, understanding and cognising is replete with visual metaphors:

seeing things from another viewpoint;
from another perspective;
in the mind's eye;
seeing what somebody else means;
getting a glimpse of what's at issue;
it was a real eye-opener;
to cast one's mind back.

The language and discourse we employ to discuss the mental is saturated with the lexicon of the visual. We don't find it at all difficult to employ expressions such as 'I can see your argument' and 'can't you see it from my point of view'. The collocation of discourses of vision and the mind (in-sight) helps us understand why the kinds of ideas which underpin visual imagery research turn out be very similar to those of perceptual psychology. Some display a preference for asserting that the higher-order visual areas (of the brain) participate in both perception and imagery (e.g. Moscovitch 1994). Others argue that the representations which underpin mental images are entirely propositional and little different from those that underlie language (Pylyshyn 1981), that is psycholinguistic conception of language which is very much a cognitive and categorical process. For the most part the study of visual imagery over the last fifteen years has concentrated on the internal representations that produce the experience of 'seeing with the mind's eye' (Kosslyn and Ochsner 1994). Early impetus for this kind of research was inspired by a series of studies on mental imagery carried out by Shepherd and Metzler (1971), using shapes similar to those pictured in Figure 2.1.

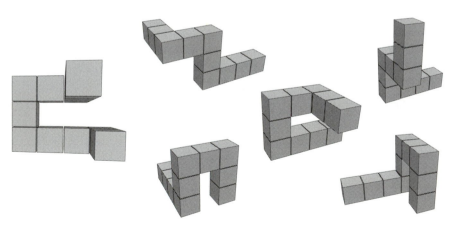

Figure 2.1 Imaging mental rotation

In these studies people are shown such images (for a brief period of time – usually between 1 and 2 seconds) and then asked to judge whether the pairs of objects are the same or different, or which face of the object are they looking at. Making a judgement in a short space of time requires 'mental manipulation' of the imagined object, i.e. by the time they have to decide, the object is no longer present in front of them. Shepherd and Metzler (1971) found that there is a linear increase in reaction time for judgement, as a function of the degree of rotation of the figures. To quote Lachman et al. (1979), 'these results show a remarkable correlation between the physical characteristics of the spatial figures and the mental operations performed on their visual images in the short-term store' (p. 251). From this earlier work a host of issues regarding mental imagery have emerged, with theories of imagery come in various guises. For example some argue that mental imagery involves top-down activation of perceptual representations (Shepherd and Metzler 1971); there are dual-code models which say that image generation involves two distinct elements, the visual and the semantic (Paivio 1991), and as we might expect, variations on the 'mind's-eye' hypothesis – seeing as if from the 'inside' (Pylyshyn 1981). In the more recent work much attention has turned to neuropsychology, not surprising given the seductive nature of 'imaging' the brain when asking people to imagine viewing objects, events or whatever. The main questions centre on whether the same areas of the brain appear active during visual and imagery tasks (Roland and Gulyas 1994; Farah 1985), and notwithstanding the potential value of brain imaging, one can detect a somewhat uncritical enthusiasm for MRI technology reminiscent of late nineteenth-century phrenology.

A moment's reflection on what is involved in the traditional mental rotation studies raises the question of what exactly constitutes the object of enquiry. In those studies similar to the original Shepherd and Metzler (1971) study, people are presented with such figures in brief millisecond presentations and then asked to make a judgement on the 'mental image' trace left after the presentation disappears. We might note that such figures are already imaginary in the sense that they are objects only ever encountered in such experiments or in the pages of problem-puzzle magazines. People are then asked to imagine how they would look when they are rotated such that they present a different face to the perceiver, which in effect involves an imaginary comparison between two imaginary objects. Then, in light of the observation that there is a correlation between how long it takes to make an appropriate judgement and how many rotations the object has gone through (from initial presentation), inferences are made about the 'vision-like' nature of image processing. What is glossed over is the fact that the very selection of such objects predicates certain assumptions about the nature of 'veridical' perception, and the nature of internal representations. The notion of rotation around an imaginary object is never considered as a problematic task to ask someone to carry out, even though in this context the act of imagining such objects being 'transformed' in the process of rotation is an interdependent aspect of making similarity

judgements. Shepherd (1990) suggests that we can avoid philosophical per-
plexities surrounding this issue by exercising care in talking about mental
imagery, i.e. instead of speaking of a person 'rotating the image of an object'
we should prefer 'imagining the rotation of an object', and 'thereby avoid all
the puzzling issues raised by the former formulation' (p. 370). It would seem
that researchers of imagery in cognitive psychology are reluctant to critically
reflect on the theoretical assumptions informing the supposed relationship
between perception and imagery. And part of the reason for this is the failure
to recognise the significance of language for any discussion of perception.

LEARNING HOW TO SEE: THE INTERDEPENDENCE OF SENSATION AND CULTURE

In an essay on how culture conditions the way we perceive colour, Eco (1996)
makes the point that when we use a colour term we are not pointing to a state
of the world, a process of reference, but instead connecting that term with a
cultural unit or concept:

> The utterance of the term is determined, obviously, by a given sensation,
> but the transformation of the sensory stimuli into a percept is in some way
> determined by the semiotic relationship between the linguistic expression
> and the meaning or content culturally correlated with it.
>
> (Eco 1996: 152)

Leaving aside those studies of early visual preference in infancy which call
attention to babies' attraction to the human face (e.g. Carey 1982), consider
what is involved in understanding how we come to 'see' anything. From
around the age of six months or so, young infants can sit up and respond to
the world around them, such that the adults around them comment on what,
they have reason to believe, the baby 'sees'. For example, imagine an infant
sitting on her parent's knee out in the garden together on a sunny day.
Suddenly some seagulls making a lot of noise swoop past overhead and the
infant looks up quickly in their direction. On doing so, the parent exclaims,
'Oh, look! Look at the seagulls' and in the immediate context links the sight
of the birds with the sounds in his/her language which denote birds. The
baby's phenomenal experience (as far as such experiences can be inferred by
others) of 'seeing' the birds, is interdependent with hearing their names,
sensing the intonation or pitch used when they are pointed out, all taking
place within a certain time, place and context of history, including the interaction history of the infant and parent. And so it goes on. Everything we see
has a name, and the name itself only has meaning with respect to all those
other 'name-sounds' which make up the structure of a language. As adults, we
certainly cannot somehow jump outside the realm of language onto an idealised neutral domain of objectivity.

In a sense we need to be mindful of a distinction between perceiving and recognising something. At best under certain conditions we feel justified in inferring that pre-linguistic infants 'see' the world around them, through our observing their actions and responses to the world. However, to claim that a young infant recognises something presupposes operations of a cognitive or conceptual nature. To recognise a thing is always to recognise it *as* something. In other words, when out walking in the meadow, I don't see daisies, I see these particular flowers *as* daisies, i.e. belonging to that category of terms embedded in, and constituted by, language. To paraphrase Harrison (1974), what a young child has to learn in acquiring her native language is not just a set of correlations between names and patterns of stimulation (e.g. flying seagulls), but an array of operations, procedures and social practices which form the foundation upon which the conceptual scheme of language is constructed. It is very difficult, for example, to talk about colour perception. As children we had to learn a whole host of 'sortal principles' which encapsulate the conditions under which we learn that this is blue, that is violet, another example is purple and so on. To quote Harrison (1974):

> Particular shades of colour (hues displayed in determinate degrees of saturation and tonality) can be arranged in orderly sequences, or series. The making of such sequences is a publicly checkable operation: if in constructing a sequence of progressively darker blues I put a lighter blue out of its proper sequence other people will be likely to notice and correct me. Moreover, such sequences connect anything that can be called a colour with anything else that can be called a colour. In the practice of constructing such sequences, then, we have a publicly checkable procedure or operation, the limits of whose applicability coincide with the limits of the category colour. Whatever can be ordered by that operation with respect to others things so ordered is a colour.
>
> (p. 134)

This consideration of the relationship between perception and language is derived in part from existential philosophy. This philosophical outlook rejects the Cartesian–Kantian view of cognition in favour of an orientation which focuses on our 'being-in-the-world', where an understanding of our existence should not entail turning away from our everyday experience. At the same time, we should recognise that any answers or glimpses of understanding will be inherently paradoxical. On the one hand our experience is that we 'live' in bodies which are quite categorically 'real', but on the other hand the very recognition or comprehension of self, body and 'other' is interdependent with our use of language (conceived here very broadly as encompassing all sign systems). And language itself produces versions and visions of reality as codes and conventions embedded within particular cultural contexts. Existential philosophy stresses that we are not neutral observers [in the world] but rather, situated participants in an ongoing, open-ended, socio-historical drama. It claims that truth comes into being in our concrete co-existence with others and cannot be severed from language and history.

(Langer 1988: 19)

Language as a social practice exists before any of us are born and thus, although it might be argued that we share some kind of 'pre-reflective bond' with others (Merleau-Ponty 1962), in our everyday lives we are always participants in the shaping of our world including the multiplicity of discourses (re)produced and extended in a continuous and negotiated dynamic construction of 'reality'. DeBernadi (1994) reminds us that the argument that language shapes its speakers more than its speakers shape language is one that repeatedly recurs within the social sciences. Sapir (1921) and Whorf (1956) were strong proponents of the view that language shapes world view, i.e. if you want to learn about my culture, then learn my language.

How then are we to understand the relationship between that which is said to constitute the basis of our perception and sensory experience, and our seeing, visualising and imagining the world? Regarding mental imagery Wittgenstein (1953) has pointed out that the concept of the 'inner picture' is misleading, given that the concept uses the 'outer picture' as a model. He notes that the uses of the words for these concepts are no more like one another than the uses of 'numeral' and 'number'. Arguably, within psychology there remains considerable ambiguity between what constitutes the 'inner' and the 'outer'. Where exactly, for example, does the boundary lie? In perception, the 'incoming stimulus' on the retina is said to form the basis for emerging constructivist processes whereby we 'see' whatever is being perceived. What is 'outside' provides the basis for the 'inside' experience of perception. To 'see' is also to categorise, and yet what underpins or motivates categorical imposition on the sensory information is surely language, social practice and cultural convention.

A partial answer to some of these issues comes from the work of the phenomenologist Merleau-Ponty. In his proposals regarding the phenomenology of perception Merleau-Ponty (1962) argued that perception is neither simply sensory imposition (of information), nor categorical imposition of 'top-down' cognitive processes. Instead he emphasised what he called a 'pre-reflective' bond between perception of the world and anchorage and embodiment within it. Langer (1988) notes that Merleau-Ponty concentrates on the fact that both external perceptions and internal imagery, including our innermost feelings and reflections, are the products of, 'a ceaseless dialectical interaction between the phenomenal body and the pre-objective world' (Langer 1988: 26).

Consider how curious it is, for example, that we can treat our own bodies as external objects, using one arm to lift a 'dead-leg'. In such situations our subjective experience is one of inhabiting the object we are 'acting upon'. Again, why do many of us tend to wince when we nearly scrape the side of our car against another, as if it is now an extension of our bodies? Images of what constitutes the 'inner' and the 'outer' are blurred on many occasions, pointing to the very contradictory nature of being both perceiver and perceived. Langer (1988) has summarised this position succinctly where she notes:

> The perceiver is concurrently perceived and perceiving . . .[this] would suggest that in belonging to the perceived world, the perceiver shares its fundamental texture while retaining the distinction of existing as a perceiving being – and a human one at that. Further, Merleau-Ponty's tracing of meaning to a pre-reflective exchange between incarnate subjectivity and pre-objective being suggests that the emergence of meaning has to do with this paradoxical difference-in-sameness.
>
> (p. 32)

Merleau-Ponty's argument is that we are primordially of the natural world and thus very much at home in it. Significantly, it is with other people that we constantly shape our world and our perception of it, and thus, both perceptual experience and mental imagery are interdependently embedded within our social-cultural, and particularly linguistic, practices. With language we construct narratives, accounts and descriptions about all that is said to be external and internal to human participation.

CONCLUDING COMMENTS

It is hard to avoid the suspicion that contemporary approaches in the study of mental imagery do not help us comprehend our everyday experience of 'internal imaging'. In other words, if our aim is to understand the whole host of images, imaginings, reflections, musings, internal feelings, aesthetic responses and whatever else is involved when referring to 'that which is inside', then mental imagery research will not really help us. For cognitive psychology mental imagery remains a representational process which involves the manipulation of symbolic entities according to abstract formal operations (information processing), or a 'brain-like' neural-network process of associated excitations (connectionism). Although the relationship between imagery and perception is analytically differentiated from the content of mental images themselves, the constructs, language and pre-theoretical assumptions of the research field rest solely on the dominant ideas within contemporary visual theory. It might be noted that mental imagery research has almost nothing to say on mental images that are 'non-visual', i.e. sound, tactile or kinaesthetically based image sensation, a curious omission given that being touched by, or touching, someone can give rise to rich imagery and associations.

  At the outset one aim of this chapter was to highlight relationships between contemporary views in perceptual psychology and those in mental imagery research. Always in the background was the suspicion that the metaphors, models and theories which inform perception (and cognition) constrain the study of mental imagery. Doubtless, adherents to these approaches may find many of the comments and observations made in this chapter unconvincing. However, the aim of this book is to outline what a psychology of the image could be. For the most part, there remain very few points of contact between mental imagery research in contemporary psychology and the more everyday ideas we have about the images we see around us and how they might influence our lives. Academic psychological research on images and 'imagery' remains constrained by the theoretical frameworks found in the study of perception (although see Barlow et al. 1990 for an exception).

We need to remind ourselves that the orienting philosophy of contemporary visual perception research is both Kantian in conception and functionalist in persuasion. From the early days of Hubel and Weisel's (1979) research on the visual cortex of cats, perception has been at the forefront of the emergence of cognitive science. Issues of representation, symbolic information processing and the neuropsychological possibilities of 'mind–brain' symmetry inform and dominate the discipline. But does the dominant position of these approaches in psychology necessarily work against articulating a psychology of the image more sensitive to people's everyday experience? First, and following Foucault (1977), it is not difficult to recognise that those discursive formulations which serve to (re)produce dominant ideologies bring with them institutional status, resources and credibility. Twentieth-century psychology has carved out a distinctiveness from other social science disciplines, by carefully emphasising methodological (natural science) practice, and by adopting those ideas commensurate with such a perspective. Post-war behaviourism was swiftly replaced by the computational/communication science metaphor, not in line with the mythology of Popperian hypothesis refutation, but as part of the emerging discourse of computational science. It is as well to recognise that psychology is hardly likely to embrace ideas within post-structuralism and critical theory. This might undermine its growing status in the sciences, no matter what their critical potential might be.

Second, and to extend this point, the psychology of perception, along with neuropsychology, is viewed as being one of the most 'hard-science' topics of psychology as science. Here, researchers employ the same discourses, procedures, practices and accountability criteria as colleagues in biology, medicine and other similar parts of science which adhere to the metanarratives of scientific practice. Within such a context, to phrase questions such as 'under what conditions can one justifiably infer that a pre-linguistic child can see x?' is rarely viewed as part of the enterprise. And in fact to do so would invoke those assumptions and presuppositions more akin to social semiotics or the philosophy of the later Wittgenstein. This is a pity as there is much in post-structuralism and critical theory that could be of value to psychology.

Third, the methodology employed in mental imagery research, in particular the social practices within which people are asked to respond to this or that mental image, serve to produce an account of internal processes presupposed on a philosophically debatable account of perception. There is no escaping the impression that those who produce this research believe either that the mind is a kind of serial-like information processing, or a parallel distributed neuronal, system. Either way, the level of abstraction proposed only extends the gap between the study of mental imagery and our experience of everyday images. Finally, the notion of mental imagery in psychology is interdependent with that of 'internal representation'. The idea of representation found in cognitive psychology and cognitive science has a distinctly 'picture-like' quality, a portraiture or iconic depiction. This reading of the term owes its allegiance to the metaphors of nineteenth-century perceptual philosophy and the manipulation of internal drawing-like entities.

Essentially, and in conclusion, there does not appear to be a potentially fruitful link between contemporary mental imagery research in psychology and a semiotically informed psychology of the image. The main reason is that mental imagery research remains predicated on unexamined assumptions about perception and the relationship between perception and imagery. For the most part to question the dominant cultural ideology of 'perception-representation-knowledge-imagery' is left to the margins of psychological theory and critical psychology (Fox and Prilleltensky 1997). Questions surrounding relationships between language and perception are in large part ignored and there is an increasing shift towards theorising imagery and associated cognitive representational phenomena in neuronal or neuro-imaging terms. Commenting on the conceptual distance between neurophysiological and social theoretical conceptions of vision, Sharrock and Coulter (1998) go as far as to note:

> there is no need to 'fill in' any putative 'middle ground' between sensory-neurophysiological inquiries into the physical mechanisms facilitating our ordinary visual capacities and perceptual activities, and the ordinary, commonsensical depictions of what can be seen . . . Neurophysiology can pursue its casual-conditions theory while ethnomethodological and related inquiries can investigate the workings of our (rule-governed) perceptual activities and the ways in which concepts are used in giving accounts of what is visually available in and through such activities.
>
> (pp. 162–163)

For a psychology of the image it is the way concepts are used which serves as the starting point. Language is first and foremost a social practice, and in our everyday talk with one another we employ appropriate models, metaphors and concepts in the service of communication. We are only beginning to examine under what conditions such concepts derive their import and significance for people. It is clear from the foregoing that our ideas about mental imagery continue to be dominated by the metaphors and ideas of visual perception. Apart from ecological psychology, the traditional view of imagery is that it is vision-like and supplemented by knowledge or representational processes, always internal and separate from the outside world in some way.

Psychology has yet to seriously consider the proposition that it is through language that we differentiate the inside and the outside. To describe the world is to theorise about it, and psychology as a discipline, unlike phenomenology, seems particularly resistant to accommodating, never mind embracing, the inherent contradiction of 'being in the world' and using language.

3   Sound imagery

INTRODUCTION

We have established that mental imagery is often taken to mean some form of internal visual-like representation. The emphasis on the visual in Western culture makes it difficult for those not visually impaired to recognise that the world of sound is an event world, while the world of sight is an object world (Ong 1971). Reflecting on the relationship between sound and imagery provokes the observation that ours is a visually dominant representational culture. There is no reason to believe, however, that sound perception is any less complicated than visual perception, and as we noted in the previous chapter, the relationship between perception itself and discursive representations of that experience remains philosophically problematic. Although we understand scientific descriptions of auditory perception, phenomenally we don't 'hear' acoustic signals or sound waves, we hear events: the sounds of people and things moving, changing, beginning and ending, forever interdependent with the dynamics of the present moment. We 'hear' the sound of silence.

From an evolutionary perspective sound has at least two distinct qualitative dimensions: one nurturing, supportive and indicative of comfort, care and safety; the other dissonant, disruptive and likely to provoke anxiety. Nurturing sounds might include blood flow (from our time in the womb), rhythm, intonational prominence and all those many sounds associated with the presence of others involved in our care. The preference new-born infants display for their own mothers' voices has been well documented (De Casper and Fifer 1980). Parents in many cultures spontaneously produce 'baby-talk' when soothing infants, a form of speech characterised by rhythmic intonational patterns, short sentences, often spoken softly (Snow and Ferguson 1977). In adult life the beneficial effect of meditative or calming mood music is promoted as an aid to reducing stress, and sufferers of insomnia know the value of listening to music or a late-night radio discussion show in order to lull themselves to sleep. The inherent rhythm to the sound of speech can have a comforting or soothing effect on us when we're anxious (although not all the time, e.g. Baker et al. 1993).

In contrast, it makes evolutionary sense that we have a high sensitivity to those sounds that might indicate the presence of potential predators, not dissimilar to our keen visual sensitivity to the detection of movement in peripheral vision. Some sounds appear to be intrinsically appealing and pleasurable, others discomforting and annoying. We are very easily disturbed by loud and disruptive noises. In particular, sounds in our environment which presuppose danger in some way, such as screeching car-tyres from behind as we walk on the road, are exceptionally attention-grabbing, and for good reason. In what sense, however, do we 'imagine' the cause of the sound or the sound-event? When woken in the night by a scratching noise we might quickly decide that we are listening to the sound of a mouse or rat under the floorboards or behind the wall. But consider, it is on hearing the noise that we then imagine that the sound is the kind of noise a rodent might make when scraping or scratching around for food. Our knowledge of such sounds has come from the cultural repertoire of all those available imaginable sounds; so we don't in reality have to have seen a rat or mouse making such a sound, a great deal of our knowledge comes from the available cultural discourses about sounds and their causes. Again, in the same way that visual perception of an event is interdependently linked with labels, names, discourses about that event, so it is for sound. We might even say that there is no such thing as silence, except an imaginary silence – a pure, abstract absence of sound. Arguably we cannot jump out of our discursive representational knowledge of sound into a 'soundless' void.

In this chapter I begin by comparing the traditional approach to sound (auditory) perception within psychology with more recent attempts inspired by Gibson's (1979) realist metaphor, and which focus on sound as event. After some discussion on the differences between these approaches, I then consider the relationship between sound, affect and our earliest experiences, and this is followed by a look at specific contexts where sound effects are deliberately manipulated in service of the imagination, such as film and radio. Reflecting on our response to sound in such contexts provokes a brief look at the role of affect and sounds that evoke particular meaning or significance for us. By way of conclusion, towards the end of the chapter a number of comments are made regarding the cultural basis of auditory perception, i.e. sound as 'meaning and event' within a particular social-discursive context.

SOUND AS PSYCHOPHYSICAL OBJECT

Psychology studies the nature of sound as the psychophysics of wave form analysis. The essential focus is on the nature of the computation said to take place as a result of sound waves creating vibrations in our eardrums. In line with other areas of sensory perception, the more dominant theories of auditory perception focus on how the cognitive system constructs appropriate auditory representations; that is, given the potentially confusing, degraded or redundant information made available to the ears. In light of the observation that sound waves from any source will reach each ear at a different time, the question of how sound is located is normally framed within a 'deprivation' model. The established practice of viewing auditory perception in terms of sound waves underlies the rather curious image we have where humans can only 'hear' sounds within a certain frequency range, and dogs, bats, porpoises and other mammals are able to hear much higher frequencies. As sound wave frequency increases, pitch increases, providing the template for Western musical scales, and interestingly one of the earliest theories of pitch perception (pitch is described as the prime quality of sound measured on a scale of high to low), proposed that the ear contained a structure formed like a stringed instrument:

> Different parts of this structure are tuned to different frequencies, so that when a frequency is presented to the ear, the corresponding part of the structure vibrates – just as when a tuning fork is struck near a piano, the piano string that is tuned to the frequency of the fork will begin to vibrate. This idea proved to be essentially correct; the structure turned out to be the basilar membrane, which unlike a set of strings, is continuous.
>
> (Atkinson et al. 1990: 143)

Even such a cursory examination of the images, metaphors and ideas informing current theory in auditory perception reminds us that the scientific study of sound is linked in a very particular way with what is said to constitute, subjectively, our perception of sound events in the first place. Consider, for example, what must influence the calibration of any instrument for measuring the intensity of sounds in decibels (Table 3. 1).

Table 3.1 Decibel ratings and common sounds

Decibel level	Example
0	Lowest sound audible to human ear
10	Quiet library, soft whisper
30	Quiet office, living room, bedroom away from traffic
40	Light traffic at a distance, refrigerator, gentle breeze
50	Air conditioner at 20 feet, conversation, sewing machine
60	Busy traffic, office tabulator, noisy restaurant
80	Subway, heavy city traffic, alarm clock at 2 feet, factory noise
100	Truck traffic, noisy home appliances, shop tools, lawnmower
110	Chain saw, boiler shop, pneumatic drill
120	Rock concert in front of speakers, sandblasting, thunderclap
140	Gunshot blast, jet plane
180	Rocket launching pad

Source: adapted from Atkinson et al. 1990.

The index on the left hand side of the table is qualitatively linked to sound experiences, but clearly these do not map onto the scale in some sort of additive fashion; thus the difference between a soft whisper and a refrigerator is hardly perceived as the same sound scale difference as that between heavy city traffic and a chain saw. It should not escape our attention that one of the most often employed dependent measures within the psychophysics of sound is the 'JND' (a just noticeable difference), an amusing example of the transformation of a social-cultural practice into an objective measure (Krueger 1992; Drake and Botte 1993). People in psychophysics experiments are invited to indicate when a difference between two sounds is 'just noticeable', thereby providing the basis for the measuring instrument.

Essentially auditory perception research is dominated by sound as 'abstracted information' in the information processing sense of cognition. To hear is to perceive (albeit in a subconscious way) sound wave frequencies, pitch intensity and so on. The measurement of relevant parameters concentrates on the sensory qualities of sound (loudness, tone, intensity, timing and pitch), where the 'brain–mind' transforms the neural excitations, caused by sound wave pressure into sound perception in an as yet unknown way. A reading of such work leads quickly to the conclusion that the psycho-acoustics of sound will have little bearing on developing a theoretical understanding of the relationship between sound perception and images, leaving aside one or two studies in marketing psychology which look at this relationship in advertising (Halpern 1988; Miller and Marks 1992).

We only have to think of our everyday experience of sound to see why there are major difficulties in developing a psychological theory of sound imagery. Consider how we might explain our experience of sound and associated imagery processes when we are listening to music through headphones, particularly headphones where there is no experience of pressure on our ears. Although we know the source of the music is external to our bodies, our phenomenal experience is of music playing in our heads, sounds and images intermeshed with thoughts, reflections and associated responses to the music. What is *inside* and what is *outside* becomes unclear, an observation which should remind us that to listen is not the same thing as to hear in a passive sense. We can then ask, how are we to conceive of sound as event?

PERCEIVING SOUNDS AS EVENTS

In the comparatively recent past psychologists have taken note that the relationship between the 'outside' and 'inside' nature of sound perception (imagery) is not simple. Gaver (1993a), for example, criticises the overemphasis on the computational approach in auditory perception. He points out that we hear *events* in the world rather than hear sounds, noting that it remains unknown how sounds close to the ear can indicate remote physical events, e.g. hearing the sound of distant traffic through a closed window. In developing his proposals Gaver (1993a) contrasts everyday listening with musical listening, as in Table 3.2.

Table 3.2 Everyday and musical listening

Everyday listening (perception of sound-producing events	*Musical listening* (experience of sounds themselves)
• hear a sound in terms of its sources	• hear a sound in terms of its sensory qualities
• rarely addressed in psychology	• traditional approach in psycho-acoustics
• reports research which focuses on people's perception of 'everyday' sounds	• sounds do not convey enough information to specify their sources: must be supplemented by memory, unconscious processes and problem-solving

The traditional approach in psycho-acoustics, as noted earlier, has been to study sound with regard to measurable sensory qualities – waveform, pitch and so on – and it is unsurprising to note that the primary focus within the psychology of music has been musical perception, tonality, pitch and so on (Boltz 1998; Krumhansl 1991). Again, and in line with the constructivist approach of visual perception, the sound information in perceiving music is said to be impoverished in some way, i.e. not adequate to specify the source of the sound. Top-down cognitive processes supplement the raw primary data activating the senses.

In contrast, our experience of listening to sounds in everyday life is in terms of the sources that produce them; the whirring of a fridge, rustling of leaves on the road and so on. To hear a sound is often to hear the cause of the sound. The wind is a good example particularly as it is the effect of 'the wind' on objects which constitutes the sound of the wind as an event or events; for example, compare the sound of leaves blowing with the intermittent but continual sound of a door swinging and banging – both caused by the wind.

Gaver (1993a) calls for an approach in auditory perception which focuses on the consistent structure of the world that allows sounds to relate reliably to their sources. Two distinct questions are raised. *What* do we hear, and *how* do we hear sound(s)? In answer to what, he develops a framework for describing ecologically relevant perceptual entities in the dimensions and features of events that we actually hear (this could be viewed as a content question). In answer to how do we hear, Gaver (1993b) developed an ecological acoustics, one that describes the acoustic properties of sounds conveying information about the events we hear (a perceptual structure question). His proposal relies on an 'analysis by synthesis' method which attempts to formalise the relationship of dimensions of physical objects to how they are perceived as event-sounds. The theoretical procedure involves an iterative process of analysing the sound of an object, e.g. a hammer hitting metal, and then synthesising a duplicate on the basis of the sound patterns (spectrograms composed of frequencies, amplitude and time dimensions). Subsequently the analysis data can be systematically reduced, and the resultant synthesised sound compared to the original. If there are no perceptible differences between the original and the synthesised versions, then the discarded data are considered irrelevant for perception. By proceeding in this way, an understanding of the aspects of a given sound crucial for perception of that sound can be obtained (Gaver 1993b: 289).

This attempt at formalising an ecological approach to auditory perception resonates with similar work within geography. Rodaway (1995) in particular has incorporated Gibson's approach in his analysis of what he calls auditory geographies. He asks us first to consider that within North American/ European culture, we focus on the visual to the extent that even our labelling of sound events emphasises the nature of the object making the sound, rather than the phenomena. For example, as a description we are more likely to say, 'the bell sounds' rather than 'the sound bells' – in the former the focus is on the bell, in the latter on the sound itself. In addition, he notes that with sight or vision there is always a phenomenal sense of being at the edge of our visual field, and thus viewing our perceptual landscape in front and to the sides of the direction we're facing. Not so with sound, where we are always at the centre of the perceptual experience; that is, we are at least as sensitive to sounds behind us as to those in front. While vision is an object world, sound is an event world. Auditory experience is always of a flow of sound, constant at times, rising or falling in intensity, noticeable when absent or excessive, but never truly 'silent'. The relationship between sound and attention becomes important whenever we use the terms 'background' or 'foreground' noise.

Noting the extension of the visual metaphor in the image of the landscape, Schafer (1977) provides a framework for understanding sound as event, with his notion of the soundscape. Soundscapes 'surround and unfold in complex symphonies or cacophonies of sound' (p. 86), and his framework emphasises the fact that we inhabit the centre of our soundscape. In one sense we might say that we feel more detached from the visual world. Sound experience is always a sensuous experience at one level, an interdependent time/space geography of constant and continuous dynamic events. Even in circumstances where you might imagine the experience of complete silence, a moment's reflection highlights the nature of such a fantasy. Consider for example that if you were sitting in a sensory deprivation chamber, at the very least you would nevertheless hear the sound of your own blood flowing through your veins and the beating of your heart. Auditory experience is a special sensory key to interiority, and, as noted earlier, when listening to sound through earphones one quickly realises that the borders between the 'external' and the 'internal' are as much determined by language and discourse as they are by phenomenal experience.

In thinking through the complex nature of auditory perception, Rodaway (1995) provides a helpful classification of phenomenal experience in his outline matrix describing an auditory geography (Figure 3.1).

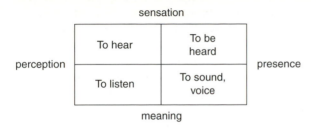

Figure 3.1 Dimensions of an auditory geography (from Rodaway 1995, with permission)

Classifying auditory experience in this way may help clarify the position or rather the conceptual relationship between sound and imagery. On the one hand there is a dimension spanning perception as raw experience with presence and embodiment. At the same time a second dimension distinguishes simple auditory sensation from sound event as meaning. Rodaway (1995) points out that hearing (to hear) may be described as the basic passive sensation, the condition which makes it possible to ask 'What's that sound?' Listening (to listen), however, implies active attentiveness to auditory information, and the very act of listening draws attention to our desire to establish or mark out meaning.

Correspondingly, however, and with respect to the second dimension of presence, we are organisms which acquire a knowledge of auditory information about the environment that surrounds us. People, animals and things all emit sounds even when they are unwelcome (such as when your stomach begins to rumble during an important interview for a job). We also, through sound, project ourselves into the auditory soundscapes of those around us – we have a voice capable of denoting our presence in the world and specific 'meanings' interdependent with the projection of 'our sounds' denoting our presence. It becomes easier to understand why we feel more detached from the visual than the auditory world. Our experience of sound is often emotional and Rodaway (1995) suggests that while sight paints a picture of the world, sound(s) (along with touch, taste and smell) is life itself. We might ask, where does our sensitivity to sound begin and what form does it take?

IN THE BEGINNING WAS THE 'SOUND'

While we can applaud the attempts by ecological psychology to draw attention to sound event perception, it remains unclear why we do not have conceptually rich theories for understanding the relations between sound and imagery. This is rather surprising and may in part be due to what Beloff (1994) has called psychology's overemphasis on written language (i.e. text). Language is first and foremost sound, or at least the business of making meaning through the use of sound. Consider for a moment though, how the study of language acquisition is conceived in psychology and linguistics. The central constructs within child language research focus on the 'lexicon', syntactic structure, lexical processing and so on, all terms predicated on a view of language as formal (often written) object. In other words, what underlies the very definitions which inform the study of language acquisition are notions of structure and language as 'text/object', an approach which derives from formal linguistics, despite the fact that Saussure's (1974) structuralism grew out of his analysis of the segmentation of sound in the vocal tract. In contrast to the formalist emphasis of psycholinguistics, from the child's viewpoint what she hears are sounds (not words), and one of her first tasks is probably to learn what sounds to pay attention to (mother's voice) and what sounds to ignore (background noise of traffic outside the window).

Alongside touch, sound perception is wrapped up with emotional response and affect. Dore (1983) argues that the earliest attempts at overcoming separation and anxiety are centred on the infant's sound-making attempts. And as the child grows her main task is to learn under what conditions making this (and not that) sound, will lead to those around her responding to her 'soundings' as intentional communicative acts. Some work within developmental psychology has mapped out the circumstance where the interactive structuring of the infants' early sounds (by parents) leads on to their making accountable (word) sounds (e.g. Golinkoff, 1883).

It would be a mistake, of course, to think that parent and child are focused solely upon intentional communication above everything else. Our emotional development is deeply embedded within 'sound-sensitive' contexts. The child's whole sensual environment is infused with sound. Folklorists and psychoanalysts have studied the nature of early lullabies sung by mothers, noting the unique (usually but not always), positive intonational contours of nursery rhymes (Sircar 1997; Bowey 1990). Infants spend considerable time playing with the sounds they make, displaying amusement and interest when others copy their noises (Romeflanders and Cronk 1995). Repetition, sound play and noise experimentation all appear to be important aspects of the child's pre-linguistic development, despite the absence of any direct correlation between early sound use and later language development (Kuhl and Meltzoff 1996; Ingram 1985). We continue to find it difficult to remember that children learn language as accountable sound performance, and only later learn that these noises are described as words, sentences and all other such constructs which derive from the invention of writing.

The significance of the first sounds for early affective development has been stressed by developmental psychologists and psychoanalysts. Sabbadini (1998), for example, argues that the earliest exposure to sound patterning has profound effects on later psychopathology. She notes:

> Let us come back to the nursery. Silent feeding sessions with a mother never addressing sounds or words to her baby may be distressing for the

child and could amount to perceptual and emotional deprivation, possibly leading to future problems in the development of linguistic and musical skills, or to overt psychopathology.

(Sabbadini 1998: 5)

While noting it is unlikely that any direct evidence linking sound deprivation with later psychopathology will ever be forthcoming (for methodological if not any other reason), we need to keep in mind that the infant's primary sensation environment is tactile and auditory before it is visual. We feel and 'sound' our way into the world before we perceive that world visually.

FACILITATING THE IMAGINATION IN SOUND MEDIA

Moving on from reflecting on our primary sensory experience, if we aim to examine contexts where the relationship between sound and imagery is paramount then we only have to turn to two influential communication media, film and radio. One might expect that a consideration of the sound techniques and practices deliberately employed within film should highlight certain aspects of the assumed relationships between visual and auditory perception. And where one strips away dependence on the visual within a communicative context (radio production) the relationship between 'image production' or the imaginary should come to the foreground. We can begin with sound and film, confining our discussion to the relationship between music and film. Dialogue as 'sound' in film serves as the primary vehicle for narrative construction and may be secondary to music when it comes to techniques for facilitating and manipulating the audience's imagination.

Sound and film

A consideration of sound imagery would certainly be incomplete without discussing the interdependence of imagery domains in film (sound and visual). Film directors and producers work hard at representing (re-presenting) our acoustic world in film. To paraphrase Balasz (1985), the acoustic landscape in which we live is often revealed through the sound film. He comments that all that has speech beyond human speech, all that speaks to us with the vast conversational powers of life and incessantly influences and directs our thoughts and emotions, is made available in the medium of film. From the muttering of the sea to the din of a great city, from the roar of machinery to the gentle patter of autumn rain on a windowpane, all are recognisable in an instant given the richness of our imagery associations and rememberings. The sound film can encapsulate the significant sounds of life, in a way that seems much more direct than, say, the lyrical poem.

We can also note that the sounds heard in a film do not need to be explained. Balasz (1985) makes the point that the timbre of a sound changes in accordance with the gesture of the visible source of the sound observed in the film, in a way akin to the way the shade and value of a colour change according to what other colours border it in a painting. In a sense the acoustic and optical images are effused together in a single 'sound–vision' picture. And the intimacy of sound can be manipulated quite deliberately in the sound film,

> We are all familiar with the 'acoustic' close-up where we are made to perceive sounds which we would never normally hear (e.g. in building up the atmosphere in a horror movie). And of course subtle associations and interrelations of thoughts and emotions can be conveyed by means of very low, soft sound effects. Such emotional or intellectual linkages often play a decisive dramaturgical part. They can be anything – the ticking of a clock in an empty room, a slow drip from a burst pipe, or the moaning of a little child in its sleep: we possess such an array of deep associations of the most common everyday sounds. We have learned a language of sound imagery, where we simply seem to know 'immediately' what any given sound 'means'.
>
> (Balasz 1985: 121)

Such observations should remind us that there is a considerable difference between our visual and acoustic education. One reason for this is that we often see without hearing (e.g. through a window) but we very rarely hear the sounds of nature and of life without seeing something, if not with the eyes then with the imagination.

There are a number of more formal approaches to the study of music in film (Neumeyer 1997; Steinberg 1997; Lipscomb 1997). Lipscomb and Kendall (1994), for example, propose that any given musical and visual relationship can be represented in a two-dimensional space representing the degree of abstraction of the musical and the visual dimensions (see Figure 3.2). Motion pictures as audio-visual composites can be placed within such a grid, where,

> one extreme of the musical dimension might be exemplified by the use of 'La Marseillaise' and 'Deutschland über Alles' in the bar scene from 'Casablanca'. Each melody is associated with the country which it represents (HIGHLY referential). The other end of this dimension might be represented by musical sound that has no conventional association, yet is perceived as organized simply because of the relationship of one tone to the others or because of the superimposition of musical sound on a sequence of visual images.
>
> (Lipscomb 1997: 2)

Lipscomb and Kendall (1994) raise two considerations concerning the combination of musical sound and visual images, attempting to take into consideration what they call the referential and syntactical aspects of the motion picture experience. In Figure 3.2, they place Norma McLaren's *Synchrony* in a position of high visual and musical abstraction. The film is a piece of experimental animation where abstract shapes appear on the screen at the same time as identical images pass over the (idealised) photoelectric cell of the 'sound track' portion of the film celluloid, 'the resultant tones are not intended to have any conventional association for the viewer' (Lipscomb 1997: 2). In contrast, Lipscomb (1997) places the final scenes from Zwick and Horner's *Glory* (1989) in a much more extremely 'concrete' visual and musical position on the grid. In these scenes a troop of soldiers prepare to march off to war, and the themes and motifs associated with the various characters throughout the film are heard on the soundtrack, 'the scene is extremely concrete (i.e. a low degree of abstraction) in its representation of human drama while the music is referential both stylistically and thematically' (p. 3).

Lipscomb and Kendall's (1994) main point is that an effective film score, in its interactive association with the visual element, need not attract the audience's attention to the music itself. Lipscomb (1989) goes on to argue that most successful film composers have made a fine art of manipulating audience perception and emphasising important events in the dramatic action without causing a conscious attentional shift. It remains uncertain, however, whether formalisms of the kind proposed by Lipscomb and Kendall (1994) will provide a sufficiently rich theoretical framework for understanding the relationship between music and film. Although a two-dimensional representation of this kind can help place or position a film within a particular genre (concrete/abstract), as a theory it leaves us in the dark when it comes to explaining why we might 'see' an image on hearing a piece of music (or vice versa). In Chapter 8 we consider audience reception theory in more depth, noting, however, that a convincing account of this phenomenon has not yet emerged.

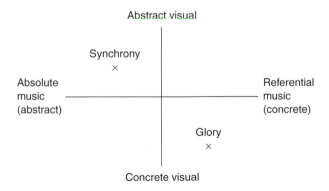

Figure 3.2 Composition dimensions for film music

Radio

Unlike film, where sound helps to widen representational space by extending the 'film-frame' on screen, radio is what Beck (1998) calls the blind medium – confined to sound alone. There is no way in which the visual scene, the 'positioned perspective' of the viewer, can be enhanced through the simultaneous employment of sound and image. Radio plays, in particular, stand on their own and have to create the unique impressions associated with engaging the listener in the 'act of sound imagining'. A number of writers in radio drama and criticism have drawn attention to the poetics of radio drama and provide interpretative tools for a systematic analysis of production systems in radio drama (Rodger 1982; Drakakis 1981; Beck 1997; Chion 1994). One idea within this work, the construction of a 'point of listening', helps articulate certain kinds of metaphors or ideas we hold regarding the nature of 'external' and 'internal' auditory experiences. Ferrington (1993), for example, interprets the effect of listening to a radio play, claiming,

> An effectively designed audio work may facilitate a listener's integration of life-based experiences into a 'movie' created within the 'theatre of the mind'. Each individual becomes his or her own movie director with no two people having the same imaginary experience.
>
> (Ferrington 1993: 45)

Building on the work of Chion (1994), Beck (1998) summarises three important elements involved in the production of a point-of-listening: the sound frame, acousmatic sound and the listening zone. Asking how is it that radio manages to create the equivalent of 'on-screen vs. off-screen', Beck notes that every sound event in radio drama requires an acoustic, a context and a verbal description to fill out the situation for a listener. Producing sound events that are 'in-frame' (rather than out-frame) involves balancing together the sounds with explanations for their occurrence within a 'sound perspective' based on what we would normally expect with our everyday acoustic environment, i.e. sounds close by us. In contrast 'out-frame' sounds are produced as if external to the immediate present (for the participants in the drama), e.g. the sound of a dog barking in the distance, seagulls and so on.

Commenting on the second category of sound, Chion (1994) calls this 'acousmatic sound': a sound you hear without seeing its cause, such as railway station and other loudspeaker announcements, a bomb exploding at a distance, the voice down the telephone line, the noise in the attic, someone coming up the stairs, the knock at the door, and what is overheard in the next room. Beck (1998) points out that in radio drama acousmatic sound is categorically different from film,

> because we hear every sound event in radio drama and connect it with its cause, within an overall sound space. Here, the acousmatic inhabits an area

beyond the main frame of the sound picture, and it is 'out' and 'unseen', but of course is still bound by the sound space's 'outer frame'. I use the terms 'main frame' of the sound picture and 'outer frame' of the overall sound space.

(Beck 1998: 23)

Notice the distinction made here between 'sound picture' and 'sound space', the first more object/image-like, the second event-determined and, needless to say, both in relation to an interpreting listener. Underpinning the idea of a 'point of listening' rests the question, from where does the listener listen? There are at least two aspects of this positioning as Chion (1994) describes them – one a spatial sense, in the space represented in the soundtrack, the second a subjective sense involving the positioning of the listener with the relevant character at a given moment in the narrative, i.e. which character is hearing what I hear? Beck (1998) points out that the listener is always positioned at the centre of the sound which determines the mixing and balancing of sound technically. The task for the director is to transform potentially confusable hearing into active radio 'listening', which involves of course retention, interpretation and an immediate reliance on short-term memory.

The listener, however, occupies a corresponding 'listening zone', which Gray (1991) claims is the imagination, the creativity of the mind or, to paraphrase Beck (1998), this is the second play in the audience's head, where the listener is the 'final actor' and 'director'. Here at least is one context where the relationship between sound and imagery is articulated with deliberation and aesthetic consideration. Commenting on the historical and social practices which surround the activity of radio listening, Beck (1998) comments that radio listening zones are personal and not socially ritualised in the same way that cinema or the theatre is,

> Listening to radio plays is rarely now a collective activity. Each listening zone has its own disattention factors, extraneous noise and accompanying activities, and in spite of these, radio listening is accessible and pleasurable. Does being a solitary listener incline one to strong or weak identification? Surely the environment influences our reception. The fact is that many Radio 4 afternoon plays have domestic plots, what in America are called 'hearth' plays. These cross over to the domestic zones of the listeners and suggest at least a relationship with the – usually – strongly sympathetic protagonists.
>
> (Beck 1998: 5)

The second 'subjective' aspect of the listening zone is reflected in the technical notes of radio drama scripts (and indicated as 'thoughts'). A subjective point-of-listening is produced where the listener is (as if) given an internal dialogue of what a character might be thinking. Again, Beck (1998) notes that technically the actor-speaker for 'thoughts' is always close to the microphone rather than in the normal position (about arm's length or further). In such a close position the voice sounds very different, more detailed, intimate and 'as if' we are voyeuristically inhabiting the speaker's mind. This production convention has been termed 'interiorization', what Beck calls radio's 'fourth dimension', through which a particular complicity with the listener can be established, 'a process as familiar as our own inner ruminations' (p. 6).

To summarise, in both film and radio drama we can identify particular aspects of the relationship between sound and imagery (or the imagination). In fact, presupposed in the design and use of the technical procedures for 'sound imaging' in these domains, exists an idealised conception of the spectator/listener's imagination processes. Radio in particular makes manifest important distinctions of auditory perception (internal 'thoughts', sound distancing, point of listening), ideas which inform our understanding of sound imagery.

AFFECT, IMAGERY AND THE SIGNIFICANCE OF SOUND MEMORY

We hear sounds as events but at the same time many of the sounds we hear conjure up particular memories, associations and images of significant moments in the past. There is a particular kind of relationship between certain sounds we hear and their significance in our lives. Developing insights into the social significance of sounds outlined by Ferrington (1995), Thorn (1998) points to the 'marking' significance that some sounds can have in our daily life. The associations of sounds made by people accomplish what he calls the 'marking off' of social boundaries in everyday life, constituting a largely unremarked part of our soundscape, or to give some examples of such 'sound marks' provided by one of his respondents,

> . . . 'dad's razor being scraped night and morning, giving me a sense of security',
> . . . 'the sound of the key in the front-door meaning dad was home and everything was all right',
> and
> . . . 'the sound of family moving about the house after I'd gone to bed giving me a sense of security and belonging'.
>
> (Ferrington 1995: 23)

Such references to notions of security are good examples of the deeply emotional and personal associations that people give in response to questions about the significance of sound. As a further investigation of such associations, in a recent pilot study of the relationship between sounds and affect (Forrester 1998), I asked students attending a university class in England what kind of emotional responses they have to particularly significant sound marks. Their responses included,

Example 1: 'The sound of a recorder – when I hear it now I get images of myself and old school friends practising in our music room – I feel the whole presence of the school and that era at that time. I can actually feel what it was like to be 8 years old again.'

Example 2: 'The sound of a lawnmower in the summer somewhere in the distance. Brings back memories of the summers playing in the garden and staying out as long as possible at our cottage.'

Example 3: 'Piano music – my sister and I trying to get our practice done so that we could go out and play.'

Example 4: 'Cross-channel car ferry horn. This meant great excitement at going on holiday, the start of an adventure, or feelings of safety and comfort on the way home after the adventure.'

Example 5: 'Grandfather's clock making a noise every hour. Whenever I heard it I was filled with joy that I was there. Usually happened in the morning.'

Example 6: 'Parents arguing – emotional worry and stress. School bell – pleased happy time to go.'

Example 7: 'Noises of children playing at playtime in school – associate this with fun . . . . Conflicting music and speech from the radio. My three older brothers all liked different music, my mother listened to Radio 4 and my father watched television. A cacophonous sound, indicative of my family being all together.'

Example 8: "A train whistle – steam train noises were very exciting. Reminds me of playing very freely in our "garden" and was closely involved in our fantasy games, e.g. train could be bringing "Cowboys".'

We can see that in these examples, simply remembering significant sounds serves to reproduce particular images and associations for people. And the images themselves are often infused with affect (examples 4 and 5), point to important aspects of past relationships (examples 6 and 7), and appear to have the potential to make people 'feel again' sensations from the distant past (examples 1 and 8). We perceive sound as event and through sound we can relive earlier associations and feelings, good, bad and indifferent. Sounds can act as signifiers for conscious and unconscious meanings.

COGNITION, SOUND AND CULTURE

Beyond recognising that there seems to be something of a theoretical vacuum in the study of sound imagery in psychology, critically reflecting on the nature of sound imagery may have implications for our ideas about cognition more generally. Rodaway (1995) points out that the Inuit do not conceptualise space and time separately but instead perceive any situation as a dynamic whole. Commenting on an early study by Carpenter (1973) into the navigational abilities of the Inuit, he notes that people are often astounded by the Inuit ability to follow a trail across an apparently featureless tundra waste, suggesting that the idea of a 'map' was for them quite alien since their world was much clearer in auditory than in visual form,

> This was an auditory world of events, processes and actions, not the visual world of places, patterns and objects. The wind was more important than the vista, offering environmental information from its noise, force and direction, and from its olfactory content as well. The long periods of darkness in the tundra winter and the snow and ice expanses where sky and land and sea merge make visual sensitivity less useful, especially when the individual is hidden well into his or her parka to keep out of the cold and biting wind.
>
> (Rodaway 1995: 110)

Arguably, for psychology knowing is predicated on the visual, reflected in the metaphors we use when discussing whether we comprehend or understand each other (e.g. I see what you mean; can't you understand my perspective; she seems to have second sight; and so on). We can speculate as to the kind of knowing derived from auditory perception. Gell (1995) argues that the Umeda of Papua New Guinea possess a quite different model of the relationship between perception, language and cognition (compared to Western presuppositions and assumptions), noting his own 'methodological deafness' which caused him to fail to appreciate

> the auditory domain, including natural sounds, language and song, as cultural systems in their own right, and not just adjuncts to culture at large, but as foundations, thematic at every level of cultural experience.
>
> (Gell 1995: 233)

We can also recognise that what we mean by silence is culturally embedded given Imada's (1994) observation that for the Japanese, silence can have a very particular suggestive force. In a brief introduction to Japanese ideas about sound, Imada (1994) points to the suggestive force of the absence of discernible sound, through two illustrations. The first is of people gathering to listen to the sound of the bloom of a lotus flower at a pond in Tokyo. The blooming actually occurs at a pitch below the level of human hearing, but people 'wanted to listen to that phantom sound. The experience was a kind of communal auditory hallucination' (Imada 1994: 5). We are reminded of John Cage's musical experiment with his 4' 33" piece of silent music. Cook (1990) cites the occasion when the pianist created havoc when he 'played' his silent piece to considerable effect. As an event, the pianist approaches the piano, opens the instrument as if to play, then sits in complete silence for 4 minutes and 33 seconds precisely. The effect as a 'performance' is to draw the audience's attention to the accompanying sounds being made by them as they await the playing. To paraphrase Cook, the piece creates a musical event from whatever is heard, and does this by creating in the listener an openness to the qualities of sounds heard for their own sake, an awareness normally absent in our everyday surroundings. Anything can be music if the listener chooses to hear it in a particular way, and the opposite can also be true – nothing can be music unless it is heard as such.

Second, in describing a sound installation in a garden, Imada (1994) draws attention to the delay between water being introduced to the *suikinkutsu* and its effect on being heard. He says that not only did people 'appreciate the sound of the suikinkutsu itself, but also the time spent creating the sound'. The delay 'had the effect of directing [their] listening to other environmental sounds in the garden' (p. 7). We are reminded that sound is not only an event, it is always an event understood within specific cultural discourses which define the meaning of a particular sound as 'the sound' for x, y, or z. We have yet to formulate a socio-psychophysics of sound perception.

CONCLUDING COMMENTS

Attempting to think of a sound as a sign may be possible only in rather specific social-cultural contexts, for example, the sound of a hooter blowing denoting the end of the working day. If anything, it seems that only when sounds are inscribed as 'text' (phonetically, musical scores, sound-wave patterns or whatever) do we find it easy to formalise the language of sound as a semiotic enterprise. Representing in text the speech event as communicative meaning makes semiotic analysis realisable, and explains in part why linguistics and psycholinguistics are dominated by formalist accounts of language. But focusing on language in this 'object'-like way, we may lose sight of the fact that speech is sound first and 'text' second. In this chapter we have seen that it is rather difficult to formulate an understanding of sound as imagery where we only have rather impoverished theories of auditory perception as our conceptual starting point. The work of Rodaway (1995) and others reminds us that there is a conceptual gap between the 'sensation of sound' as perceptual experience and the recognition of sound as 'event and meaning'. Within this gap we have inserted discourses of sound, and thus a 'sound as sign' can only be understood with respect to the cultural discourses within which the sound is embedded. And the answer we give ourselves to the question 'what's that sound?' will often rest upon our imagination, in the sense that hearing a sound as belonging to a recognisable category will engender imagining the cause of whatever produces that kind of sound. We cannot yet talk of a theory of sound imagery, but we can at least begin to articulate conceptions of sound which move away from psychology's overemphasis on auditory perception.

4 Dream images and conceptions of the unconscious

INTRODUCTION

One definition to be found in the Oxford English dictionary under the term *dream*, reads 'A train of thoughts, images and fancies passing through the mind during sleep' (OED 1989: 1036). Continuing our exploration of internal image domains, this chapter focuses on the question: How do we understand the experience of dreaming and the images it contains? Making sense of a dream, and the images which constitute it, is something we are all familiar with, yet not without a sense of contradiction or surprise, disbelief or dismissive disinterest. Our experience of dreaming is akin to entering a self-contained world where the images, sensations and thoughts are 'other worldly' or at least slightly alien. On the one hand we recognise that dreaming, or more precisely our memories of what we experience on awakening, signifies an aspect of our mind somehow separate from conscious reflection, yet at the same time potentially understandable, given that we can recognise and remember the images, sensations and feelings of dreams in a way similar to experiences we have when awake. Freud (1976) emphasised the same point, citing Hildebrandt's (1875) observations:

> Whatever strange results they [dreams] may achieve, they can never in fact get free from the real world; and their most sublime as well as their most ridiculous structures must always borrow their basic material either from what has passed before our eyes in the world of the senses or from what has already found a place somewhere in the course of our waking thoughts – in other words from what we have already experienced either externally or internally.
>
> (Freud 1976: 68)

Consider how we learn to talk about dreams as children. During our early pre-school years on awaking and spontaneously discussing, often in a rather garbled fashion, what we have just been experiencing as dreaming, our parents will provide an account which serves to reassure both us, if we are frightened, and themselves (their child is not speaking in an incoherent way for no reason).

'Oh, you've been dreaming have you?' and so on. More often than not, parents soothe their children, talk over what they 'saw', telling them that everything is fine and it was 'just a dream'. Over time, we then enter into breakfast-time discussions about having dreams, recounting narratives about 'what happened' in the dream state. Parents generally believe it is a good thing if children can recount their dreams, 'get them out of their system', and for the most part encourage them to talk about them, providing an appropriate language for making sense of the experience. We have to learn to speak appropriately about dreams within such discourse, parents being quick to decide whether a dream 'really happened' or not, and in doing so we are encultured into the models and metaphors about dreaming held by the particular society we belong to.

As adults, we continue our discursive production of dream narratives, accounts, interpretations and reflections on what it was we remember experiencing during a dream on awaking. However, we tend to do so only within particular kinds of contexts. We often prepare ourselves for an extended period of listening, and maybe with a certain sense of tedium, when we hear a friend say to us, 'I had this dream the other night, and do you know what?' We recognise that prefacing an account, or dream narrative, with such an assertion gives our friend some considerable poetic licence. We also know there is a certain necessity or at least drive to make sense out of our dreams by recounting them in narrative form. Certain dreams appear to have such a vividness and significance to us that it is only in part by being able to recount them to another that we then appropriate them in some way. Furthermore, when they are disturbing or confusing we may hope that through discussion we will understand what their 'real' meaning might be. One's experience of such recounting and interpretation points to the potential therapeutic value of dream interpretation. Understanding the processes whereby the narrative construction and (re)production of a dream in the psycho-therapeutic context can trigger associations and feelings central to the analysand's work within therapy.

This chapter begins by looking at contemporary theories of dreaming which concentrate on establishing an empirical foundation for the study of dreaming, where the latter is viewed as primarily a cognitive activity. We then go on to consider a second aspect of contemporary research and the major theoretical framework for the study of dreaming, namely, psychoanalysis. There is little doubt that our cultural ideas about dreams have been profoundly influenced by Freud and psychoanalytic theory. One aim of this chapter is to provide an overview of the psychoanalytic approach to the study of dreaming. Given the emphasis throughout the book on understanding the social semiotic underpinnings of image recognition and production, our discussion then turns to the relationship between structuralism (particularly semiotics) and psychoanalysis, before concluding with an examination of Freud's original theory of dreaming.

DREAMS AS PROBLEM-SOLVING

Contemporary interest in dream psychology within psychology departments (e.g. Hars et al. 1985; Blagrove 1992; Buellens 1996; De Koninck et al. 1990) focuses primarily on whether what we experience in dreams is something to do with solving problems in waking life. The general idea is that dreaming can be likened to such conscious cognitive activities as imagination, analogical reasoning and creativity (Blagrove 1992). These mental states are then used to explain instances of problem-solving during dreams. It is not just dreams which serve such a purpose, the psychiatrist Buellens (1996) commenting on nightmares notes, 'From a psychophysiological point of view nightmares are possibly derailed attempts of problem solving, of overcoming frightening experiences' (p. 12). The enduring idea here is that dreams are adaptive and functional, and given such an orientation, physiological measures of activity during sleep have long played a role in mapping out the parameters of the dream world, particularly the use of the electroencephalograph or EEG recorder, a technique for recording brain wave patterns.

Since the earliest studies of sleep, when it was noticed that there is considerable electrical activity in the brain and corresponding eye and muscle movement, a kind of folklore has grown up around the 'mind/brain' activity of a sleeping person. The early electroencephalographers described themselves as blind men trying to guess the workings of a factory by listening outside the walls (Hassett 1978). Such a metaphor has provoked further commentary; for example, Gray (1991) has stated that:

> You can't tell how the machines inside a factory work by listening outside the walls, but you can get some idea of the total amount of activity. You can tell, for example, when things have partly shut down and when they are going full steam ahead. If you listen long and hard enough you may begin to make finer distinctions than that, and if you also observe the factory's outputs you may be able to determine which sounds correspond with which outputs. Similarly, by correlating the types of ink squiggles recorded in the EEG with subjects' overt behaviour or reported moods, researchers have developed a basis for using the EEG as a rough index of psychological states.
>
> (Gray 1991: 221)

More recently, researchers in this area have distinguished between a *true dream* and something else simply termed *sleep thought*. The distinction arises from narrative accounts people provide on being woken up during REM sleep. The dreamer typically has the experience of moving around in or viewing a real environment, however bizarre, where events and actions relate to each other in at least some minimal way. In contrast, when woken up during slow-wave sleep (non-REM), people admit to some sort of general mental activity, but activity which tends to lack the sensory hallucinations familiar to the true dream. Often describing dreaming in terms of adaptive function, the kinds of theories proposed by researchers in sleep laboratories are somewhat prosaic. Essentially, dreams are viewed simply as side-effects of physiological changes taking place during REM sleep, changes which ensure that nerve cells in the brain get enough exercise during the night (Foulkes 1985; Hobson 1988; Edelman 1987).

Analysis employing REM measures, comparing and interpreting accounts from people woken during REM and non-REM sleep, may as much tell us about prevailing cultural ideas about the purpose of dreaming, as uncover specific scientific facts concerning dream functioning. First, REM sleep has little bearing upon what is normally understood as information processing within cognitive psychology. Horne (1988) has demonstrated that REM activity is a more general factor concerning arousal of the nervous system of humans and animals alike. Second, we dream in REM and in non-REM sleep and in a sense the issue is thus quantitative, not qualitative. Third, it remains unclear whether the association of REM with cognition is interlinked with the numerous hormonal changes going on during sleep. Nevertheless, one only has to consider the following passage from an introductory psychology textbook to be reminded of the prevailing ideas regarding the nature of dreaming:

> REM sleep is sometimes called paradoxical sleep; internally the body is aroused while externally the body is calm. Even more intriguing . . . is what the rapid eye movements announce: the beginning of a dream. Even those who claim they never dream will, more than 80 percent of the time, recall a dream after being awakened during REM sleep. Unlike the fleeting images of Stage 1 sleep, REM sleep dreams are often emotional and usually story-like. (People occasionally recall dreams when awakened from stages other than REM sleep, but these dreams usually contain a single image, such as 'I was trying to borrow something from someone.').
>
> Are the eye movements linked to a dream's visual aspects? Is the dreamer 'watching' the dream as if it were a private movie projecting in the mind's inner theatre? Most researchers believe not: the darting eyes, like the occasional twitching of muscles, may merely reflect the overflow of the dreamer's nervous system.
>
> (Myers 1998: 214)

The phenomenon called REM sleep is itself perceived as a puzzle – if there is electrical activity then the mind is said to be aroused, yet the body is calm. Leaving aside the observation that there are no studies which look at the social practices prevalent in a sleep laboratory, i.e. what constitutes an appropriate account of a dream on being awoken from sleep, it is notable that dreams are judged on a qualitative dimension of 'image' content or frequency. Emotional, story-like dreams have more status than simply statements or assertions. And finally, we can recognise the more dominant metaphor underpinning much of this research: dream activity as an energy release procedure.

Alongside this essentially psychophysical approach where dreams are viewed as simply the side-effects of neuronal activity, one finds the problem-solving perspective of cognitive psychology and the hydraulic metaphor central to the psychoanalytic account, where dreaming acts as a safety valve for unconscious excitations. Given that extensive reviews of this literature can be found within psychology and psychoanalytic journals, the aim here is simply to focus on the more general concepts or metaphors which underpin much of this work.

In a critique of the problem-solving approach, Blagrove (1992) distinguishes between the three types of problem-solving dreams. Dreams of one type are said to be adaptive for waking life, a second type exhibit creativity and novel problem-solving within the dream but are of no relevance on awakening, and a third type are said to reflect adaptive strategies known in waking life. His general thesis is that problem-solving dreams are very rare. Our waking concerns, but not our cognitive abilities, are translated into the enigmatic dream representation: meaningful but not adaptive. For Blagrove (1992) what is at issue is not whether dreams can provide a stimulus for problem-solving, but rather whether the process of examination of the dream provides whatever solutions are forthcoming. The idea that dreams help us to solve the problems we have in daily life derives some support from those few occasions where we realise something, on waking, as a result of trying to make sense of what we have just been dreaming.

Most of the time, however, our experience of dreams, and the language and ideas we use to explain dreaming, paints an image of the 'dream world' as an environment where we are more likely to encounter puzzles than to solve problems. Arguably the main reasons why psychologists conceive of dreams as problem-solving phenomena rest on the dominance of the cognitive–computational metaphor in psychology (Montangero 1991), and the desire to link together research from psychophysiology with broader themes in cognitive science. It is clear, however, that there is some considerable distance between the psychophysiological approach to dreams and the perspective taken in cognitive psychology. Rather than conceiving of dreams as being some sort of background 'problem-solving' repository, a place where solutions automatically occur in a way unknown to us, the classic position is that, when we are awake, we can use our memories of dreams to reflect on problems we suspect are beyond our everyday comprehension. Of course, the minute we talk of what we remember from our dreams when waking, then we have already moved to dream interpretation and thus to psychoanalytic perspectives.

PSYCHOANALYSIS, STRUCTURALISM AND SEMIOTICS

Any discourse on understanding the images we encounter (report) in dreams is already informed and engendered by psychoanalytic thinking. Freud hinted at the semiotic nature of dream analysis in his book *Interpretation of dreams*:

We are thus presented with a new task which had no previous existence: the task, that is, of investigating the relations between the manifest content of dreams and the latent dream-thoughts, and of tracing out the process by which the latter have been changed into the former. The dream-thoughts and the dream-content are presented to us like two versions of the same subject matter in two different languages. Or, more properly, the dream-content seems like a transcript of the dream-thoughts into another mode of expressions, whose characters and syntactic laws it is our business to discover by comparing the original and the translation.

(Freud 1976: 277)

From a structuralist perspective, psychoanalysis serves as a prime example of structuralist methodology, given the essential reliance placed on the function of language in our lives. As the talking cure, psychoanalysis is linguistic through and through, but the process of analysis highlights the fact that all sign-systems place boundaries on our attempts at self-expression. Through the process of analysis both analyst and analysand recognise that trying to express, through language, whatever is underneath the concerns or trouble initiating the analysis, is often difficult and forever partial. In trying to understand the images we encounter in dreams the question arises as to why semiotics and structuralism might have any bearing on our endeavours. A number of structuralists have argued that one of the most important functions of semiotics is to provide a method whereby people can become aware of ways of reading signs around them, and coming to see how a society's meanings may be manipulated by those who wish to influence others (e.g. Sturrock 1986: 94). One of Peirce's most ardent followers, Morris, considered semiotics as crucial to the education of the young, arguing that

a truly democratic society would aim, as a matter of principle, to enlarge and diversify the sign capacities of its members. Only in such a society would semiotics be given a basic place in the educational process, so that the individual would be prepared to resist the exploitation of himself by other users of signs, to avoid pathic signs in his behaviour and to make his contribution to the constant correction and creation of signs upon which a healthy society depends.

(Morris 1971: 289)

It is important to recognise the significance of semiotics for dream interpretation and the relationship between such analysis and the associated discourse of psychopathology. The general point about avoiding 'pathic' signs in one's behaviour (Goffman 1959) is of interest when considering the role of dreams and semiotics. The observation that a number of familiar mental conditions can be described in semiotic terms, given that they find expression in the 'linguistic performance' of the person concerned, has particular significance for dream interpretation. The claim has been made that all mental illnesses or disturbances can be described as defects in the sufferer's semic or signifying powers. Certainly, as Sturrock points out, if the integrity of the 'semic act' is threatened in some way because one party is semically disadvantaged and fails to display and use common (conventional) signs, then this can lead to a loss or difficulty with sociability and communication.

Consider in this regard the nature of the psychotherapeutic situation. The therapist is presented with somebody who considers that their communicative capacity, with themselves and often also with others, is being affected somehow by disturbed feelings, emotions, irrational behaviours and so on. The analyst's role is to somehow make good the breakdown or distortion of communication by identifying those signs which might be understood as symptoms of bodily malfunctions, disturbing dreams, irrational phobias or whatever. The task of the Freudian analyst is to recover contents that have been successfully *repressed* by the client. As presented by the client, these symptoms either are without content or have been given a content with which the psychoanalyst will be dissatisfied, believing that their 'real' content is other than what it appears to be. So, for example, the client might be reporting that other people find him/her very arrogant and aggressive, leading to difficulties in social interaction. This behaviour, however, turns out to be a defensive strategy against potential feelings the client might experience if he/she was rejected by somebody when they were simply being themselves or expressing what they really felt. As Sturrock (1986) notes, 'the Freudian psychoanalyst is thus the very model of a semiotician . . . Freud's own description of the method which he evolved was that, in its early days psychoanalysis was above all an art of interpretation' (Sturrock 1986: 95).

In semiotic terms Freud extended the area of recognised significance in human life quite dramatically, by bringing people to admit as signs phenomena which would previously have been thought trivial or meaningless. Jokes, slips of the tongue, *double-entendres* and dreams are the staple diet of Freudian analysis or 're-reading', where they might become charged with a new significance. However, it is important to recognise that for semiotics, and structuralism more generally, it is not the nature of the interpretations which psychoanalysis specialises in that are of interest, rather the methods employed to produce them. A fundamental premise of these methods is that dreams, or acts of forgetfulness, are not interpretable as isolated entities but as events within a certain psychic system, the relations between the parts being the essence of Freudian thought. And essentially the psychic system is made up of the tripartite differentiation between Ego, Id and Superego. Sturrock (1986) again:

> The old idea of the Self as a unitary principle or force that is absolute master in its own bodily house has found it hard to recover from Freud's tripartite division of the psyche into Ego, Id and Superego; these three elements would certainly seem to form a structure since they are unthinkable in independence one from the other and are constituted by the relations

which join them. Their respective 'values' within any individual shift constantly, and psychic 'health' is taken to depend on their preserving a certain 'equilibrium'.

(Sturrock 1986: 96)

To understand the role of dreams with regard to this image of the psychic system requires a more detailed examination of Freud's theory of dreaming.

FREUD'S THEORY OF DREAMING: A CENTRAL ASPECT OF PSYCHOANALYTIC THINKING

Numerous writers within and beyond the boundaries of psychology and psychoanalytic studies have commented on the significance of Freud's mature theory of dreams culturally, scientifically and with regard to clinical and therapeutic practice (Sulloway 1979). Freud's analysis of the psychology of dreaming can be viewed as having three main features: the state of sleep itself; the processes of censorship and regression; and the dream-work. Together these elements form a framework within which the process of how dream-thoughts transform into dream-contents becomes a central theoretical construct. Freud's explanation of how the one is turned into the other depends greatly on the syntactical operations that he called 'condensation' and 'displacement'. Condensation occurs whenever a single signifier or expression in the manifest 'dream-content' is shown by analysis to have multiple signifieds or contents in the latent 'dream-thoughts'. This phenomenon is sometimes described as 'over-determination', and 'displacement' occurs whenever what the analyst believes to be the 'true' content of a manifest expression is found in other than its rightful place in the sequence of such expressions, lurking, that is, behind a false signifier. In order to get a better idea of how these ideas fit with one another we can use Sulloway's navigational map of the (mature) theory of dreams, as in Figure 4.1 (after Sulloway 1979)

There is little doubt that this conception of dreaming has had a significant influence within and beyond psychology, for example in film studies and art, and continues to inform contemporary theories of dreaming. Closer examination also highlights the conceptually rich nature of the theory, something of a marked contrast to alternative theories of dreaming discussed earlier. This conception of the many processes said to be involved in the dream state has to some extent become part of our cultural outlook, certainly such that we rarely step back to consider why, when we talk of our dreams, and indeed waking thoughts, our ideas are presupposed on this Freudian framework. First, it is important to recognise that within this scheme of things, no matter what we believe about our identity and our everyday experience of who we are, our minds are somehow not really our own. There is always a disproportionately large part of our being which is unknown to us, unconscious and somehow motivated to undermine, displace, disrupt and generally usurp our conscious

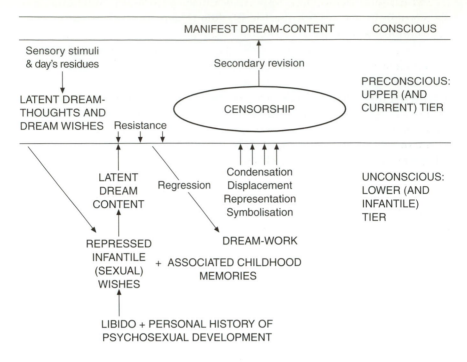

Figure 4.1 Freud's mature theory of dreams (after Sulloway 1979)

sense of experience and ego-identity. Viewed positively, in line with Darwinian thinking, it is essential for our survival, never mind acceptable societal conventions for behaviour, that certain primary developmental processes and drives become overlaid with inhibitory processes (such as repressing sexual desire for close relatives). Considered negatively, this is a concept of the mind forever divided, at least at one level, where what is unacceptable, frightening, incoherent, unsavoury and in large part bound up with our early experiences, constantly seeks to express itself through the life-force (libido), and is always a threat to our sense of identity.

Of course, the socially unacceptable nature of our unconscious drives is resisted by our conscious self or ego: we are forever expending energy in repressing that which is primitive, uncontrollable, distasteful in our own psyche. Freud, and to an even greater extent Lacan, emphasised that the child's introduction and enculturation into society through learning language leads to the formation of ego-identity, while at the same time repressing all those many desires within the child considered unacceptable. In becoming a positioned subject (through language) we enter into a lifelong process of repressing all that is understood to be anathema to ego development. During dreams, however, when the normal defence mechanisms associated with conscious thought (awareness) are loosened, unconscious desires, associations and repressed wishes seek to find expression and generally 'come to the surface' of our awareness. Thus in Figure 4.1 we find the driving force of the libido seeking to express repressed infantile wishes (often of a sexual nature) acting upon the preconscious tier of the mind. On then encountering resistance from the preconscious tier a process of regression takes place leading to what is termed the dream-work.

Sulloway (1979) highlights the nature of censorship and regression in Freud's theory, noting with regard to the former that the power of censorship (over the unconscious) is not totally abolished during sleep. The 'censor' is meant to ensure that the state of sleep is not seriously disturbed by wishes which are constantly emanating from the unconscious, generating intolerable ideas and would-be affects. Censorship acts upon such troublesome desires in distinct ways: first, the preconscious greets the wish with an initial round of censorship and simply prohibits its entry into consciousness. The unconscious wish is thus forced back (regresses in a backward direction) and obtains visual representation by 'cathecting' (energising) the perceptual system. With respect to regression Sulloway (1979) notes:

> This regressive process is the reverse of the normal, daytime flow of energy from the perceptual system to consciousness . . . Associated memories that have been aroused by the dream wish become visually cathected in this regressive process, and the dream wish itself is subjected to considerable distortion by the dream-work. These disguised dream thoughts now make their second attempt to enter consciousness, at which time another, but less severe, round of censorship may occasion gaps within the final, manifest content of the dream.
>
> (Sulloway 1979: 335)

Two points are worth emphasising here. The notion that infants and children have a sexual life or even desires is very troubling for parents and adult society in general. This partly arises from the very conception of sexuality as something that mature adults hold (more often than not directed at and involving another). For children, however, sexuality may be better understood as their predisposition for self-exploration, taking pleasure from their bodies and the whole host of feelings and sensations which arise from the gradual awakening of corporeal sensation. Yet at the same time, we recognise and understand that when parents discover their offspring displaying or performing self-oriented pleasurable acts, condemnation or at least prohibition is appropriate and required. In some sense, then, we need to conceptualise repressed infantile desire as the repository of memories, feelings, associations of primitive pleasures prohibited by those around us in the myriad of everyday interactions in our personal histories. Becoming an adult involves our accepting the many prohibitions we encounter as children.

A second thing to note in this account involves the particular misunderstandings which surround the term regression. In an everyday sense we understand regression to mean a going back to an earlier stage of life or development, indicative perhaps of failing to come to terms with some current situation. Laplanche and Pontalis (1988) draw our attention to the fact that for Freud the term regression had to be understood as something involving the flow of energy through psychical systems, i.e. in a topographical sense:

> Freud introduces the idea of regression in order to account for an essential characteristic of dreams: the dream thoughts arise for the most part in the form of sensory images which impose themselves upon the subject in a quasi-hallucinatory fashion. The explanation of this trait calls for a topographical conception of the psychical apparatus which views it as made up of an ordered succession of systems. In the waking state these systems are traversed by excitations in a progressive direction (travelling from perception to motor activity); during sleep, by contrast, the thoughts, finding their access to motor activity barred, regress towards the perceptual system. It is thus above all in a topographical sense that regression is understood by Freud when he introduces the idea.
>
> (Laplanche and Pontalis 1988: 386)

This regression of the latent dream content, now combined with both sensory stimuli and the previous day's residues (of images), results in the dream-work, the complete set of operations which transform all this raw material so as to produce the manifest dream, distortion being the result of dream-work. Some comment is required on the mechanisms which constitute the dream-work – condensation, displacement, representation and symbolisation – but it is important that we keep in mind the observation that the dream-work is in no sense 'creative' (i.e. based solely on a unique transformation of the images experienced), or to paraphrase Laplanche and Pontalis (1988), it is the dream-work and not the latent content which constitutes the essence of the dream: the dream is in essence the work it carries out.

As the name suggests, condensation is where a dream-image is some kind of composite of a variety of other important images. By allowing the summation of cathectic energies from different ideas and images, condensation is said to facilitate the dream's regressive path toward perceptual representation. The important point here is that condensation ensures that the manifest content of a dream is always much smaller than its latent content. Freud provided a flavour of what he meant by condensation in *The interpretation of dreams*, noting:

> It may operate in various different ways: sometimes one element (theme, person) is alone preserved because it occurs several times in different dream-thoughts ('nodal points'); alternatively, various elements may be combined into a disparate unity; or again the condensation of several images may result in the blurring of those traits which do not coincide so as to maintain and reinforce only those which are common.
>
> (Freud 1976: 83)

The image of condensation is as a process which Freud accounts for in eco-nomic energy terms; psychic energies which have been displaced along different associative chains accumulate upon whatever idea is situated at their point of intersection, 'If certain images – especially in dreams – acquire a truly exceptional intensity, this is by virtue of the fact that, being products of con-densation they are highly cathected' (Laplanche and Pontalis 1988: 83). So, for example, during analysis the analysand may report seeing a particular person in a dream and something about the person disturbs or unsettles him/her. By exploring the associations and ideas associated with the person, it becomes apparent that although the content of the dream might simply be represented as the image of however the person is, the recounting and re-reading of this condensed image brings out a whole host of deeply disturbing emotions, affect and long-repressed psychic elements.

Displacement is the second principal mechanism or governing agent of the dream-work. This occurs where a latent dream-thought is replaced by some other idea that is distantly related to it along the pathways of psychical asso-ciation. 'Displacement, like condensation, serves the purpose of dream distortion by modifying the affective content (degree of interest and intensity) given to the latent dream-thoughts in the manifest dream-façade' (Sulloway 1979: 336). The third aspect of the dream-work has particular significance for our understanding of images in dreams. Here, Freud's proposal was that the psychic system responsible for dream-work demands that all meanings, even the most obscure and abstract thoughts, are expressed primarily through visual images. Laplanche and Pontalis (1988) note that speech, talking to oneself or conversations enjoy no special privileges, their role in dreams constrained to that of meaningful elements in the dream. In other words, there is no sense in which the meanings of conversations in dreams bear any relation to the sense they might have in ordinary spoken language:

> the transformation of thoughts into visual images may be in part the result of the attraction which memories couched in visual form and eager for revival bring to bear upon thoughts cut off from consciousness and struggling to find expression. In this view a dream might be described as a substitute for the infantile scene modified by being transferred onto a recent experience. The infantile scene is unable to bring about its own revival and has to be content with returning as a dream.
>
> (Laplanche and Pontalis 1988: 390)

Turning to the fourth element of the dream-work, Sulloway (1979) focuses upon the crucial role of symbolisation, arguing that it deserves special notice:

> A symbol is something that depicts, and stands for, something else, sim-ilar to – but distinct from – an allusion, a metaphor, a simile or a highly indirect representation. Unlike representations, however, symbols are not created during the dream-work, since they already exist in the unconscious

and are merely seized upon during dream formation. The dreamer, more-over, knows nothing of symbolic meanings, which therefore escape censorship while subserving representation. Freud considered symbolisa-tion as being, along with censorship and the dream-work, an independent means of distortion in dreams.

(Sulloway 1979: 337)

We should note, however, that the term symbol has come to mean very dif-ferent things in psychoanalytic theories of dreaming, particularly as a result of the work of Lacan. Freud's idea of the symbolic restricted it to mean all the symbols which have a constant meaning and, in part, constitute the products of the unconscious. They were essentially conceptual entities and may or may not be linguistic. Lacan, however, has written extensively on the structuralist nature of psychoanalysis and emphasises what he calls the 'symbolic order': the domain of language which client and analyst must enter into. Client and ana-lyst meet like any two other individuals who share a sign-system, within the symbolic order, even though the language they use does not exhaust the con-tents of their psyche: the incommunicable or ineffable remains as what cannot find admission to the 'symbolic order' but is the unique psychic possession of the individual. There is always more than language. This inexpressible realm is not to be identified with the unconscious, because the Lacanian uncon-scious can be brought to expression: it is that which is either missing from the exchange between client and analyst, or that which enters the exchange in a perverted form: 'the unconscious is that chapter of my story which is marked by a blank or occupied by a falsehood: it is the censored chapter. But the truth can be recovered; most often it is already written elsewhere' (Lacan 1977: 124).

   It is quite difficult to recognise what this conception of the unconscious means for Lacan, and the place of dreams within this perspective. One way to think about this, is that Lacan wanted to dispense with the idea that the unconscious is a place, a sort of psychic 'cave in the mind' where all our worst fears, instinctual drives and so on reside, ready to (re)present themselves in part through the dream-work. And part of the difficulty we have in understanding images of the unconscious is derived from the 'store-like' or compartmentalised idea we have of memory. If we move to thinking of memory as something much more dynamic, amorphous and linked to the particular history of every individual as a series of events, we can begin to picture that which we call the 'unconscious' as interdependent with the long history of activities, feelings, anxieties and pleasures we have experienced. From birth there has been a con-stant nurturing of our expressivity by those around us – the projection of desire of the Other which constitutes part of our being, accompanied however by an ongoing repression of all that is considered undesirable, inappropriate, irrelevant or simply unnoticeable. In other words, our parents, in their desire for us to become healthy human beings, implicitly project through their lan-guage an idealised notion of who we are, and what we should become. At the same time, every interaction during the early years of our lives has involved (explicitly or implicitly) the repressing of that which the 'Other' considered undesirable. This Other is expressed in the language which constitutes our self-positioning, through the social practices presupposed in the structuration of everyday life, and through our own (often obscured) recognition of some essential gap between our phenomenal experience and the constraints of language (including self-dialogue). Again, the enduring idea is that what has been repressed will eventually come back – again articulating the dominant nature of the psychic energy metaphor pervading psychoanalytic thinking.

Finally, the last component of Figure 4.1 is secondary revision. Our experience of dreams is that they can be bizarre, weird, involving terror and despair or inexpressible pleasure, but often with a sense that we have been somewhere that defies explanation. On waking up after dreaming, it is normal thinking, not the unconscious or the dream-work, that demands some degree of intelligibility. Laplanche and Pontalis (1988) define secondary revision or elaboration as the 'rearrangement of a dream so as to present it in the form of a relatively consistent and comprehensible scenario' (p. 412). It would be a mistake, however, to think of the secondary revision as part of the dream-work. In a sense, this process acts independently of the dream-work, always with the purpose of fulfilling 'conditions of intelligibility'. Probably a good way to think about this process is to recognise that when we are near to waking, or where we have to recount (as if in narrative form) the contents of a dream, the very process of articulating an account can only be accomplished in light of what a 'rational explanation' might be. Quoting Freud on this point, Laplanche and Pontalis (1988) emphasise that secondary revision resembles rationalisation in the sense that the system is required to come up with a relatively coherent account or construction of events such that intelligibility of the material is realisable. The idea is that somehow the process of secondary revision provides us with something much more akin to a day-dream than psychotic disunity. For Freud the dream-work was initiated by certain events and experiences during the previous day which triggered unconscious wishes, 'when sleep finally sets in, the pace of the dream-work is merely accelerated. A dream, Freud explained, is like a firework which takes hours to prepare but goes off in a moment' (Sulloway 1979: 339).

We can pre-empt concluding comments on Freud's mature theory of dreaming by reminding ourselves that the upper tier of Figure 4.1 focuses upon the current form of the dream and includes the preconscious day's residues and the latent dream-thoughts, as well as their final night-time product, the manifest content of the dream. In contrast the lower tier is organised around the dreamer's repressed childhood libidinal impulses and associated childhood memories. This tier contains the ultimate motivation and meaning of the dream. Dream interpretation is focused on revealing these two major levels of significance.

CONCLUDING COMMENTS

For a psychology of the image, this short journey into the ideas, theories and proposals surrounding dreams and our understanding of them can only touch upon the complex nature of the phenomena, and the language which surrounds it. There is little doubt that psychoanalytic thinking continues to inform, if not define, the ideas and concepts regarding dream images. Psychophysical perspectives remain rather simplistic and fail to do justice to the significance that dreams have for us in our daily lives. Probably only very few of us refrain from reflecting on the content of our dreams, even when only dismissing them as curious outcomes of something which happens when we sleep. Possibly the influence of Freudian thinking is so culturally pervasive that we find it hard to believe that somehow dreams can be understood as a 'cognitive' activity, at least in the sense that they involve rational or critically reflective components (Blagrove 1992). Within and beyond psychology the 'mind' is forever split against itself in some way, and dreams provide the fabled 'royal road to the unconscious'. More than anything else, the reason why we might feel we would have had to invent the concept of the unconscious, had Freud not done so, is the loss of conscious control or volition we experience when dreaming. Having said that, one other enduring image of the dream is that somehow the dream state always belongs to another world or dimension (Karon 1996; Clark and Loftus 1996). Dream therapists, or at least those of certain marginalised schools of dream analysis, go as far as to say that within dreams we obtain messages from other worlds, noting the long historical and cross-cultural belief that the gods, spirits and alien creatures communicate to us through dreams (Schweitzer 1996).

The social-cultural basis of dreaming, our experience of dreaming as such, the images we recognise when dreaming and the discourse we use to interpret our experience, are often glossed over or ignored (Lippman 1998). The enduring idea we have of dreaming is that it is the private and internal image-creating process *par excellence*. However, it is clearly impossible to claim having experienced or perceived something in a dream that does not already exist as a semiotic object. Even to claim that one has seen an unrecognisable 'thing', nonetheless invokes that semiotic category – the class of all unrecognisable objects. Perceiving dream images may in a sense be no different from recognising objects and images when awake, and as we noted in Chapter 2, there are enduring difficulties in conceiving of perception outside of language and description. What is different is the language or discourse we have for talking about the experience of images and events in dreams.

Theme II

Interdependent images

Inside and out, or outside and in?

PREFACE

Earlier chapters on the nature of mental imagery, sound imagery, dreams and conceptions of the unconscious, have highlighted the prevailing emphasis in psychology on the differentiation between internal and external image worlds. For the most part discussion has focused on the diverse accounts within psychology and psychoanalysis aimed at understanding the images, impressions and associations said to constitute mental life as such. However, as noted previously, differentiating the internal from the external relies on particular philosophical ideas regarding cognition, consciousness, phenomenology of being and the situatedness of having a body in the world. The psychology of the image proposed in this text aims at developing richer theoretical frameworks for studying images in psychology, and at highlighting the importance of our everyday exposure to images, and focuses on giving due respect to people's own experiences and understanding of images.

The next three chapters look in more detail at the boundaries between internal and external images, in order to better understand the relationship between what within psychology are commonly taken to be quite separate domains. Three topics will be examined in order to investigate whether our understanding of images is interdependent with our exposure to particular social semiotic systems: images of the child and the developing self; the self-image and public reputation; and images of that most compelling form of display, gender.

These three areas within psychology are particularly interesting and relevant because they lend themselves to either internal or external explanatory frameworks; for example, what it is to have a sense of self-consciousness compared to taking care of one's public image. Identifying specific debates between theoretical perspectives within each area highlights issues that a psychology of the image can address, over and above the fact that conflicting viewpoints draw attention to the disparate nature of the discourses which inform these areas. The topics themselves are selected because of the interrelationships between them: ideas of the developing self can themselves be gendered (Bem 1983), self-image is said to depend upon certain stages of a developing self (Brooks-Gunn and Lewis 1984), and self-identity is arguably interdependent with the display of gender (Goffman 1979). We turn first to images of childhood and the developing self.

5 The developing self

IMAGES OF CHILDHOOD: THE EXPECTED BABY

The images and associations which surround the word 'development' are varied, diverse and sometimes ambiguous. The notion of development underpins the idea of learning in a progressive fashion, the attainment of knowledge, finding 'oneself', discussions of maturity, and many other ideas and associations which presuppose change as an 'onwards and ever upwards' process. However, it remains unclear precisely what we mean by development, that is, outside of descriptions and discussion which focus on measuring change in the structure of physical bodies, cognitive skills, social competencies or whatever. Developmental psychology has at times reflected on the nature of its central definitions, particularly in light of the criticism that what constitutes the discipline is not explanation, but description. Burman (1994), for example, argues that the discipline promotes very limited and constraining (and indefensible) views of the universal nature of development. It concentrates on the significance of the individual, the downplaying of the socially based nature of child 'production', and has an ethnocentric focus on individualism which detracts from the difficulties and concerns of child-rearing.

Ideas of childhood are certainly diverse and redolent with positive notions of innocence, play, carefreeness, amusement, nurturance and care, alongside negative associations of dependency, irrationality, aggression, mess, control, worry and ever-present demands. Historians have pointed to the sociological and economic circumstances which surrounded the 'production' of childhood as a state of being and an emerging social class (children) from the late twelfth century (Higonnet 1998; Schultz 1995). Sociologists have noted that the construction of childhood as a social category has led to a disparagement of children's own productive labour, within and outside the home, and a refusal to recognise that they may have rights of their own (Morrow 1996; Alanen 1989). We also have an enduring image of childhood as time, positively as the fantasy we have of that period when we were free of responsibility (all that entails with attaining adulthood). In contrast we hold negative images of childhood as that time full of fears, rejection, abandonment, misunderstandings, frustrations and hidden unfulfilled desires, resulting in memories which undermine our current attempts to sustain happiness. We talk of 'acting like children' regressing to a state of infancy, behaving like an adolescent or juvenile. Our language is permeated with discourses on, and of, childhood as that state/time which cannot be regained, and yet something to which we can apportion 'blame' for our current problems (at least in part).

As a way of framing the following discussion on images and ideas of the developing self, we can begin with some observations on those discourses which inform our understanding of the child before birth. Notwithstanding the idea that the birth of a second child can be radically different (for parents) than that of the first, for many people the very knowledge that a child is imminent engenders a whole host of ideas, fears, beliefs and anticipations and, importantly, social practices which serve to position the child in a particular way before she/he exists. In other words, before the child is born a position or space for him/her is produced by those around him/her. And this 'position' is in large part produced in light of the ongoing social-discursive practices regarding childhood which prevail in a given society. These practices are embedded in the immediate close family, and lay beliefs about the nature of the children themselves, and understood with reference to academic theories of development which underpin social and educational policy. Consider, for example, an image taken from a pregnancy magazine describing the development of the foetus (Figure 5.1). Note first the image clarity of the foetus compared to the mother. Not only is the mother's body only partial, it is 'faded' somewhat and clearly of secondary importance to the 'baby within' – except that is for the breasts, with the nipples marked out as a 'baby-relevant', highlighted aspect of her body. Whatever else the mother's body is, first and foremost it is a container for the foetus. If anything, one is left with the impression that the baby has somehow taken over and 'possessed' the mother, an interpretation born out by feminist analysis of the repressive discourses on childbirth in Western medicine (Thomas, J. 1995). The associated text accompanying the image further highlights the cultural presuppositions informing this discourse:

> *What's*
> *happening . . .*
> *to your baby*
> Your baby's brain wave patterns are maturing, and she's becoming more aware of her surroundings.
>
> Her eyelids will remain sealed until the end of this month when she will start opening and closing her eyes.
>
> Her nostrils have opened and the air sacs in her lungs have developed. But they will have to mature more fully to prevent them collapsing when she breathes air. However, if she was born now, your baby would have a good chance of surviving.

She can suck her fingers and thumb and may have hiccups from time to time. This is believed to be caused by her swallowing the amniotic fluid.

She is becoming very active. To avoid the umbilical cord knotting or kinking and cutting off her air and food supply during all this movement, it is covered with a substance called Wharton's jelly.

She is about 34cm (13.5in) long and weighs about 0.6kg (1.31b).

Week 34

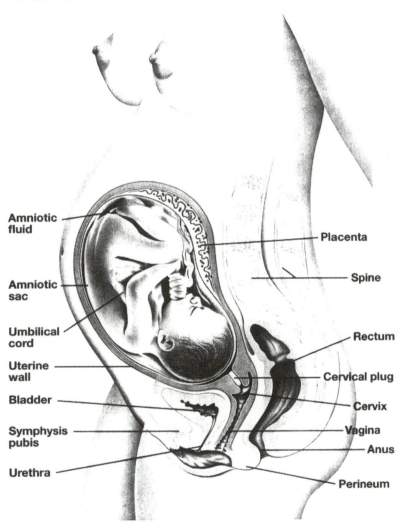

Figure 5.1 Baby during one of the nine magical months. Reproduced with permission from Mother and Baby Picture Library

In this text, there is no question or doubt over the status of the foetus as agent, "she's becoming more aware". She is active, conscious and somehow intentional. The discourse is predicated on constructs of separation (she is a separate being even though inside the mother), agency, intentionality and a conception of development as a journey. The text also addresses the assumed fears, beliefs and interests of the audience: chances of survival, the potential collapsing of the lungs, the knotting of the umbilical cord, what the baby can do and so on.

Compare this everyday or lay discourse with that of the medical student. The images and text for the same time period from *Gray's Anatomy* are informed by a quite different set of assumptions and ideas (Figure 5.2(a)). Here the mother's body does not exist at all. The foetus is not only an object of scientific enquiry (its very 'objectness' emphasised), but is presented in a series of images depicted to highlight an embryological perspective on development – the foetus itself represents the measurement index on such a scale. We might also note the somewhat curious expressions on the faces of the foetuses in Figure 5.2(b). One reading of the changes in the types of expressions used, is that the foetus is moving from being an 'alien' to something akin to a human infant, yet uncertainly so (and unsurprisingly male in this example).

The related text serves to underscore the objective (scientific) sense of the discourse:

> *Remaining lunar months.* Throughout the remaining lunar months of normal gestation the covering of vernix caseosa is prominent. There is a progressive loss of lanugo, except for the hairs on the eyelids, eyebrows and scalp. The bodily shape is becoming more infantile, but despite some acceleration in its growth the leg has not quite equalled the arm in length proportionately even at the time of birth. The thorax broadens relative to the head, and the infraumbilical abdominal wall shows a relative areal increase, so that the umbilicus gradually becomes more centrally situated. Average lengths and weights for the eighth, ninth and tenth months are 40, 45 and 50 cm and 2, 2.5 and 3–3.5 kg.

In contrast to the earlier text, in this scientific/medical description, notions of agency and intentionality with respect to the foetus are entirely absent. Notice also that presupposed in this description is a particular model of human proportionality and symmetry (third sentence). The phrase 'even at birth' articulates the particular medical criteria underpinning what constitutes normal development after the baby has been born. If nothing else, a comparison of such images and the discourses which accompany them highlight the wide variety of views and assumptions informing ideas of development.

In a recent volume entitled *Deconstructing developmental psychology*, Burman (1994) considers parenting magazines and other child advice literature, noting

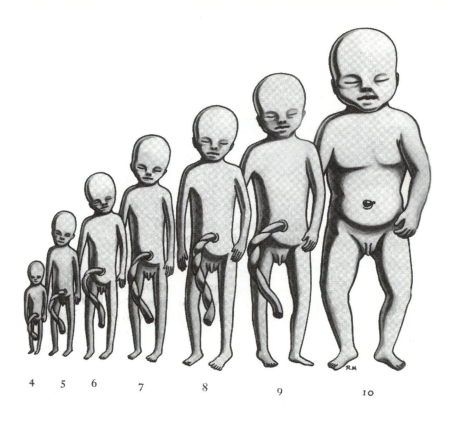

Figure 5.2(a) Changes in relative size at the foetal ages (lunar months) indicated

that the idealised accounts of mothering, the family, pregnancy and child care work against those who cannot attain what is considered conventional or appropriate. Our worries and concerns for our children (e.g. timing of their first steps) derive from conceptually impoverished accounts of development, discourses which have only occasionally been the target of post-structuralist critique. Essentially, developmentalism consists of the production of, and reliance on, explanatory statements concerning natural regulation of changes in the human life-span. Similarly, citing Walkerdine (1993), and in line with post-structuralist thinking, Morss (1996) argues that the very idea of development is not natural and universal, but a very specific European patriarchal story, a metanarrative that occludes other marginalised stories. In contrast, their anti-developmental approach 'involves the critical scrutiny of developmentalism, and the search for systematic alternatives to developmental explanation' (p. 51). Morss (1996) also notes that to a surprising degree Marxists have treated childhood as a kind of pre-history, as a biological phase

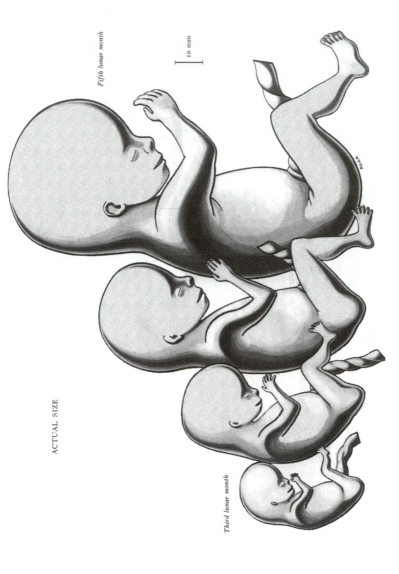

ACTUAL SIZE

Fifth lunar month

10 mm

Third lunar month

Figure 5.2(*b*) Progressive changes in foetal size and proportions over three months

prior to the individual's entry into the social world. He also argues that Freud, alongside his traditional approach to evolution and development, espoused an anti-developmentalism, not least through the continuous revision, restatements and reformulations of his work. In *Beyond the pleasure principle* he argued that what might look like development is really a strategy of constant repetition and replacement. Morss comments on Freud's ambivalence to developmental explanations, 'We must not be deluded by the appearance of progress in developmental change. People may repeat previous experiences, may seek to reinstate previous situations, but it would be misleading to say that people "develop"' (Morss 1996: 105).

THE CHILD IN PSYCHOLOGY: IDEAS AND IMAGES OF LEARNING AND DEVELOPMENT

Before moving on to consider in detail ideas of the developing self, we can look briefly at three of the more popular ideas on learning and development, those of Piaget, Vygotsky and what has become known as the theory-of-mind tradition. Extensive reviews of these theories, the findings which support them and the status they hold in developmental psychology can be found in Smith et al. (1998) and Durkin (1995). For now I simply want to consider some of the images of the child which emerge from these perspectives.

Probably more than any other person, Piaget has had considerable influence in developmental psychology. Piaget was first and foremost a genetic epistemologist and was interested in identifying what he termed the biological substrates of knowledge. He was critically concerned not with content, whether a child knows x or y, but with the underlying cognitive structures which make knowledge possible, and how these structures function in relation to the environment. Piaget's earlier ideas, although somewhat diffuse, emphasised the importance of representation and egocentrism, while his later work is best understood as a mathematical model of cognition (called the Grouping). This theory was Piaget's attempt at capturing the essence of the child's cognitive activities. It is not simply a kind of list (of what a child can and cannot do) but an abstraction which describes basic processes – from which one can infer the evolution of a comprehensive and integrated structure. The image we have of the child is of somebody who finds it difficult to understand the point of view of another person during the earlier stages of development, subsequently acquiring the requisite level or complexity of internal knowledge structures in order to act competently in the world.

One noticeable shortcoming of the Piagetian approach is that it derives from a logical mathematical conception of human cognition, an orientation appropriate only for particular kinds of representational processes and cognitions (e.g. problem-solving, inferential processing, number manipulation, solving physics problems). The emphasis is on particular forms of knowledge which most people might only consciously engage in less than 10 per cent of the time, and children considerably less. Attempts at utilising the Piagetian perspective for the study of development outside of a restricted set of cognitive tasks have met with only partial success (Chapman 1986; and see Forrester 1992 for a review). We are left with the distinct impression that Piagetian 'knowledge structures' are highly abstract idealised conceptions of what it is to think, reason and engage in hypothetico-deductive inference. The enduring image one is left with is that before the child reaches adolescence he/she is essentially only partially human.

Moving to Vygotsky's (1934) views on development, this increasingly popular perspective can be considered as a particularly unique combination of Marxist, Darwinian/evolutionary and structuralist/semiotic ideas, as various researchers have noted (Sinha 1988). The social interaction context is the starting point, and social-cognitive development consists of a progression from the social to the individual, from the inter-psychological to the intra-psychological. Thus through a child's interactions with other people, initially spontaneous behaviour comes under increasing self-regulated control. For Vygotsky what was important was to identify the initial conditions for, and the development of, self-regulatory behaviour, particularly given that becoming aware of one's own behaviour is the first step towards attaining the status of an independent individual. Consider here how the 'external' becomes the 'internal' through social interaction:

> any function in the child's cultural development appears twice or on two planes. First it appears on the social plane, and then on the psychological plane . . . [it appears] . . . between people as an interpsychological category and then within the child as an intra-psychological category.
>
> (Vygotsky 1934: 93)

And,

> The very mechanism underlying higher mental functions is a copy from social interaction: all higher mental functions are internalised social relationship.
>
> (p. 164)

This process of internalisation transforms the process of development, changing cognitive structure and function. In other words the translation of 'outside' social interaction scenarios into 'inside' internal cognitive structures can itself alter the nature of knowledge structures and the way they function. While it is clear that this idea of development is more sensitive to the reality of every-day interaction, it remains unclear whether it is the 'knowledge mechanisms' which are being internalised, or the knowledge mechanisms and their contents, or whether the internalisation is giving rise to associated 'generalisation' abilities. We are left in the dark about who precisely is 'carrying out' the transformational process, and looking at development in this way presupposes a 'biologically pure' originating epistemic subject. As Sinha (1988) notes, this simply evades the issue of whether development should be conceived as the transformation of the social to the individual, or the individual to the social.

Alongside Piaget and Vygotsky, recent development theory is dominated by computational conceptions of development. One such example, known as the 'theory of mind' approach, gives precedence to the representation/computational role of the child's 'mental states'. Formal cognitive definitions of 'theory of mind' emphasise the link between intentional action, mental states and everyday reasoning, particularly about the behaviour of other people. A theory of mind is said to be a common-sense or folk psychology, and children's theory of mind underlies their ability to give explanations and predictions of behaviour by ascribing mental states to themselves and others. Mental states are expressed in speech acts, and in this view social interaction is an interaction of minds mediated by language. Within this view it is proposed that only older children (aged 5 or more) have metapragmatic understanding and can comprehend the role that language plays in social organisation (Baron-Cohen et al. 1985; Perner 1992; Russell 1996).

Arguably this approach (e.g. Leslie 1987) rests upon a somewhat negative orientation of the child's actions. His/her cognitions are perceived as 'abuse by reference' (object substitution), or 'abuse by existence' (use of imaginary objects). The way in which this model is conceived starts from a particular and, for some, already compromised set of criteria bearing on what representation might be (see Descombes 1980), then offering the suggestion that the only way the child's difficulties (i.e. their lack of ability as implied by the model) can be overcome is by positing meta-cognitive 'de-coupling' mechanisms. Whatever else, we are left with the impression that the development of the child's mind entails a progressive separation of cognition from experience. One is left with the suspicion that this is a conceptually incoherent idea, as how can one be in the world and yet be separate from it?

IMAGES OF THE DEVELOPING SELF

In part, the somewhat anti-developmental critique implicit in the above questions the extent to which developmental psychology has responded to, or even considered as worth addressing, the growing influence of postmodernism in those disciplines bordering psychology (sociology, linguistics, social anthropology). One way of situating and prefiguring the potentially divergent nature of contemporary developmental theory is through considering that most essential (modernist) or contentious (postmodernist) topic: the self or, specifically here, conceptions of the development of the self. The whole nexus of associations surrounding the concepts of agency, subjectivity, identity and individuation have become the focus of critical concern within postmodernist and poststructuralist thinking (Kerby 1991; Giddens 1991; Ricoeur 1992). Correspondingly, there is some evidence that the concept of the logocentric self is becoming an ideologically contested construct within psychology (Gavey 1989; Gergen 1991; Smith 1994). Given this background, clarifying the theories, assumptions and methodological practices which underlie the study of the developing self should help us understand the prevailing discourses which inform theories of the self, and the extent to which such discourses produce or contribute to the contemporary emphasis on an internal/external divide in psychology. In the remainder of this chapter I wish to concentrate on the ideas and metaphors which surround the notion of the developing self.

CONTRASTING ACCOUNTS OF SELF-DEVELOPMENT

A cursory glance at contemporary models of the developing self reminds us of the distinct agendas of sociology (the ideological self), education (the progressive/constructivist self), psychology (the conceptual self) and psychoanalysis (the problematic self). Within developmental psychology Piagetian accounts (e.g. Case 1991) can be found alongside affective–moral approaches (Emde et al. 1991). Arguing that the concept of self follows on from the appropriate level of cognitive development, Case (1991) suggests that children's explicit sense of self, 'derives from their ability to take themselves and their representations as objects of direct reflection' (p. 227), while Emde et al. (1991) propose that emotionally engaging experiences, stored as procedural knowledge, contribute substantially to an affective core of a dynamic self. Given that understanding young children's active engagement in, and participation with, the social world is interdependent with comprehending cultural metaphors for the attainment of selfhood (personhood), articulating the tenor, significance and underlying assumptions of contemporary approaches should aid our understanding.

Here, I wish to concentrate on two approaches to the development of the self, the psychoanalytic perspective of Lacan, and the conceptualist approach found in various guises in contemporary developmental psychology (subsuming computational, symbolic and social-cognitive interpretations), the knowing subject-self. Lacanian self-idealisation continues to have considerable influence in domains beyond psychoanalysis (advertising, film studies, cultural studies), providing a major theme for postmodern criticism, while contemporary developmental psychology appears to be moving either closer towards a neuro-psychological based conception of self, agency and intentionality (Russell 1996), or further extending earlier ecological/contextual accounts (Neisser 1988, 1993). For the present it is clear that the conceptual self remains dominant within psychology (and see Chapter 6). The points of contrast which will serve as a background frame for discussion are (1) the philosophical framing of the self, (2) the self–other distinction, and (3) the relationship between language and the self.

Philosophical framing of the self

We can begin by noting that across perspectives the philosophical status of the subject is rather different. The semio-psychoanalysis of Lacan formulates the originating condition of the self as existentially problematic, to paraphrase Morss (1996), gaining subjectivity more as a fall than as an achievement. The child is born into an experience of 'lack', the forever irreconcilable condition of existence as disunity, incompleteness and loss. At one level, the project is doomed to failure (the child can never again be reunited as one with the mother), irrespective of the strategies invoked to overcome his/her emerging recognition of disunity, and precarious identity. In contrast, the epistemic status of the self in developmental psychology is assured from the beginning. The Kantian inspired version of the conceptual self is motivated by metaphors of progress, advancement, constructivism, and ever-increasing knowledge leading ultimately to possible self-contentment and wholeness (e.g. Kohlberg's sixth level of the moral self – Kohlberg 1976). Separability is itself conceived quite differently. In one, Lacanian individuation is coterminous with social-semiosis and entry into the symbolic order (the entry into language use), in the other, the proto-self subject 'inside the child' strives to communicate so as to facilitate the acquisition of the objective self, a certain level of cognitive ability being necessary for such progression (e.g. Brooks-Gunn and Lewis 1984). The self constructed through and positioned in language can be contrasted with the self learning to use language as a tool serving intentionality. The images of the developing foetus analysed earlier provide an example of a discourse which helps position the baby/child prior to birth. In much the same fashion that images of the child can be interpreted in contrasting ways, so too can discourses of the child in academic accounts of development.

The self–other distinction

Interpretations of the self–other distinction provide a second contrast. The Lacanian developing self begins to emerge only on recognising the existence of a (separate) image reflected back through the Other's desire. In other words, the child is provided with an image of who they are (and *that* they are) through the talk, response and affect directed at them from the mother. The parents' desire for the infant to *be* a child finds expression in what they do and say to him/her. Furthermore, between 9 and 18 months, Lacan's mirror phase, the primary means of the child establishing a difference between him/herself and the world is constructed. Through identification with the body of another, seeing itself (another body) in the mirror, the child responds jubilantly and answers 'That's me!' In saying 'that's me' the child is in effect saying 'I am another.' Lacan considers that the subject can only conceptualise him/herself through the reflected image directed back from the position of desire (the mother's).

Forming a self-conception presupposes separation and alienation. We need to recognise that Lacan's mirror is a metaphor for the imaginary (that which can be identified with me), and it is the ideal of the image which brings the self into being and, at the same time, irretrievably splits the subject-being from itself (image vs. real). In other words, the phenomenal experience of being in a body, and yet seeing an image-reflection out there in the mirror, initiates a sense of identity alongside an awareness of the pain of separation. This is an important idea for a psychology of the image as Lacan's conception of the relationship between the external – that which is projected back to the child from those around him/her – and the internal – whatever sense of identity the child fictionalises as a result of recognising that what is 'reflected back' constitutes part of who he/she is – constitutes the whole notion of identity in the first place. It is essential to remember that for Lacan the mirror is a metaphor describing the formation of identity through the process of interaction.

The nature of the self–other distinction for the cognitive or conceptual self is much less problematic in mainstream developmental psychology. A generalised interest in others emerges during the middle of the second year, evidenced in patterns of looking and gaze-direction, i.e. fulfilling conventional criteria for what sustained interest constitutes (Camioni 1994). Where theorists do place significance on the role of the other (e.g. Neisser's (1991) interpersonal self), a cognitivist orientation on the self still underpins such extensions, 'they *realise* that the person in question is attending to them as well' (Neisser 1991: 206 – my italics). Realising presupposes an entity who can reflect, think and consider. Key moments in the stages of the emerging self are correlatively linked to cognitive and social-cognitive developments (e.g. around the middle of the second year). Self-recognition awaits, and follows from, the development of the cognitive system.

The relationship between language and the self

When we turn to the presupposed relationships between language and the developing self, particular tensions between modernist and postmodernist perspectives become clearer. At risk of oversimplification, the more traditional modernist view considers language as a formal object, a system of signifying relations which exists as a predetermined formal structure, functioning as a communicative tool (and a largely unproblematic neutral entity amenable to analysis). For the most part, the study of language in cognitive and developmental psychology rests upon this orientation (although see Howe 1993). From Chomsky (1957) to Pinker (1996) innateness remains the core explanatory construct underpinning cognitivist-linguistic, and computational, structuralism. In contrast, postmodernist accounts of language focus on language as both system and social semiotic practice (Fairclough 1992; Hodge and Kress 1993), subsuming distinctions reflected in terms such as discourse, discursive practice, speech genre and register. Accordingly, language segments the world according to culture and context (Lee 1992), and in doing so

produces different versions of that reality: ideological interpretations potentially repressive, contestable and always deeply insidious (Foucault 1972).
Language cannot be a neutral context-free entity: as social practice and productive semiosis, whether talk or text, language interpenetrates all forms of
analysis, folk-hermeneutic and formal-analytic. We noted earlier the ways in
which language provides the context for interpreting different images of the
foetus, and it is clear that images do not exist separate from the broader discursive contexts they are embedded within.

With respect to language and the developing self, for Lacan the self goes
through at least two major self–other divisions. The first division is via looking in the mirror, or more precisely the mother's reflective desire, and the
recognition that 'I am another'. Here, the imaginary self takes shape: only in
the Gestalt of the image in the mirror is completeness possible, and the self of
being and the 'other' in the mirror mark the initial division. In acquiring language, a second division becomes superimposed on the first. For Lacan, the
significance of emergence into the symbolic order was coterminous with arguing that the notion of the self is embedded in language. The subject, in fact,
is constituted in language, 'It is a vicious circle to say that we are speaking
beings, we are speakings' (Lacan 1977: 284). The use of the word *I* or uttering
one's name, reminds us that the subject of the enounced and the subject of the
enunciation never fully come together, the subject not one in its representation
in language.

It is difficult to get an idea of how this might come about for the infant.
However, consider a young child quietly helping herself to some jam unknown
to her mother (in the kitchen). On entering the kitchen later, her mother
turns and utters:

'So, you've been at the jam have you?'

Leaving aside the issue of whether the child recognises that he/she is being told
off, more significantly, how do we know whether the child understands that
the mother *didn't* know he/she was helping him/herself to the delights of the
cupboard. The notion or idea of 'separateness' is produced or created in language, and similarly the ontology of the child's being is constituted through
language (you've, have you, and so on). It is well known that when parents are
talking to language-learning children they refer to themselves as mummy
and daddy specifically, instead of the potentially more ambiguous pronoun
forms, as if aiding the children into their allotted position (Snow and Ferguson
1977). For Lacan, the child's realisation of self, attained through the experience
of her positioning in language, is interdependent with a growing sense of the
gap between them: identity of self in language as substitution for the loss of
union (completeness) brought about by birth and separation in the first place.

In developmental psychology the cognitivist self is a mental-state(s) construct, or mental-event representation (Nelson 1996), to which language is
'hooked on' or attached in some way. The existence of a cognitive entity is

inferred (by others) from patterns of orderly behaviour exhibited by the child, and language is a tool or instrument at the service of this (privileged and private) subject. In structuralist inspired individualist accounts of language acquisition (Chomsky 1957), the self and related cognitive constructs remain separate or underlying. Consider for example developmental psycholinguists' proposals regarding the acquisition of the conventions for using pronouns between 2 and 7 years. Karmiloff-Smith (1979) argues that children do not acquire full adult use of the pronominal system until their cognitive capacities are sufficiently developed. Such systems are formally conceived, external entities appropriated over time, essential tools for communication acquired by the cognising subject-self. Notwithstanding accounts of language acquisition that emphasise the significance of social interaction (Howe 1993; Ryan 1974), for the most part the importance of first attaining a certain level of cognitive ability is emphasised in standard accounts. Within developmental psychology modularisation of affective, cognitive and language-skill domains remains a powerful idea. As Emde et al. (1991) put it, 'in general we assume that the child gradually adds language, cognitive understanding and shared meaning to ongoing affective–moral procedures, and that many action tendencies thus become rationalised' (Emde et al. 1991: 265).

Possibly, a realisable psychoanalytic-semiological account of language acquisition is itself a paradoxical notion. As Lacanian 'speakings' we cannot be anything other than that which, as positioned subject, the symbolic Other constrains or determines us to be: we don't acquire language, rather as positioned entities in the already existing semiotic system we are interdependent 'speakings' embedded within the language that we acquire. In the postmodernist view(s) of language, it is implied that we can never jump out of discursive practices onto some idealised neutral ground. For the cognitivist, modernist self, while the ability to learn language is seen as an innate predisposition, language will always remain a formal object out there to be acquired and used, the contrast reflecting the conceptual distance between post-structuralist and structuralist formulations of language – social semiosis versus formal object, Foucault versus Chomsky. We can turn at this point to consider one important domain which might contribute towards children learning how to portray appropriate images or versions of themselves, that being through narrative.

NARRATIVES AND THE SELF

As in other areas of the social sciences, the study of narrative has gathered pace within psychology (Hambleton et al. 1996; Hyden 1995). Construing three distinct typologies of narrative – temporal, text-cohesiveness and social-cultural – Mishler (1995) argues for a more inclusive research strategy combining all forms. Despite such proposals for the development of conceptually rich theoretical frameworks (e.g. Mancuso 1996), the focus within the discipline is upon narrative as methodology, that is, using procedures and methods derived from linguistics and critical theory for analysing extended texts, accounts or autobiographies (Somers 1994; Zwaan 1996). Employed in areas as diverse as psychotherapy, health psychology and human–computer interaction (Friedman 1993; Plowman 1996; Sarbin 1985), narrative is generally understood as an additional method for formalising accounts of human action. Occasionally it is also viewed as a predictive procedure for establishing the nature of causal relations (Trabasso et al. 1989). In so far as human action presupposes narrativisation, causality presupposes activity and telos.

The theoretical frameworks and methods of analysis within the study of narrative are likely to be of particular importance to an emerging psychology of the image. We noted in the previous chapter that accounting for our experience of images in dreams rested in part on being able to provide a coherent narrative to ourselves or those around us on waking. Similarly, as parents we spontaneously produce narratives about our children and construct artefacts and processes to service such activities (e.g. baby's first activity diaries, family photograph albums, video-recordings of the school play and so on). As adults, our own parents often locate their ideas of who they think we are within family narratives which have evolved over time.

Within developmental psychology we find four approaches to the study of narrative: analysis of children's story-telling abilities (Blum-Kulka and Snow 1992); children's comprehension of narrative (Nelson 1990); the relationship between understanding narrative and temporality (Engel 1986; Nelson 1996); and the study of relations between memory and narrativisation (Fivush and Hammond 1990; Hudson 1990; Tessler 1991). In addition, there are a small number of theoretical accounts which emphasise the more general role of narrativisation for cognitive and moral development (Bruner 1986; Day and Tappan 1996). For the most part, these approaches to narrative in developmental psychology rest upon formal theory, either grammatical or representational. In other words, narratives are always something external to the child, structural and representational phenomena which he/she has to acquire and understand, before using them in context. And it is within such narratives that one finds the models, metaphors, ideas and images of children and childhood.

For now we can consider the question of the versions of self made available in the talk that infants and young children are exposed to. Although this issue has yet to be addressed empirically, there are different lines of evidence that support the proposal that the sense(s) of self we acquire is in large part determined by the models, metaphors and constructs of self made available in the discourse around us. We can, for example, consider the quite different notions of the 'child-person' presupposed in the social relations central to participation in conversation. Ochs's (1988) work on Samoan caregiver patterns illustrates how the organisation of turn-taking procedures is linked to beliefs and expectations regarding the nature of children. In particular she contrasts the Western predilection for inferring intentionality on the part of the parent with the Samoan emphasis solely on the social consequences of action. Significantly the pragmatics of everyday conversation are determined by the pre-determined status position of participants, and thus for both the Samoan and the Kaluli people (Schiefflein and Ochs 1981) adults do not consider the infant worth speaking to, instead communicating to them through older siblings. If a young child addresses a parent then the parent will reply to an older child, who then speaks to his/her sibling. Thus, the subject positions realisable in conversational contexts are part and parcel of the cultural norms and conventions regarding participation. This is also highlighted by Blum-Kulka's (1993) analysis of American and Israeli families telling stories at mealtimes. In particular, she notes that while all her recorded narratives foregrounded individual selves, the Israeli families are more likely to discuss events where the family ('us') is the main protagonist. With respect to implicit expressions of participant power relations, she notes,

> the parental conversational demands imposed on children index parental power: they set the terms for entry into the hegemonic, adult world of discourse. Simultaneously though, parents engage in socialising practices to ease the children's passage into discourse.
>
> (Blum-Kulka 1993: 365)

Another indication of the intricacies of the positioning of the subject-self in discourse is with respect to the acquisition of the pronominal system in different languages. Investigating the young child's acquisition of 'I–You' pronominal shifting in English, Oshima-Takane (1988) notes that children who have less opportunity of being addressed directly take much longer to learn the skills required for pronominal shifting. If you don't know the practices of subject positioning, and how they operate, you'll find it more difficult to participate in talk. Similarly, Hollos (1977) has noted that children from different social settings (urban vs. rural contexts) show distinct patterns of acquisition for the pronominal distinctions employed in Hungarian. In this language the pronoun terms used communicate criteria such as deference, intimacy, solidarity and distance, and learning to employ them appropriately depends on exposure to particular types of contexts (different terms are used depending on the formality of the interaction). In other words, learning the syntax of the pronominal system is interdependent with understanding the institutional status of the 'self–other' positioning employed by those around the child. The 'I' made available for the enunciating subject is already predicated on a specific formulation of the participant's status position, an orientation formulated explicitly in Japanese (Harada 1976) and Tamil (Brown and Levinson 1978).

It is also the case that in many cultures parents exhibit distinct preferences for the public version of the 'child-self' they wish their own offspring to display. Children are tutored quite specifically about appropriate behaviours and attitudes when interacting with adults in different contexts outside the home

(McHoul 1978; Wells 1981). Through such tuition the child is introduced to the set of practices which constitute his/her subject position in context. And for the most part, such positioning remains implicit in the talk, that is, pre-supposed by the models and metaphors of whatever 'self' is embedded in the parents' discourse.

What is important about exposure to a social life within the conversational context is the invitation (by virtue of one's humanness) to participate in its pro-duction. Exposure to, and participation in, talk both provides the young child with lessons in how conversational structures are parameterised, and also tutors him/her in the appropriate discourses for that cultural niche. These will include discourses on 'being a self', 'having a character', displaying inten-tional agency and so on. In her analysis of children's fantasy play activities, Whalen (1995) demonstrates the considerably sophisticated nature of the dis-course genres endemic to participation. Children's play in particular may provide one centrally important context for 'trying out' the various role posi-tions reflecting different discourse genres (e.g. schoolroom vs. home-cooking), where different stagings (and characterisations of self) can be enacted. Tutoring of subject positioning, and its associated accountable consequences, would be part and parcel of the child's early engagement in talk with her peers. Whatever else is going on, it seems clear that narrativisation is interdependent with the construction of selfhood.

CONCLUDING COMMENT

In the earlier sections of this chapter we looked briefly at examples of dis-courses which inform our understanding of children and development. The subsequent analysis of theories and metaphors of the developing self indicates that developmental psychology has yet to engage with key ideas within post-modern thinking, particularly critiques which articulate the relationship between ideology, power and discursive formulations. We need to be careful, however, to distinguish between discourse as text (e.g. from the parenting magazine) and discourses which are part and parcel of ongoing interaction (talk). When children are learning how to take up the 'subject positions' of the situated self in context, this is very much a dynamic, ongoing and, to some extent, contestable social practice. Certainly, the discourses of the child repre-sented in magazines, books and academic theories will inform the content of what participants say during such situations, but the active, practical and potentially open-ended nature of interaction itself should caution us against assuming that we take up positioned 'selves' in some sort of causally deter-mined fashion. Our capacity to simultaneously orient to contradictory versions of our 'selves' in context cannot be overlooked. With this thought in mind we can turn to consider images of the self more directly.

6　Self-image and social identity

INTRODUCTION

Discussing what we mean by the self appears banal and significant at one and the same time. On the one hand acquiring the language we speak presupposes a 'self', positioned in the very act of talking and listening: we don't have to question the existence of that which seems to constitute our very nature. In post-war Anglo-American culture we also have a language of 'self-indulgence', a derogatory discourse for those who engage in over-examining that primary assumption of Western thinking, the self that simply exists as the initiating state of being (i.e. the self-same identity of personhood). At the same time, the self is a profoundly significant notion in contemporary culture. We are encouraged to search for our 'real' selves, we talk of adolescence as a period when our sense of self-identity is fragile and incomplete, we aspire to self-fulfilment and are encouraged, whatever else we do, to be our (true) selves.

We are very familiar with the elaborate discourse surrounding this polysemous word: self-esteem, selfishness, self-identity, individuation, ego, higher-self, self-centred, self-actualisation and self-consciousness. The list is endless but of course not exclusive to the abstract and reflective, as self-catering, self-service, self-taught, self-select and self-destruct remind us. Unsurprisingly, academic discourses on the self reflect conflicting philosophical positions on this central idea. Compare for example social constructionist views (Sampson 1989) with cognitivist (Neisser 1991), evolutionist (Gallup 1998) and culturalist (Cole 1980) perspectives. Psychology, as the science of mental life and behaviour, has a long tradition of theories and images of the self. At one time the enduring image of the self was of some overall coherent 'predisposition' which incorporated different aspects of mental and emotional life in a highly stable and organised way. Cattell (1964), the personality theorist, spoke of the ideal self, the real self and the self sentiment, all underlying factors which cohere into a unified entity. The humanistic school promoted images of the 'actualised' self and the quest for individuation through the 'Gestalt self' (Rogers 1968; Maslow 1962). The history of psychology is replete with models, metaphors and images of the self.

We might contrast this obsession with the self in Western psychology with certain 'no-self' doctrines of Eastern philosophy and religion, particularly Buddhist beliefs about existence, karma, the 'self' and the removal of suffering through overcoming desire, becoming unattached and disinterested in personal gain. Within this framework the individual is nothing more than a series or sequence of thrown-together thoughts, sensations, volition and material elements (Huebner and Garrod 1991). To exist at all is by definition a position based on past failures (previous lives) and one should aim to progress or develop such that the 'self' is annihilated. The doctrine places emphasis on detachment, on the idea that only by letting go of all desire, material, self-ish, and pleasurable, can one put an end to suffering. Detachment is also the basis for true compassion, given that self-concern is always compromised:

> Whereas in Western theories, compassion is feeling for another while maintaining oneself in connection with him, in Buddhism compassion is feeling with another so much that one's own self is forgotten or left behind. There is, then, nothing to connect with others, only self-less concern to give them. This means, prescriptively that self-sacrifice is always called for . . .
>
> (Huebner and Garrod 1991: 350)

Noting in passing that such detachment is viewed by some as morally reprehensible (Gilligan and Wiggins 1987; Noddings 1989), we are interested here in the idea of the self-image, an amorphous term but one which focuses on a conception of the self always in relation to others: essentially self-image discussed with reference to how others view us. Any idea or understanding we have of who we are (or think we are) is formed interdependently with the social context we grew up in, the long history of our interactions with others, alongside whatever constitutes the situations or contexts we now find ourselves in. In line with the suggestion that our internal imaginings, conceptions, representations and images are intimately connected with the myriad sign-systems experienced and produced externally, three elements of the self-image warrant consideration. The first perspective focuses upon the dramaturgical metaphor of Goffman (1979) and his suggestion that the self-images we project amount to role performances, where we are compelled to display versions (images) of ourselves during interaction. We noted earlier that Goffman's psychology was about the relations between an individual and 'ritual' interaction, and his concern was to investigate the procedures and practices through which people organised, and brought into life, their face-to-face dealing with other people. It should be noted that this way of thinking about the self-image emphasises the significance of agency: there is always a 'someone/agent' behind the various 'faces' we are compelled to project during interaction with others.

A second and more contemporary perspective is known as social identity theory. This social-psychological theory of the self emphasises a socially constituted sense of self-identity, one mediating the relationship between self-concept and membership of social groups. In contrast to Goffman's (1979) focus on agency, this image of the self rests in part upon the predominant ideas within mainstream psychology, particularly the central constructs of information-processing psychology (e.g. cognition as categorisation). This perspective deserves critical scrutiny, given that it remains committed to an individualistic 'self-concept', yet at the same time seeks to incorporate important aspects of social relations, emphasising a socially mediated and interchangeable self-image.

In the last section of the chapter we touch briefly on notions of reputation and embarrassment, two areas where the idea of maintaining or warding off threats to a self-image is paramount, before considering the phenomenological approach to the self. This perspective raises questions regarding how external and internal self-dimensions relate one to the other. We conclude by commenting briefly on whether self-image and identity are better considered as narrative representations, part and parcel of the stories we tell ourselves about who we think we are.

GOFFMAN AND THE DRAMATURGICAL SELF

Throughout his work on the nature of the self, Goffman (1959, 1979) advanced the proposal that human action is akin to theatrical performance. The self is a kind of social process where in different contexts we all act 'as if' we are this or that particular kind of person. Paraphrasing Tseelon (1995), central to this dramaturgical metaphor is the idea that people possess a repertoire of 'faces', each activated in front of a different audience, always for the purpose of creating and maintaining a given definition of the situation they are in. At one and the same time Goffman (1959) argues that displaying an appropriate version of the self is a culturally specific phenomenon, yet this ability or predilection is a human universal, 'the construction of "fronts" and the threat of being caught in embarrassing situations is a human constant' (Tseelon 1995: 40).

Goffman had a somewhat marginalised status within the disciplines of psychology and sociology. Psychology considered his writing to be too sociological – that it didn't lend itself to experimental methodology and quantitative analysis – while sociology viewed his approach as over-individualistic with little attention to macro-sociological processes. While Goffman's psychology concerned the relations between an individual and 'ritual' interaction, his micro-sociology should be seen as an attempt to tread a middle course between 'relativity and objectivity'. Drew and Wootton (1988) emphasise that Goffman's concern was to:

> investigate the procedures and practices through which people organized and brought into life, their face-to-face dealing with other people. To investigate this domain required finding means of access to these

procedures and initially ways of conceptualizing these resemblances between different occasions.

(Drew and Wootton 1988: 6)

The value of Goffman's work for our thinking about the self-image is twofold. First, the conceptual sophistication of his 'doctrine of natural expression' serves as a critical commentary on theories which overemphasise cognitive or 'self-categorisation' processes. Displays of what constitutes the self are interdependently anchored to the social context. Second, his emphasis on role-performance highlights an often overlooked aspect of self-image research, that displaying the self is always a dynamic process. This aspect of his theory provides a much needed antidote to conceptions of the 'self' which uncritically assume the centrality of a 'core', static internalised self-concept.

In an essay on the gendered nature of advertisements, Goffman (1979) outlines what he calls the 'doctrine of natural expression':

> We assume that among humans a very wide range of attributes are expressible: intent, feeling, relationship, information state, health, social class and so on. Lore and advice concerning these signs, including how to fake them and how to see behind fakeries, constitute a kind of folk science.
>
> (p. 7)

With regard to the semiotic nature of expressing attributes, he suggests that in our everyday life we routinely seek information about properties of objects (animate and inanimate) that are enduring and in some way read as naturally basic – information about the characteristic or 'essential nature' of people and objects. The fact that such information as 'signs' both exists and is displayed, is a central idea of Goffman's perspective. In an essay on the recognition and display of that essential characteristic 'gender', Goffman (1979) notes that although this most cherished distinction is taken as the prototype of expression, 'something that can be conveyed fleetingly in any social situation and yet something that strikes at the most basic characterisation of the individual' (p. 6), it is nonetheless complex. He comments:

> The human objects themselves employ the term 'expression', and conduct themselves to fit their own conceptions of expressivity; iconicity especially abounds, doing so because it has been made to. Instead of our merely obtaining expressions of the object, the object obligingly gives them to us, conveying them through ritualisations and communicating them through symbols.
>
> (p. 7)

There are at least three things to note about this framework. First, given that there must be a potentially unlimited number of personal attributes which could be attended to, it cannot be the overall structure of performance or display which is expressed but rather specific situationally bound contextual elements. 'Structural' aspects of individual expression are interdependent with the dynamics of any ongoing participation context. Second, this process of expression is intrinsically social, and not reduced or explained away by appealing to the notion of instinct:

> expression in the main is not instinctive but socially learned and socially patterned; it is a socially defined category which employs a particular expression, and a socially established schedule which determines when these expressions will occur . . . individuals do not merely learn how and when to express themselves, for in learning this they are learning to be the kind of object to which the doctrine of natural expression applies, if fallibly; they are learning to be objects that have a character, and for whom this characterological expressing is only natural.
>
> (Goffman 1979: 7)

What is important here is that these configurations of what we take to be natural expression are not elements passively processed in an everyday fashion, but instead are an integral part of what we produce or what can be generated in social situations.

Third, the distinction between 'biological elementism' and human display in Goffman's thinking needs to be emphasised. As others have noted, biological sex determination must be distinguished from gender display, or as Goffman (1979) puts it:

> These acts and appearances are likely to be anything but natural indexical signs, except insofar as they provide indications of the actor's interest in conducting himself effectively under conditions of being treated in accordance with the doctrine of natural expression. And insofar as natural expressions of gender are – in the sense here employed – natural and expressive, what they naturally express is the capacity and inclination of individuals to portray a version of themselves and their relationships at strategic moments – a working agreement to present each other with, and facilitate the other's presentation of, gestural pictures of the claimed reality of their relationship and the claimed character of their human nature.
>
> (p. 7)

This quotation exemplifies Goffman's position regarding the production of images of the 'self'. Such projections are said to be 'gestural pictures' of the claimed status and reality of the participant's own 'inner' nature. These signs, symbols, displays or expressions of our 'personhood' on the one hand are to be read as evidence of our real selves, yet on the other can only be recognised as such with respect to the semiotics and language game germane to the kind of individual one is claiming to be. In a sense such displays can be seen as the production of membership category devices: specific discourses of the self which are only recognised as such within the minutiae of the ongoing interaction and always presupposed on participants displaying a mutually agreed orientation to their production and relevance (Sacks 1992; Antaki and Widdicombe 1998). And the process can be both subtle and complex. To paraphrase Giddens (1988), individuals who *act out* roles cannot be just like individuals who *act at* roles:

> Role distance can be a way of demonstrating supreme confidence in the performance of tasks involved in a particular role. By demonstrating to others that he or she does not fully 'embrace' the expectations involved in a role, the individual might actually validate rather than cast doubt upon its authenticity.
>
> (Giddens 1988: 260)

In other words, precisely because roles are not displayed and carried out in stereotypical ways should alert us to the fact that their very 'spontaneity' or flexibility becomes an important element in their recognition (by others) as displays of authenticity. If you wish to appear convincing in playing a partic-ular role then don't try to do it perfectly, rather act out the part alongside occasional hints that you are aware you are acting in line with the appropriate conventions.

While employing a dramaturgical metaphor, Goffman did not support the idea that reality was essentially constructed. His unique contribution was the application of a kind of social determinism constrained by the structural real-ities operating at the micro-behavioural level. And one expression of such structural realities was his notion of 'frames'. Working on three levels (the physical, social-ecological and institutional), frames are not cognitive objects or mental rules, but rather behavioural scenarios tied to the dynamics of unfolding conversational contexts. These are alignments to situations such that there is a compulsion to behave in some, and not other, specific ways. And where the constraints at one level of a 'frame' are breached or extended there remain in place others which allow for change only in predictable and recog-nisable ways.

Goffman defended the 'realist' view that the physical world exists and has a primary reality (first frame): situations are something that participants arrive at, rather than merely construct. The mental realm, he points out, is not 'a free-floating realm but a derived realm' and 'it is out of the basic physical frame that the mental emerges, always anchored to it' (Goffman 1981: 95). The second social-ecological frame emphasises Goffman's evolutionary position where the importance of 'display' is paramount and so, 'When nothing event-ful is occurring persons in one another's presence are still nonetheless tracking one another and acting so as to make themselves trackable' (Goffman 1981: 103). The third, institutional frame exemplifies the 'institutional' nature of talk, in a way however which again does not imply a causal dependency. Collins (1988), commenting on the notions of frames, notes:

> The rituals of social life should not be regarded as an 'expression' of the properties of institutions; it is a form of activity established 'in regard' of those institutions. There is only a loose coupling to the qualities of the institutions themselves.
>
> (Collins 1988: 53)

Given our interest in a psychology of the self-image, we should note that participants can be in several complex layers of self-definition at the same time. Images or versions of the self can be simultaneously held even where they are contradictory, and this despite our belief that somehow we are always maintaining a consistent, cohesive 'self-concept'. Further, the suggestion that these layers have a structure in relation to one another is for Goffman support for the argument that they are not simply created by the observer, a point often ignored by those who favour the idea of the mutual construction of worlds of 'intersubjectivity'.

With the individuated focus of contemporary psychology and the long-held significance of a core 'inner self', it is not particularly surprising that we often overlook the fact that producing, maintaining, projecting or defending images of the self is an active dynamic process. This brings us to a second element of Goffman's analysis which can inform our understanding of the self-image, and his emphasis upon the dynamic conversational context, and in particular its sense of immediacy:

> Talk creates for the participants a world and a reality that has other participants in it. Joining spontaneous involvement is a unio-mystico, a socialized trance. We must also see that a conversation has a life of its own and makes demands on its own behalf. It is a little social system with its own boundary maintaining devices.
>
> (Goffman 1967: 113)

Giddens (1988) comments that participation itself, 'presumes and calls forth a monitoring of each individual of the other's responses in relation to the context' (p. 258). And so on occasions where someone does something odd, this is recognised in an 'immediate' sense by those around precisely because such events or behaviours are taken as a display or sign that the person is not quite under control. Again:

> We are clearly seen as agents of our acts – there being very little chance of disavowing having committed them; neither having given nor received messages can be easily denied, at least among those immediately involved . . . in the presence of another . . . every case of interaction thus has a confrontational nature, but it is one typically balanced and managed by the resources individuals mutually apply to ensure respect and consideration for one another.
>
> (Goffman 1963a: 16)

In light of such observations, it is a little difficult to argue that we simply decide to 'hold off' or claim 'time out of' participation while we engage in fairly complex sets of computational activities and inferences. Such an assumption is central to social identity conceptions of the self, as we shall see.

One final important way in which Goffman stressed the 'immediacy' and confrontational character of conversational contexts was through his suggestion that individuals are compelled to 'chronically display' agency to one another, and similarly, it has been argued that the underlying 'self' has no enduring description, but is simply the human capacity for negotiating various performances and transformations:

> We are compelled to have an individual self, not because we actually have one but because social interaction requires us to act as if we do . . . The self is only real as a symbol, a linguistic concept that we use to account for what we and other people do. It is an ideology of everyday life, used to attribute causality and moral responsibility in our society, just as in societies with a denser (e.g. tribal) structure, moral responsibility is not placed within the individual but attributed to spirits or gods.
>
> (Collins 1988: 50)

Goffman might have claimed that the self is much more akin to a subset of pre-dispositions or expectations of particular role scenarios. In contrast to Lacan, however, for Goffman there is always an agent or subject who is staging the performance, an issue we will return to in the final chapter.

THE COGNITIVE SELF AND SOCIAL IDENTITY THEORY

Turning to cognitive or rather social-cognitive ideas of the self, a long-cherished lay belief or folk model about self-image and self-identity is that, whatever it is, it is derived in part from the social groups we are members of, grew up in, identify with, belong to and so on. The social psychologist Tajfel (1972), providing one of the earliest definitions of social identity, argued that it is 'the individual's knowledge that he belongs to certain groups together with some emotional value and significance to him of that membership' (p. 31). As a psychologist, for Tajfel (1972) the emphasis was on the individual's knowledge rather than role-performance. Similarly, Hogg et al. (1995) argue that the social category into which we fall:

> provides a definition of who one is in terms of the defining characteristics of that category – a self definition that is part of the self concept. People have a repertoire of such discrete category memberships that vary in overall importance in the self-concept. Each membership is represented in the individual's mind as a social identity.
>
> (Hogg et al. 1995: 264)

What underpins this concept of the self-image is the significance of group processes. In a sense the 'group' is taken as an axiomatic entity, and inter- and intra-group processes considered fundamental to whatever idea of the self one holds, or as Abrams and Hogg (1988) put it, the primary process being:

> how [society] constructs individuals through the mediation of groups represented by normative and consensual practices, and how in turn individuals recreate these groups . . .[and] . . . the central tenet of this approach is that belonging to a group is largely a psychological state which is quite distinct from that of being a unique and separate individual, and that it confers social identity, or a shared/collective representation of who one is and how one should behave.
>
> (Abrams and Hogg 1988: 2–3)

On the one hand then social identity theory is committed to the existence of a 'core' subject self, yet at the same time claims that individuals represent multiple mutually co-existing social identities as separate distinct psychological states. The very process of 'self-categorisation' is interdependent with stereotypical representations germane to specific groups. Turner (1985) clarifies this process of self-categorisation where he claims:

> group behaviour is assumed to express a change in the level of abstraction of self-categorization in the direction which represents a depersonalization of self-perception, a shift towards the perception of the self as an interchangeable exemplar.
>
> (Turner 1985: 100)

Conceptually, social identity is a social construct said to mediate the relationship between the individual and society. In that sense one would imagine the central concern is with understanding the relationship between beliefs and ideas about specific group membership and individuals' role performance, the question being, in what way is any self-image projected or maintained by a person linked to culturally specific images germane to this or that group. In this account we act the way we do because we see ourselves as belonging to a particular group, the salience of the 'group' changing depending on the context we are in. However, as Hogg et al. (1995) note, research in social identity theory has over-emphasised cognitive factors or belief structures, leaning if anything towards a 'psychologisation of behaviour' (p. 264). Deaux et al. (1995), for example, argue that social identities are linked to internal cognitive attributes, themselves interrelated with other related attributes in personal identities. For a research tradition concerned with social psychological theory there seems to be a significant overemphasis on individual cognitive factors.

What social identity theory amounts to is a highly complex (and abstract) notion of internal self-categorisation where as yet unknown cognitive processes operate together in the construction and maintenance of a rational and coherent conception of self. And this conception simultaneously holds to a private (cognitive) self alongside multiple possible, but essentially still cognitive, social identities. Correspondingly, on looking closer at how the structure of self-knowledge is said to be organised, one finds the dominant metaphors of mainstream cognitive psychology (e.g. Swan and Wyer 1997). The work of Higgins (1987) represents the recent emergence of connectionism, and the proposal that discrepancies between internal social identities are best represented and understood as an associationist network, a suggestion that moves the identity aspect of social identity theory even further away from the social world. The concept of self/mind in social identity pays only lip service to the relationship between language, self-image and social identity (e.g. Giles and Johnson 1981).

Comparing social identity views on the self with Goffman's (1979) dramaturgical model, what becomes clear is that the very different conceptions of the self-image reflect in part the adoption of either a 'cognitive dominant' or 'language dominant' perspective on thinking, attribution and self-categorisation. One can argue that there are two general approaches to the mind–language relationship found in psychology: the cognition-dominant orientation, which takes the view that concepts, cognitive states and categorisation processes generally constrain and support thinking and language, and the language-dominant view, where instead, it is our language which determines the order of our experience and the world.

Within psychology the 'cognitive dominant' view has been the preferred option. This is no great surprise given the importance laid upon ideas about individuation, thinking and ego-identity in Western thought and culture over the last three centuries. Essentially, it is the 'existential status' accruing to the existence of propositional attitudes which support the view that concepts underlie language. A propositional attitude is said to describe the relationship between an intentional stance and mental states, a fundamental assumption being that mental states are essentially representational, and psychological concepts 'objects' of intentional stances. So, in order for mental states to exist at all they have to be the end product of a 'cogito' which permits the existence of critical judgement in the first place. The starting point is the assumption of the existence of propositional attitudes, and the status of individuation is assured by the foundational criteria of a 'cogito' or an epistemic subject. Concepts and categorisation processes are then superimposed on to this propositional framework. And one such set of concepts will be those underpinning identity, self, personality and all those essential categories and ideas which are said to underpin our knowledge of the self. Social identity approaches to the study of the self rarely question the epistemic status of the 'core' self-concept, and to that extent remain very much part of the modernist project which is contemporary psychology.

THE 'TURN TO LANGUAGE' AND THE STUDY OF THE SELF

In contrast to cognitive orientations to the study of the self, postmodern perspectives in psychology lean towards the study of language, and an analysis
which focuses on particular social, cultural and institutional practices. In this
way of thinking, if one treats language as a formal object for analysis, then the
rationale for doing so will always rest on certain assumptions regarding what
it is to be objective, value-free, analytic, and all that is entailed in adopting a
scientific approach. Of course these assumptions, when expressed through
social action, are themselves understood as interdependent with the language
you use, the practices you ascribe to, and the historical precedents provided by
prior research, i.e. the procedures deemed appropriate within the particular
cultural context you are in.

   Critical psychology has been drawing attention to the fact that throughout
the later half of the twentieth century, philosophy has been particularly concerned with the problematic status surrounding notions of truth and identity
(particularly European philosophy). This critique is beginning to exert some
influence upon contemporary psychology (e.g. Kvale 1992; Fox and
Prilleltensky 1997), and correspondingly, the social-constructionist orientation
to the study of the self emphasises social practice and social semiosis; the
signs, discourses, performances and actions which represent in one way or
another what it is to 'have a self' or 'display a self-image'. In this view the comprehension of *any* communicative phenomena must rest upon sets of social
practices, and related 'forms of life' without which representational processes
would remain unrealisable. The most significant of these social practices is language, which of course is interdependent with whatever we understand as a
realisable conception of self and other.

   A language/social practice perspective on the self owes part of its allegiance
to existential philosophy. This philosophical outlook rejects the
Cartesian–Kantian view of eternal or absolute truth in favour of an orientation
which focuses on our 'being-in-the-world', where an understanding of our
existence should not entail turning away from our everyday experience. At the
same time, there is a distinct recognition that any answers or glimpses of
understanding will be inherently paradoxical: on the one hand our experience
is that we 'live' in bodies which are quite categorically 'real', but yet our very
recognition or comprehension of self, body and 'other' is interdependent with
our use of language (conceived here broadly as social semiosis). And language
itself 'produces' versions and visions of reality as codes and conventions embedded within particular cultural contexts. However, we are also participants in
the shaping of our world including the multiplicity of discourses (re)pro-
duced and extended in the continuous and negotiated dynamic interpretation
of 'reality'. With this in mind we can turn to phenomenological ideas of the
self.

THE PHENOMENOLOGICAL SELF

Adopting a phenomenological approach to the self entails a significant shift from thinking of the self as a network or mosaic of cognitive associations to an experiential awareness of the body or 'bodiness' as incarnate intentionality. Whatever makes up our understanding or awareness of the self, it is crucially interdependent with our experience of being in a lived-in body. The body is no longer an object somehow separate from thinking or awareness, or to quote Langer (1988):

> Bodily space envelops my limbs in such a way that I know where they are without having to think about them or look for them. Moreover, my awareness of my body is inseparable from the world of my perception. The things which I perceive, I perceive always in reference to my body, and this is so only because I have an immediate awareness of my body itself as it exists 'towards them'. The body image thus involves a primordial, pre-reflective orientation and motility insofar as I am immediately aware of where my limbs are as my body projects itself towards the world of its tasks.
>
> (Langer 1988: 85)

Compared to the cognitivist formulations of social identity theory, this is a much more diffuse and dialectical way of thinking about the 'self-body'. In addition, thinking of the self in this way also highlights the problem of uncritically assuming a cognitive constructionist view of perception (Chapter 2). We seem to forget that it is the very act of taking up a position in a 'lived-in' body which makes it possible to conceive of objective space in the first place, that is with respect to external positions and spatial positioning (in front of; behind and so on). To see at all, is always to see from somewhere and always being in a body, relative to external objects and the 'taking up of a position'. Central to the development of the phenomenological approach was the work in perception of Merleau-Ponty (1962). Langer (1988) points out that Merleau-Ponty concentrates on awakening us to an awareness that all our so-called 'external' and 'internal' perceptions – even our innermost feelings and seemingly self-subsistent thought – are the products of a ceaseless dialectical interaction between the phenomenal body and the pre-objective world. This approach questions the 'mind–body' dichotomy and the differentiation or contrast between the 'internal' and 'external'.

   A phenomenological approach to the self also holds to the idea that the world is not 'ready-made' in some everyday sense. What constitutes the world, the objects within it including the lived-in body, is constructed in an ongoing and dynamic way through the gradual acquisition of habitual actions. Bodily spatiality, which is always inherently dynamic, is 'the very condition for the coming into being of a meaningful world . . . the dialectic movement whereby it takes shape cannot be broken into so many self-contained fragments' (Langer 1988: 57). When we begin to think of the body in this way, the idea that we have a separate 'internal' self is thrown into relief. We can ask, where exactly do we draw the boundary between the 'internal' and the 'external'– at our skin, our clothes, at the end of a walking-stick or wheelchair? As Merleau-Ponty pointed out, to learn to type, drive a car or use a wheelchair is to be transplanted into them, or conversely, to incorporate them into the bulk of the body itself. The boundary of the 'body-self' and a 'mind-self' begins to look much more amorphous or at least unclear, and to distinguish the internal from the external becomes a matter of description, cultural belief and ideology. From this perspective what we mean by 'knowing the self' may be better thought of as a form of narrative representation. In other words, the kinds of stories we construct and tell ourselves about 'ourselves' is a form of discourse first, and only secondarily something which necessarily relates to the mind (self-concept) or an actual lived-in body.

NARRATIVE IDENTITY AND THE SELF

Extending the ideas about narrative introduced in the previous chapter, it would seem that however we understand this idea of the self, describing what it is or giving an account of 'yourself' always entails constructing a narrative. 'I was born in Glasgow and I went to the local convent school, left home at age . . .' and so on. The very act of reflecting on 'oneself' entails constructing a story or narrative which, given the specific circumstances you happen to be in, provides a realisable and self-explanatory account of experience at a specific point in time. Ricoeur (1984) has argued that we tell stories, not in order to impose narrative structure on phenomenal experience, but because living means being always caught up in narratives such that whatever we call the self and the self-image – our idea of who we are – is itself an ongoing, changing and constantly (re)produced narrative account of identity. But unlike the creator of narrative fiction, we are somehow stuck with the characters and circumstances which form the raw material for our accounts. As David Carr (1986) puts it:

> We are constantly having to revise the plot, scrambling to intercept the slings and arrows of fortune and the stupidity and stubbornness of our uncooperative fellows, who will insist on coming up with their own stories instead of docilely accommodating themselves to ours. And the fact that we are ourselves sometimes among that recalcitrant audience, that each of us has his own self to convince and cajole into line, puts paid to any pretensions we might have to anything like being the authors of our own lives: not only do we not control the circumstances, so that they conform to our plans; we do not control our own plans, or even the self who plans, whose very identity is threatened in the internal dialogue whereby we become our own worst enemies.
>
> (Carr 1986: 166)

In an important sense, our subjecthood is not only embedded in the symbolic structure of language as Lacanian 'speakings', but additionally we find ourselves positioned as characters in the plots, narratives and stories of those around us. This is a process which begins early, sitting on our parent's knee and being tutored in the 'art of remembering' and the social practices of narrating (Edwards and Middleton 1988). We quickly learn to narrate our own accounts of everyday life, activity, social relationships and self-identity. And when those accounts begin to lose coherence or appear to be somewhat fragmented, we seek out contexts whereby the business of recounting can initiate or produce a more appropriate narrative account of the self (e.g. pyschotherapy, counselling or simply talking through personal self-narrations with anybody who will listen). Images, metaphors and models of the self become characterisations in the narratives we produce, including self-characterisations.

REPUTATION

Before drawing together some conclusions on images of the self we find in contemporary psychology, at least two other sub-topics on this theme warrant attention for a psychology of the image: reputation and embarrassment. The main reason why these two topics can shed some light on our analysis of the self-image is that in situations where reputation or embarrassment become important we are somehow compelled to reflect on what constitutes the self-image. For most of the rest of the time we really don't think about our self-image. Beginning with reputation, the OED provides two definitions which contrast personal and public meanings:

1   The common or general estimate of a person with respect to characteristics or other qualities,
2   The honour or credit of a particular person or thing; one's good name, good report or fame in general.

Certainly when we reflect on the meaning of the word reputation, it quickly becomes apparent that it seems to cover a multitude of subtle distinctions (Bromley 1993). Associated with the private, the personal and the 'internal' the idea that specific characteristics and attributes somehow coalesce together and provide the basis for a 'reputation' is clearly formulated on notions of accountability, convention and appropriate displays of behaviour in context. But importantly, and with respect to the first definition above, it is something which exists outside of the person. And projecting and maintaining a 'good' reputation is closely tied up with the idea of public 'face'. When we consider how this idea of 'face' might work in everyday interaction, from the perspective of pragmatics, Brown and Levinson (1978) argue that forms of politeness rest upon certain rationalist rules or social conventions of conversation that underpin the concept. They suggest that politeness phenomena exist as a protective mechanism against threats to one's 'face', where:

> Normally everyone's 'face' depends on everyone else's being maintained . . . and since people can be expected to defend their 'faces' if threatened and in defending their own to threaten others' 'faces', it is in everyone's best interest to maintain each other's faces . . . that is to act in ways that assure the other participants that the agent is heedful of the assumptions concerning face governing conversation.
>
> (Brown and Levinson 1978: 46)

The general idea is that everybody has certain wants and desires including maintaining a reputation, and the only way of achieving these needs is to be sensitive to whether other people's actions serve to threaten our interests or in turn, whether our desires are seen as potentially threatening by others. We don't just rush up and demand somebody gives us something, rather we recognise that we will increase our chances of getting something from somebody else through using language in a 'face-saving' way (e.g. 'Excuse me, I know it is a lot to ask, but I was wondering if you could possibly lend me some money'). This idea of 'face' highlights how reputation can be expressed in the micro-detail of everyday interaction.

In contrast to pragmatics, within social psychology the study of reputation (e.g. Bromley 1993; Emler and Reicher 1995) has focused mainly on dispositional or personality factors. Reputation is described by Bromley (1993) as the sum total of opinions expressed about a person or entity in a particular community. In practice, in this line of research, reputation is viewed as a set of personality characteristics that somebody possesses, and which has a direct bearing upon internal conceptions of the self. To paraphrase Bromley (1993), reputation is seen as an extension of the self, something that is uniquely one's own, encompassing the things with which we feel personally involved, family, friends, achievements and so on. As with social identity theory, this theme of research is predicated on the existence of a core self which manipulates perception of reputation in specific ways and is thus open to the criticisms regarding social identity theory outlined above. We might note that there have been attempts at transposing the metaphors and models of cognitive social-identity based reputation onto analysis of institutions and organisations (e.g. Hochschild and Young 1995), a somewhat inappropriate enterprise given that producing, maintaining and promoting an individual reputation will in part be based on any individual's fantasies regarding what it is to possess a reputation in the first place. Why researchers might believe that there is any relationship between individual and corporate/institutional reputation highlights the curious notions sometimes held about supposed relations between internal and external image processes.

Within the public sphere, reputation is seen as much more than a personalised attribute and always a potentially ambiguous discursive object.

Constructing and maintaining the right sort of reputation can be costly for business (Landon and Smith 1998), and in recent years we find the growth of reputation entrepreneurs who can reconstruct image reputation, enhancing community identity for disreputable towns (Campion and Fine 1998), resurrecting company fortunes (Elsbach and Glynn 1996), and promoting marginalised occupations (Ambrosi and Schwartz 1995). Manipulating a reputation can also have profound effects on public life. Mickey (1997) charts the way in which a public relations company exerted considerable influence over the Congressional decision to enter the Gulf War between the USA and Iraq. He notes that the testimony produced by the public relations firm in support for the 'Citizens for a Free Kuwait' group and presented before Congress was never substantiated, despite the fact that this information became the trigger for the US entry to that conflict. In line with Baudrillard's (1988) argument that the signs and symbols used by the media construct their own reality, Mickey (1997) notes:

> Public relations practitioners can manipulate the image because they know the importance people place on signs and symbols in the culture. But, since media technology today gives us the facts as presented simply because they are presented and have little or no reference to truth, one could pose the serious question of whether the field of modern public relations practice must today and in the future be held to even greater accountability and tighter scrutiny.
>
> (Mickey 1997: 271)

There are indications that within public relations research the study of reputation is moving away from psychology and adopting a social semiotic perspective. Porter (1992), for example, looks in detail at oil-company advertisements and brings together narrative and semiotic analysis to highlight how meaning is produced and constrained within such commercials. For now, it remains striking that the relationship between self-image and reputation remains relatively unexplored, and when it is considered, the tendency is to adopt the individualistic cognitivist orientation of social identity theory.

EMBARRASSMENT: MAINTAINING A REPUTATION OR HIDING THE SELF?

Moving to the flip-side of personal reputation, one might argue that embarrassment lies at the heart of the social organisation of day-to-day conduct. It provides a personal constraint on the behaviour of the individual in society and a public response to action and activities considered problematic or untoward. Embarrassment, or more precisely the recognition that many situations or events seem potentially embarrassing, plays an important part in sustaining the individual's commitment to social organisation, values and convention.

Heath (1988) suggest that embarrassment permeates everyday life and our dealings with others, and Crozier (1998) proposes that embarrassment is experienced when an individual recognises that an action can be interpreted negatively by others, even when they themselves agree with their point of view.

Notwithstanding the observation that embarrassment is in large part a culturally bound 'display' or set of display signs, there are many movements and actions we display when interacting which are seen as indications of 'being in a state' of embarrassment. Flustered gestures, blinking eyes, shifting gaze, lowering of the eyelids and even gritting the teeth have been described as constituting the essential signs of what is viewed as an emotional state (Goffman 1959; Keltner and Buswell 1997).

To what extent, however, do we think of embarrassment as an emotional state? Certainly, when feeling embarrassed, particularly when interacting with significant others (people whom you either respect, or feel deferential towards, or who you think can exert an influence on other people's impression of you), we often have an acute awareness of the possibility that signs of our embarrassment are 'leaking out' in some fashion. Whether these signs really are 'exhibited' always remains rather unclear or at least ambiguous (are my ears going red? do people notice I'm stuttering a little? and so on). It remains unclear why we begin to display appropriate signs of embarrassment; however, learning that our body can inadvertently display signs of embarrassment apparently outside our control begins early and is readily focused on by children when reporting on each other's behaviour (Underwood 1997; Bennett and Cormack 1996). For the most part, the display of embarrassment seems to be critically dependent on interaction with others – there are no reported studies on self-examination of embarrassment when alone.

One context where the 'display of embarrassment' highlights the relation between embarrassment and images of the self is in the medical encounter. The conventions which surround appropriate behaviour and display of 'the body' as both a private (personal) and public object provide insights into the semiotic nature of embarrassment as display. In an analysis of the medical consultation of general practice, Heath (1988) describes how patients adopt a characteristic pose or body posture which involves transforming their 'bodies' into objects of examination or inspection. From a video-tape analysis Heath describes how, following an initial opening phase of the interaction where the patient displays the characteristic signs of embarrassment (fidgeting, blinking eye gaze and so on), patients adopt a particular kind of pose which he calls the 'middle-distance' orientation:

> In each case the patient at the moment the examination begins, turns to one side and slightly lowers the eyelids, as if looking into the middle distance, away from the doctor yet at no particular object within the local environment. Whether the doctor is listening to the patient's chest, testing his blood pressure, tapping the body or simply inspecting a difficulty,

the patient looks neither at the doctor nor the areas of examination and seemingly becomes inattentive to the proceedings. As the examination is brought to completion, the middle-distance look is abandoned, and the patient once again orientates towards the co-participant . . . The middle-distance orientation allows patients to cope with the contradictory demands of the physical examination . . . [and] . . . also keeps self-consciousness and embarrassment at bay.

(Heath 1988: 149–150)

Thinking of embarrassment as some form of disturbed, difficult or at least aberrant behaviour (e.g. flustering and stuttering) is not borne out by this form of fine-detailed sequential analysis of actual interactions. Heath (1988) points out that when you actually examine instances where the display of embarrassment is accentuated, it becomes difficult to think of the phenomenon solely in terms of self and identity or ideas of impression management. Thinking of embarrassment and reputation as social constructs reminds us again there remains some distance between folk-psychological and academic/professional theories of the self, and self-display as social semiosis.

CONCLUDING COMMENTS

Analysing images and ideas surrounding the notion of the self highlights the problematic nature of maintaining a strict differentiation between 'internal' and 'external' imagery processes. Goffman's dramaturgical theory focusing on masquerade, display and performance reminds us of what is involved in constructing, portraying and maintaining an image of the self during participation. Social interaction both compels us to display a version of ourselves and provides us with the props, characterisations and scripts necessary for successful deception. We should note, however, there remains an active 'agent' who is playing out all the different roles and images involved. In contrast to psychoanalytic theorising on the nature of identity (always a much more problematic and potentially fragmentary self), Goffman remains committed to the idea of an 'internal' and intentional agent, even though it is an agent who is never 'off-stage', except, possibly, when alone.

In contrast, it is clear that theorising on the self and self-images in psychology is heavily influenced by contemporary and dominant cognitive metaphors. Social identities are 'sets' of psychological states, separate one from the other, yet forming part of the overall 'self-concept'. One is left with a rather confused impression of this image of the self. In particular it seems conceptually incoherent to maintain a core or central self concept which is at one and the same time composed of distinct sets of social identities. Social identity theory leans very much in the direction of an internal image of the self designed as some sort of associationist construct (Tangney et al. 1998), or as a conglomeration of schemas or scripts (Swan and Wyer 1997), and even recently a connectionist construct where the social self embraces neural network imagery (Smith 1996). One reason why this framework continues to exert such an influence within social psychology is linked to the marginalised status that branch of the discipline has had over the last 20–30 years. Social psychology in the USA and the UK has worked hard at emphasising the scientific, particularly experimental, nature of its programme and has reconceptualised many of its original themes and topics in line with the dominant cognitive-inspired metaphors within psychology.

In between the cognitive and social-practice approaches to the self we locate the phenomenological approach. In this approach the problematic nature of differentiating the internal from the external is foregrounded rather than glossed over. Whatever we call the self is interdependent with the experience of being 'in a body'. And yet the boundaries of the body are harder to specify than we would like to think (as any user of a prosthetic device will testify). It should not escape our notice that Lacan was influenced by Merleau-Ponty's (1962) writing on the phenomenology of the body. There is an important sense in which it is only when looking at one's reflection in a full-body mirror or, by chance, seeing your reflection in a shop window that you are provided with a complete and 'whole' self-image. Normally, there is no sense in which you 'feel a complete self' (whatever that might be) during everyday phenomenal experience, and narcissism is sometimes described as the process whereby one becomes captivated by the 'self-image'. Lacan's use of the 'imaginary' mirror/reflection self is a metaphor for the child's captivation in the mirror, and related to this, the notion that the ego-ideal is always an inauthentic agency functioning to conceal a fragmented lack of unity. As we noted earlier, one important aspect in helping create the 'sense of authenticity' when reflecting on the self is through the stories we hear and tell ourselves. As Kerby (1991) put it, 'we are always already caught up in narrative [and] . . . we are primarily story telling animals' (p. 12).

7   The gendered image

INTRODUCTION

Another domain where one can examine the ideas surrounding internal and external images is gender. In this chapter my aim is solely to provide a number of introductory comments on contemporary research in psychology, sociology and cultural studies on gendered images. By gendered images, I mean both the specific images and icons represented in men's and women's magazines, and also more general ideas we have about what it is to be male or female, encompassing the stereotypical prejudices regarding gender display found in many cultures. Nancy Armstrong (1988) has argued that the body functions as an image or sign which we use to help us understand social relationships, 'which include the relationship between ourselves as selves and the body within which as modern selves, we find ourselves enclosed' (p. 2). Some researchers in fact propose that it is simply not possible to talk about self-identity and self-image without presupposing gender identity (Bem 1983). Whether we think of the self as an identity construct, conceptual schema or narrative representation, our self-reflections will be closely linked to, if not interdependent with, our gender identity. Within developmental psychology this way of thinking is represented in gender schema theory, where a gender schema is taken to be a network of associations that form a fundamental part of an individual's cognitive/conceptual framework, and 'gender based schemata' processing, a central characteristic of perception. Critical theorists, however, emphasise the very ambiguity of gender categories, instead defining gender as

> what we make of sex on a daily basis, how we deploy our embodiedness and our multivalent sexualities in order to construct ourselves in relation to the classification male and female. This deployment does not arise from any 'natural' or scientifically representable idea of the body as a physical object, nor is it individually negotiable . . . Sex/gender systems, as we understand them, are historically and culturally specific arrogations of the human body for ideological purposes. In sex/gender systems, physiology, anatomy, and body codes (clothing, cosmetics, behaviours, miens, affective and sexual object choices) are taken over by institutions that use bodily difference to define and to coerce gender identity.
>
> (Epstein and Straub 1991: 3)

We understand the world through the gendered prisms of our own (mis)per-ceptions, notwithstanding those of us who experience conflict when taking on the gendered discourse we are invited or compelled to appropriate (Ekins 1993). One aim in this chapter is to consider some of the explanations for the ways in which women and men are represented, for example in the images familiar to us in the pages of fashion magazines or on television. Why is it, for example, that if you quickly scan through newspapers and magazines you are much more likely to find numerous images of women's body parts than you are of men's. Similarly it would seem that men appear to have a wider range of 'image role models' they can aspire to: the rugged sportsman, idolised pop star, intellectual, scientist, adventurer and so on. In contrast women have fewer pos-itive models and a goodly number of negative ones: hard-headed careerist, ruthless business woman, dull housewife, pop-star past her prime, to name a few. In thinking about such obvious differences we need to guard against cliché and simplistic theorising. Many images of women in women's maga-zines, for example, are constructed in very much the same 'women as object of men's desire' genre as is found in men's magazines. Without some under-standing of the ideological role of discourse, understood here as encompassing images, ideas and language, it might seem curious that women buy into the beauty myth. Women learn to position themselves outside of their own bodies, they compartmentalise, analyse and criticise their body images, rarely seeming to own them in the way men apparently do (Grogan 1998).

Another aim of what follows is to examine the discourses and images which surround the relatively recent literature on masculinities or male representa-tions. It is fairly clear that men are 'imaged' to a much lesser degree than women and more often than not with much less focus on body parts as such. As a white, middle-class, Scottish male I feel a distinct sense of discomfort writing about gendered images, a sense of unease which might accompany any commentary or discussion of images of any group I don't belong to. Nevertheless, one can ask the question, are women more 'gendered' than men? An additional and subsidiary aim of this chapter is to look at one or two attempts at formulating frameworks used in the analysis of images: specifically Kress and van Leeuwen's (1996) image composition procedure and the Lacanian informed methodology employed by Williamson (1978) in advertising. A number of summary comments on the nature of the relationship between gender identity and gender image serve as a conclusion to the chapter.

PUTTING ON HER FACE: IMAGES OF THE FEMININE

Ever since Betty Frieden's (1963) proposal that the depiction of women in magazines served to reinforce a narrow and servile image of women, a significant body of research has lent support to the more everyday observation that women tend to be portrayed as passive, conforming, sexualised and sub-ordinated people/objects. Within contemporary publications (fashion

Figure 7.1 A contemporary image of a woman found in a fashion magazine

magazines such as *Vogue*, and 'women's interests' magazines such as *Cosmopolitan*) images function largely to reflect and reinforce traditional sex-role stereotypes, in which youth and good looks are emphasised, and very often the women defined with reference to the male (either explicitly or more often implicitly).

Reviewing the changes in images in magazines over 30 years, Demarest and Garner (1994) argue:

> Their concerns [new magazines] are more with physical appearance than social equity; with individual adaptation than social action and change. Thus it would seem that despite 25 years of awareness of the 'female mystique', the image and reality of women's roles as depicted in women's magazines are still far apart.
>
> (Demarest and Garner 1994: 367)

One important contribution to recent research on gendered image production and reception is the work of Efrat Tseelon, particularly in her book *The masque of femininity*. Drawing on both Freud and Goffman, Tseelon explores the construction of femininity principally by focusing on the role of fashion, personal appearance and the body in defining the female self. Developing the thesis of 'fashion as deception' Tseelon (1995) examines cultural artefacts and practices as signifiers of ideological meaning. In doing so, she notes that from antiquity (particularly in Western Graeco-Roman mythology) the woman has been characterised as cunning, duplicitous, untrustworthy and evil. Often she is portrayed as disguising herself behind false decoration and using her beauty and finery as a vehicle to dazzle men to sin:

> the woman becomes one with fashion, and the qualities of fashion become fused with her character. From early to medieval Christianity the importance of female apparel formed part of the theological discourse. The moral language of true and false, essence and appearance has become paradigmatic in the relationship between fashion and self, particularly the female self.
>
> (Tseelon 1995: 1)

Drawing parallels between the early Christian idea that the female is 'inessential' and contemporary psychoanalytic theory which defines the 'essence' of femininity as a social construction, Tseelon comments on the notion of 'masquerade', noting that:

> The idea (based on the Freudian notion that the libido is male, 1905) is that the essence of femininity is a dissimulation of the female unconscious masculinity. It is because of her anxiety of the man's retribution for challenging his power that she disguises herself as an object of desire (the castrated 'feminine' woman) to reassure that her power is just a charade.

One finds here echoes of the church fathers' insistent demand on feminine chastity through transcending the body. This requirement implies that the woman can only equal man if she transcends her essential nature: if she renounces that which is quintessentially feminine: the flesh. And if the 'real woman' is a man, a feminine woman is a masquerade. In Lacan's formulation femininity is like a fetish: pretending to hide what is in fact not there – a castrated lack-in-being.

(Tseelon 1995: 37)

The proposal that the woman is artifice and fake presupposes a number of hidden questions, primarily, does she hide her real essence or is she only a series of masks with no essence after all? To answer this Tseelon (1995) argues that one has to establish the meaning of the multiplicity of appearances if one is to understand whether sartorial self presentation is sincere or manipulative.

Addressing the first question, Tseelon (1995) considers both Goffman's dramaturgical theory of role performance, and the more dominant research tradition within social psychology addressing the manipulation of images, impression management (after Baumeister 1986). Critically reviewing the latter, Tseelon (1995) notes that pervading the literature and discourse of impression management is the concept of the great manipulator. What is more, there is a marked division between the private, sincere 'self' and the public, much more 'deceptive', versions of that self managed as a set of impressions. Typically, impression management research lends itself to experimental studies in social psychology where impressions are to be seen as sets of resources, carefully calculated with respect to costs, benefits and so on. In line with the implicitly rationalistic models of social cognition and attribution, the private, sincere mentalistic 'self' that puts on a 'deceptive' appearance does so as a calculated cognitive act.

In contrast, as we noted earlier, Goffman's dramaturgical psychology rests on the language of dramatisation and performance. Here all projections (of appearance) are displays resting upon culturally specific knowledge of signs, signals and conventions appropriate to any staging. However, as we noted in the previous chapter, the essence of self-presentation is that appearing to possess a certain quality is just as important as actually possessing it. Goffman was concerned more with the mechanics of creating an appearance and less with the relationship between appearance and reality. From his perspective both honest and dishonest behaviours are 'staged'.

Noting in passing that the evidence Tseelon (1995) reports, based on in-depth interviews with women, appears to support Goffman rather than impression management theory, important links between stigma and conceptions of beauty can be drawn out. Traditionally, psychology refers to stigma as an attribute of a person where a clear distinction is made between normality and deviance. Elliott et al. (1982), for example, have argued that being stigmatised can have negative effects usually associated with those who lose the protection of social norms (e.g. disfigured people being perceived as deviant and disadvantaged). Goffman's emphasis on the dynamic nature of the processes of stigmatisation (endemic to interaction) is both more compelling and more subtle, given that in any interaction the underlying 'self' has no enduring description, but is simply the human capacity for negotiating various performances and transformations (Collins 1988). For Goffman the self is much more akin to a subset of predispositions or expectations of particular role scenarios, where stigma is processual, being positioned within interaction and expressed as falling short of whatever is taken to be the norms for identity. His argument is that the occasionally precarious, and the constantly precarious, form a single continuum, 'In other words, on the dimension of normality and deviance we do not occupy permanent, but transitory positions. These positions are not persons . . . but perspectives' (Goffman 1967: 37).

Further developing these ideas, Tseelon (1995) emphasises the stigmatised nature of beauty for women. Even the most cursory comparison of the ways in which men and women are represented in the media highlights the fact that we have very different expectations regarding appearance. Paraphrasing Tseelon, women are stigmatised by the very expectation to be beautiful, or at least try their best to present themselves in the 'best possible light': in other words, there is little conventional pressure on men to portray themselves in line with an endemic discourse of beauty, attractiveness and all that surrounds being an object of pleasure (men's pleasure). Irigaray (1991) argues that the very nature of language itself, never mind the discourses on beauty, is deeply patriarchal, i.e. reflecting and reproducing the dominant male perspective to such an extent that an alternative female discourse has yet to be articulated. Through the very process of acquiring a language and entering the cultural discourses available to her, the young girl appropriates, and is positioned within, an identity which regards her natural body as a stigma. If a woman is not careful she will be considered as potentially deviant, not least if she fails to display that she is at least trying to be as beautiful as she possibly can be. Tseelon (1995) again:

> The patriarchal regime . . . defines and judges her through a phantasy model of beauty, which essentially regards her natural body as a stigma. It is for this reason that the physical self becomes the centre of her conception of herself . . . for women physical attractiveness takes on a 'master status' not only when they occupy an extreme position on the attractiveness scale, but even when they inhabit a middle position. Further, this kind of stigma is not constantly negatively reinforced. On the contrary: the experience of being or becoming beautiful can be very rewarding. Rather, this kind of stigma is evident from the anxiety experienced by women in case they 'don't measure up' or are 'caught in the act'.
>
> (Tseelon 1995: 89)

At the very least, there seems to be some sort of catch-22 regarding the relations between women and images of women. Essentially, and given the idealised nature of 'beauty', most women are not beautiful but are encouraged to strive to be beautiful. However, to be seen to be doing so is taken to be artificial, untrustworthy and capricious. There is certainly another whole side to this concept of beauty, those available images of the non-beautiful women, downmarket images in pornographic magazines, the 'always ready to fulfil demands for her family' housewife, the adolescent vixen, the castrater, the silly old bag and many others besides. The whole idea of physical attractiveness, as Tseelon (1995) notes, situates the woman as spectacle, the man as spectator, and 'naturalises' all that comes with gendered image production by making it seem as if it's simply obvious, inevitable and common sense. Ideological forces are at their most powerful and insidious when they become as if invisible.

One additional aspect to this view of the gendered female image comes from the work on eating disorders and what Bruch (1978) has called the 'relentless pursuit of thinness' for women. Researchers studying the onset of anorexia nervosa often note that weight loss becomes a sign of mastery, control and virtue. To quote Garfinkel and Garner (1982):

> Pressures on women to be thin and to achieve, and also conflicting role expectations which force women to be paradoxically competitive, yet passive, may partially explain why anorexia nervosa has increased so dramatically. Patients with anorexia nervosa respond to these pressures by equating weight control with self-control and this in turn is equated with beauty and 'success'.
>
> (Garfinkel and Garner 1982: 10)

Theories about how and why women are influenced by the desire to possess an 'ideal' body shape remain for the most part predicated on cognitive/representational modes of thinking. For example, Myers and Biocca (1992) argue that the process of internalising and adopting a social ideal rests upon the construction of a mental model (Johnson-Laird 1983) that 'may involve visualising oneself in the socially represented ideal body' (Myers and Biocca 1992: p. 129). They suggest that young women 'bond' with the models they are presented with and then fantasise themselves as thin, beautiful versions of themselves. 'It is at this stage that the ideal puts its hook in the young women's self-image (self-schema) by influencing the model of the ideal self they wish to become' (p. 129). In line with many researchers in this area (Shapiro 1988; Hawkins and Pingree 1990), they call for richer and more rigorous cognitive theories to explain the 'cognitive dynamic involved in the construction of a body image or a young woman's self-schema' (Myers and Biocca 1992: 130). Such suggestions are likely to be understood by post-structuralist feminist theorists as part and parcel of the problem: a conceptualisation of, and focus upon, phallocentric individualist cognition.

Whatever other conclusions one might come to about the portrayal of female gender images, it is not difficult to suggest that any internalised image or set of images regarding self-portrayal, sartorial identity and image/role performance is going to be saturated with contradictions and ambiguities. If one recognises the validity of the emerging feminist critique about the endemic patriarchal nature of language and discourse (Cameron 1985; Irigaray 1991), then for the young female child growing up, all understandings, self-representations, incipient self-identities are insidiously contaminated by the dominant male perspective implicit in the very structure of language (Penelope 1990). The very language that she uses to express her innermost thoughts is not an idealised neutral technology for communication: the medium, unfortunately from a woman's point of view, is part of the message. Acquiring language entails appropriating the symbolic order and for the most part this remains an essentially male discourse.

In addition, beyond the language of everyday dialogue, there is a second layer of idealised discourse and representation presupposed in the numerous images within magazines and other such media. Here, even a somewhat cursory analysis reveals that male desire has become female desire. The female image so transparently represents the 'object of male desire' and perversely, in the very process of seeking to display herself in the most attractive way possible, reflects back that desire in her own projected self-image. Tseelon (1995) draws our attention to the subtle and complex ways in which women's own self-perception and the perceived look of the male 'Other' become irretrievably linked:

> The ultimate consequence of existing as spectacle is a permanent dissatisfaction with the visible self. Ample evidence suggests that women (not just pre-pubertal but as young as little girls, and not just those suffering from eating disorders) have a more distorted body perception than men do. In line with the cultural requirement to be thin, they tend to think of their bodies as heavier than they really are. The collective imagination may perpetuate itself by making people slot into age-old cultural positions unaware.
>
> (Tseelon 1995: 76)

Over and above these observations, Tseelon (1995) highlights the fact that the primary image of woman within Western thinking is that of the 'inessential' or even absent. Essentially, she points out that theology and psychoanalysis have constructed an image of the feminine which is radically 'non-essential'. Images of the self are clearly interdependent with images of one's gender yet it does seem that women are more 'gendered' in a sense than men. At the same time, and at risk of stating the obvious, it would be a mistake to forget there are significant institutional interests focused on (re)producing the predominantly Western images of women, or more precisely, interests that wish to ensure women themselves take on board the beauty myth.

IMAGES OF MEN: DOMINATION, POWER

Only in the fairly recent past has the study of gender roles, relations and images turned to masculinity, and understandably, with some theoretical suspicion (e.g. Hearn 1996). There is little doubt that there is nowhere near the same 'cultural focus' on images of men in contemporary society. For men there is nothing like the same concern with body-image as there is for women, considerably fewer of them are affected by eating disorders, and comparatively little pressure is placed on men to attain any sort of ideal body image. And only in the last few years have we seen the emergence of magazines for men containing 'idealised' images of men, images which reflect a style or genre readily identifiable from women's magazines (for example, the man in Figure 7.2 displays a very stylised body stance and gaze, described by Goffman (1979) as one example of a submissive 'body cant').

Within cultural and media studies a literature has grown up in recent years focusing on a wide range of topics under the umbrella term 'masculinities' (see Mac an Ghail 1996 for a review) with some criticism from feminist and critical studies standpoints, given that contemporary analysis of masculinity is in part a psychologisation of certain feminist perspectives. McMahon (1993) notes that:

> many descriptions of masculinity are really descriptions of popular ideologies about the actual or ideal characteristics of men. In the literature on masculinity, the ideological nature of the term is most clearly theorised by the term 'hegemonic masculinity', defined as the 'culturally exalted form of masculinity'. In popular usage, notions of masculinity (and femininity) are inextricably embedded in naturalising and policing discourse, which construct appropriate models of gendered practice, and which can be used to bring the appropriateness of an individual's gender identity into question. Thus, men may well experience themselves as 'expressing their masculinity' or experience doubts about the status of their masculinity.
>
> (McMahon 1993: 690–691)

It's certainly not difficult to find rather extreme conceptions of masculinity, for example as represented by Bly (1990) with his proposal that masculinity is that which is assumed to lie underneath cultural expressions of gender. In this somewhat defensive anti-feminist view male essence is obscured or lost due to a lack of appropriate initiation ceremonies in the modern world. Hearn (1996) notes that to begin the analysis of men with masculinity/masculinities, or to search for the existence of masculinity/masculinities, is to gloss over the fact that it simply cannot be assumed such a construct exists in the first place, given that, 'to do so is to reproduce a heterosexualizing of social arrangements' (p. 214). In other words, the very language we use serves to reproduce the divisive gender categorisations endemic to human relations. To talk of

Figure 7.2 The male body cant: appropriating an image style. Photograph by Bob Richards GQ/Condé Nast Publications Ltd

'searching' for essential masculinities, even if theorised in line with feminist ideology, simply serves to perpetuate a patriarchal discourse.

At the very least any adequate theory of masculine gender images has to have the concept of power at the centre: it has to both reflect the fact that masculinities are 'structured' in dominance and, in turn, help maintain or reproduce that dominance. It should be emphasised that in what follows we have moved away from discussing gendered images as such, and on to the more general ideas surrounding masculinity. If anything, such a rhetorical shift reflects the relative absence of attention on male images in contemporary culture. Examining the relationship between masculinity, power and identity, Edley and Wetherell (1996) provide a useful overview of four principal ways in which images and ideas of masculine gender have been theorised: psychoanalytic, social relations theory, cultural perspectives and role theory. Beginning with the psychoanalytic account, the classic Oedipal narrative describes how a natural desire of sexual interest in the mother is recognised as problematic for the male child, given that he has a rival in the form of the father. Recognising the greater power of the rival leads to a fear of castration and, over time, a move on the child's part to identification with the father. In turn, this motivates a move away from expressing sexual desire towards the mother, and directing it instead at other acceptable females (acceptable to the father, that is). Keeping in mind that the psychoanalytic account is metaphorical, and not reducible to the actual influence any two parents have over a child, the significance of the Oedipal complex derives from the fact that:

> it brings into play a proscriptive agency (the prohibition against incest) which bars the way to naturally sought satisfaction and forms an indissoluble link between wish and law, a point which Jacques Lacan has emphasised.
>
> (Laplanche and Pontalis 1988: 286)

This should not obscure the fact that whatever constitutes the actual experience of maternal desire is probably more complex than generally recognised and certainly full of ambiguity. Freud (1925) himself noted that a boy has not merely an ambivalent attitude towards his father and an affectionate object-choice towards his mother, 'but at the same time he also behaves like a girl and displays an affectionate feminine attitude to his father and a corresponding jealousy and hostility towards his mother' (p. 226). The dominant nature of the father can be seen to be underpinned by the conditions of the male's own psychological development.

During the 1960s and 1970s a feminist critique and rereading of psychoanalytic theory suggested that (if anything) it was men, not women, who were the more insecure and fragile sex. Masculinity seems to have a permanently defensive air about it, or, to paraphrase Edley and Wetherell (1996), men are in a constant state of uncertainty about their own gender identities: always in a state of having to prove themselves as men. In related contemporary work

(Frosh 1993; Hollway 1984) theorists are suggesting that a boy's 'flight from femininity' is motivated not so much by the fear of castration, nor the mother's wish for her sons to achieve an 'appropriate gender identity' but by the fact that the boy sees, from a fairly early age, that in becoming a man he becomes a member of the most powerful half of humanity.

At some risk of over-simplification, there are at least two enduring ideas of masculinity at work here – the independent, self-sufficient macho-man representing strength, fortitude and power, and in contrast the increasingly insecure post-feminist man in flight from the 'feminisation' of contemporary culture, uncertain of his position vis-à-vis women. Commenting on an interview study investigating masculinity and unemployment, Willott and Griffin (1996) find examples of the latter in the close link between discourses of public masculinity and domestic provision. In the words of Gavin, one of their respondents:

> If your partner goes to work, you're always, depending on what job she does, you're always thinking well, 'I'm unemployed like, I can't give her the things she wants, I can't buy her the things she wants.' But there's someone out there that's got a job, got money. And all he's got to do is wave a few wads in her hand like, and she'll walk away with him.
>
> Willot and Griffin 1996: 85)

In other words, the key to understanding the explanations and accounts that men provide, accounts linked to their notions of self-identity, is to be found in the defensive attempts they make to ward off anxiety, to avoid feelings of powerlessness. If this is so, power, not desire, becomes 'the motor for positioning in discourses and the explanation of what is suppressed in signification' (Hollway 1989: 60).

A second theme within the study of masculine gender identity and self-image comes from role theory. Borrowing from both developmental psychology (Archer and Lloyd 1985) and sociology, role theory rests upon the metaphor of social behaviour as adopting roles and performance. Basing his evidence on a review of work in developmental psychology, Archer (1984), for example, argues that, compared to girls, there is much more gender-role rigidity for boys in their developmental pathway to adulthood. He cites in support the work of Eisenberg et al. (1982), who found that pre-school children have an early awareness that boys should avoid gender-inappropriate activities, a sensitivity not matched in the girls' perceptions. Earlier role theorists such as Brannon (1976) argued that the male role consists of four basic clusters: the avoidance of all feminine behaviour and traits (no sissy stuff), the acquisition of success, status and bread-winning competence (the big wheel), strength, confidence and independence (the sturdy oak) and aggression, violence and daring (give 'em hell). Social learning theory underpins much of the research within this area: for example, Fagot (1974) suggests that parents tend to reinforce the assertive behaviour of young boys, while suppressing the same in their daughters.

The question remains whether the oppressive, dominant, subjugating, patriarchal 'symbolic order' implicit in the discourses and language the boy acquires corresponds with his experience growing up as a boy and becoming a man. In contrast to the acceptable conventions expressing femininity, where are men to find an appropriate outlet for their feelings of inadequacy, fears, self-loathing, rejection and so on? In that regard, role theory begs the question of why the two sex roles are defined as they are, and the only logic behind the theorisation of two distinct sex roles is by analogy with men and women as two biologically distinctive categories. Connell (1987) argues that sex role theorists buy into too consensual an image of society, portraying the process of gender socialisation as relatively smooth and harmonious, and failing to appreciate the degree of struggle and negation which lies behind the construction of gender identities: 'they fail to grasp the extent to which the construction of gender identities is based upon the struggle for social power' (p. 101). In large part trying to explain images of masculinity by simply appealing to the rather amorphous process of learning roles somehow evades the question.

Alternatively, the social relations perspective on men views masculinity as a set of distinctive practices that emerge from men's positioning within a variety of social structures – work, the family, local context and so on. Social relations theory argues that masculine identity takes its shape from the various institutions men are located or embedded within. So, if men are aggressive, competitive, emotionally inarticulate and oppressive, then this merely reflects the ways in which men are positioned within our current mode of economic production. And working-class men (because they feel more oppressed at work) will tend to dominate their families more – compared to their middle-class counterparts (see Seidler 1989). Edley and Wetherell (1996) note that the question still remains as to why men want to dominate in the first place.

One answer to the question of men's desire to dominate is provided by Jefferson (1996), who draws attention to the significant relationship between masculine expressions of power and anxiety. He argues that subjectivity is a product of various social discourses and each individual's personal biography, and in line with theories of the developing self highlighted earlier in Chapter 3, he notes:

> Foucault-derived social discourses provide the possible subject positions, and a reworked Lacanian notion of desire enables the actual choices made by particular individuals to be understood. Klein, divested of her biological assumptions, provides the crucial key. The result . . . is to make 'the inter-subjective management of anxiety' central to a theory of subjectivity.
>
> (Jefferson 1996: 158)

Jefferson (1996) calls for a more social reading of the psychoanalyst Melanie Klein (1948), particularly her suggestion that anxiety can be conceptualised as a product of human relations, not nature. The idea is that the defence mechanisms of splitting and projection are constantly implicated in the intersubjective management of anxiety; and it is 'the continuous attempt to manage anxiety, to protect oneself . . . [which] . . . provides a continuous, more or less driven, motive for the negotiation of power in relations' (Hollway 1989: 85). Again, we can understand Irigaray's (1991) criticism that psycho-analytic accounts remain predicated on masculine explanatory discourses: as much to say that, as a man, it is not really my fault that I desire power, it is the result of having to manage deep anxiety implicated in my attaining subject-hood in the first place.

In their review of masculinity Edley and Wetherell (1996) conclude that the above theories simply don't go far enough in explaining the construction and (re)production of masculine identities. They suggest that what is required is a cultural perspective which represents a background framework for under-standing masculinity. For them, masculinity is passed down from generation to generation, through a set of cultural practices carried out by ordinary people making sense of their lives:

> From a cultural perspective . . . every culture in the world must contain its own specific set of ideas or themes which relate to men and masculin-ity . . . these 'cults' of masculinity can be seen as providing members of a cultural community with a shared understanding of what it means to be a man: what one looks like, how one should behave and so forth.
>
> (Edley and Wetherell 1996: 106)

So, the task of the cultural analyst is to pick out these themes, to be able to 'read' what a culture has to say about the meaning of masculinity. The reason why this is seen as an important task is because cultural theorists insist that men become, in a very real sense, constituted through these meanings or 'ide-ologies'. Summarising their views on the relationship between the production of 'meaning' and institutional forms of life, Edley and Wetherell (1996) suggest:

> Men have dominated over women, by and large, because they have man-aged to gain a stranglehold over meaning. What it means to be a man, what it means to be a woman; what jobs constitute men's work and what constitutes women's work. It is the ability to control the ways in which society thinks about these things that has provided men with the basis for their power . . . the point is that because men have dominated many of the key institutions which help to produce and recycle meanings (namely the church, schools and particularly the media) it is usually their 'versions' of the world which 'command the greatest weight and influence . . . [and] . . . secrete the greatest legitimacy'.
>
> (Edley and Wetherell 1996: 108)

Finally it should be noted that the processes whereby men continue to possess a disproportionate share of power are discrete, subtle and complex:

patriarchy, like any other culture, does not declare its own partiality. It does not offer itself as just one sense-making system among others. Instead it presents itself as the way of seeing the world: as entirely natural, normal and straightforward.

(Edley and Wetherell 1996: 108)

These summary accounts of female gendered images, and ideas surrounding masculinity, are strikingly different given the presence of the female image, the absence of the male and the insidiously ever-present look of male desire. There is little doubt that in popular culture the enduring image of women is as an object viewed from the perspective of male desire. Correspondingly images of female sexual desire are conspicuous in their absence, that is images which pre-suppose a female 'look' not based on the conventions of male desire. We note with some interest the emergence of 'queer theory' (Minton 1997), described as an attempt to get beyond the gendered and sexed practices of the social world, a world that 'marks the death of the meta-narratives of gender which have dominated the modern world . . . . to live outside of gender' (Plummer 1996). For now, we can conclude this discussion by looking in more depth at some of the methods employed to analyse gendered images.

ANALYSING GENDERED IMAGES: A COMPARISON OF METHODS

Any critique of gendered images presupposes some level of analysis of the images themselves. Within social psychology there have been few attempts at providing critical frameworks for the analysis of gendered images, notwith-standing the work of Tseelon (1995) reported above and Beloff (1984). As such, there are no well established procedures or strategies indicating how to conduct such analysis. In this section I compare two potentially valuable forms of image analysis, both approaches found within communication and media studies. The methods are Kress and van Leeuwen's (1996) image composition approach which is based on a grammar of visual design, and Williamson's (1978) Lacanian inspired procedure for decoding advertisements. Essentially one is a formal-grammatical methodology of image composition, the other a psychoanalytically informed analysis of the 'image–spectator' relationship.

Image composition: Kress and van Leeuwen's (1996) approach

Adopting what might in broad terms be termed a social-semiotic approach to signs, Kress and van Leeuwen (1996), developing what they call a grammar of visual design, argue that representation is essentially a process whereby a sign-maker produces a representation of an object, person or thing but always within a specific interest. The nature of the interest, however, is complex, arising 'out of the cultural, social and psychological history of the sign-maker, and focused by the specific context in which the sign is produced' (p. 6). As an illustration of their approach we can turn to their analysis of various elements which make up an image. Composition of any image is said to depend on the relationship between representation (how the image presupposes criteria for the classification, categorisation and conceptualisation of the imaged object) and interaction (how the image employs conventions for indicating the social relations between the producer and the viewer of the image and the representation in the image itself). The composition relates representational and interactive elements through three elements or systems:

Kress and van Leeuwen (1996) define each element specifically as:

1   *Information value.* The specific position of elements (the participants and syntagms that relate them to each other and to the viewer) endows the picture with the specific informational values attached to the various 'zones' of the image: left and right, top and bottom, centre and margin.
2   *Salience.* The elements (participants and representational and interactive syntagms) are made to attract the viewer's attention to different degrees, manifested in such factors as placement in the foreground or background, relative size, contrasts in tonal value (or colour), differences in sharpness, etc.
3   *Framing.* The presence or absence of framing devices (realised by elements which create dividing lines, or by actual frame lines) disconnects or connects elements of the image, signifying that they belong or do not belong together in some sense.

Using an example from a women's weekly magazine (see Figure 7.3), note first that this image is polarised along lines of 'Ideal–Real', a picture of what is promised by using the product, contrasted with a smaller picture of what the products actually look like. In addition, the information format uses a 'background–foreground' placing of the image relative to the text (e.g. we see the image of the woman through the word 'RADIANCE'). With respect to salience, because the elements of the picture are not in proportion, with the largest section element being an image of a woman with the fleshtones highlighted so as to stand out from the blacked-out background, the advert gives much greater prominence to the promise rather than the actuality. The forehead is also highlighted to create a certain soft glow relative to other parts of the image. Finally, there are elements of deliberate framing, an overall division or boundary between the main image and related text (on top of the head and resting on the shoulder). The product itself is set alongside the textual element, and where 'in such pages verbal text becomes just one of the elements integrated by the codes of information value, salience, and framing and reading is not necessarily linear, wholly or in part, but may go from centre to margin, or in circular fashion, or vertically, etc.' (Kress and van Leeuwen 1996: 185).

Figure 7.3 Image composition and processes of identification

This form of analysis provides a set of procedures or criteria for analysing the choice and construction of elements in an image. The information value component of composition is determined in part by the arrangement of the visual elements in any design image. Kress and van Leeuwen (1996) detail examples of the relations between compositional elements, noting differences between 'centre–margin' and 'circular' layouts, highlighting the ways in which magazine and newspaper designers manipulate the reader's response to the information content. One such example is the 'given–new' layout in many magazine spreads, where designers exploit our familiarity with reading on a horizontal 'left-right' axis, and place elements which have to be taken as 'given' on the left-hand side of the page, and correspondingly information on the right-hand side is marked as 'new', i.e. building upon what is assumed or signified by the 'given', yet providing additional new information:

> Broadly speaking, the meaning of the New is therefore 'problematic', 'contestable', 'the information at issue'; while the Given is presented as commonsensical, self-evident. This structure is ideological in the sense that it may not correspond to what is the case either for the producer or for the consumer of the image or layout: the important point is that the information is presented as though it had status or value for the reader, and that readers have to read it within that structure, even if that valuation may then be rejected by a particular reader.
>
> (Kress and van Leeuwen 1996: 187)

While this kind of approach yields many insights into the process of image design and construction there remains a certain overemphasis or seduction with a 'quasi-linguistic' formalism. Kress and van Leeuwen (1996) themselves recognise that their approach tends towards the cold and clinical with the affective response of the image viewer representing a rather minimal element of their framework. Their concluding semiotic analysis of a painting by a 10-year-old girl questions the relationship between the affective and the cognitive in our production of visual objects, closing with the comment that the child's efforts can only be understood with respect to issues of identity and subjectivity.

Identification and the role of the spectator: Williamson's (1978) analysis

Issues of identity, subjectivity and interpretation are central to our second approach to image analysis. In contrast to Kress and van Leeuwen (1996), who essentially articulate a structural analysis of the sign-systems central to image design, Williamson (1978) asks us to 'enter the space between the signifier and signified', between what that means and what it means. The space of course is an individual subject and obviously for any image to have an effect on us, we have to appropriate it in some way, to make it our own. Williamson (1978) asks us to consider how we are constituted as active participants by (and in) those advertisements which promote gendered images. In order for these images to mean something to us we must be involved in transferring the image into feeling, in other words any response will depend in part on our co-operation with whatever is presupposed by the image. Essentially, she is asking how do we create and/or take the meaning of a product in an advertisement, how are we created by that image and in what ways do we create ourselves 'in' the advertisement?

Williamson (1978) sets out to demonstrate that in perceiving advertisements, rather than being free to choose particular products (or not), we are enmeshed within the material presuppositions that underpin the very construction of the images used, 'they invite us to "freely" create ourselves in accordance with the way in which they have already created us' (p. 42). The first point she makes is that any sign/image (to have any meaning at all) must serve as a replacement for that which it represents, and that an iconic replacement is not going to work at all unless it has some value for us. Signs and images possess what value they have through our recognising what they represent. The picture of the woman in Figure 7.3 is recognisable as depicting a desirable image, given that having skin which appears soft, radiant and somehow 'renewed' whenever the cream is used 'means' something outside of the immediate context of the advertisement:

> The advertisement cannot claim to have created that meaning, for do we not 'know' it already? However, we do not know that we know it until it is used in the ad – ideas are maintained not in the vacuum of the abstract but through their active use: values exist not in things but in their transference. Therefore, since any system of values constitutes an ideology, it is clear that an ideology can only exist in that its component values are constantly being regenerated by their transference; and the transference of values (perpetuated in monetary terms by buying and selling) means the same as replacement of meanings. In other words, where the values are ideas, they are perpetuated by our constant deciphering or 'decoding' of signs.
>
> (Williamson 1978: 43)

The argument is that if the meaning of the advertisement takes place through the transformation between signs, and this process takes place within us, then not only does this place us in the space of the signified, but it calls for an examination of how our own subjectivity is signified through such transactions. This theory highlights the relationship between external images and internal identification processes, articulating reasons why for some women there is a feeling of inadequacy, of not ever being able to fully take up the projected subject position implicit in the sign–spectator relationship. One element central to the process of positioning or embedding in the 'fantasised' depictions of the imaginary advertised worlds is appellation. Williamson (1978) points out that every advertisement assumes a particular spectator: it projects into the space out in front of it an imaginary person, composed in terms of the relationship between the elements within the advertisement. In order to understand the advertisement you have to move into this 'space' and in doing so take up the position of the spectator, where:

> The 'you' in ads is always transmitted plural, but we receive it as singular. Although the aim is to connect a mass of people with a product, to identify them with it as a group, this can only be achieved by connecting them with the product as individuals, one by one. Thus we are addressed as a certain kind of person who is *already* connected with a product: there is only one receiver of the ad, the subject 'you', already there in the address. However, this address applies to all of us, and none of us: as an individual this imaginary subject does not exist, but in that we each 'become' him or her, he/she exists as a set, a group – the totemic group centred on the product . . . We constitute a totemic set of one, we find our identity as part of a group the rest of which does not exist. We are appellated as already in a group of one.
>
> (Williamson 1978: 51)

Central to the analytic interpretation employed by Williamson (1978) are the ideas of Lacan, Lévi-Strauss and Althusser. In particular, she articulates a Lacanian analysis of the positioning of the imaginary self (or selves) presupposed by the 'subject' created by the advertisement. Her argument is that advertisements alienate our identity by constituting us as one of the objects in an exchange we are compelled to make (even minimally in the act of recognising the advert as an advert), and in doing so, 'appropriating *from us*, an image which gives us back our own "value"' (Williamson 1978: 64). Furthermore, the images and language of the advertisement play upon the impossibility of ever traversing the gap between the potentially fragmentary and contradictory self (everyday experience) and the imaginary self projected in the advertisements. And, of course, the promise of a coherent identity is represented by what the product will do for us:

> You are created by the advertisement and become its currency, in the process of using it: you are signified by the very fact that you give it significance, in the process of giving it significance. Our creation of meaning in the ad – as active receivers, and its appellation of us, as subjects, are synonymous and simultaneous.
>
> (Williamson 1978: 55)

This Lacanian-inspired analysis of advertising images stands in some contrast to that provided by Kress and van Leeuwen's (1996) formal-grammatical approach. Williamson's (1978) psychoanalytic hermeneutic approach does provide a theoretically rich account of our response to images (and the construction of our 'spectatorship' within them), however, at the risk of over-looking the formal/technical devices of image production. In contrast Kress and van Leeuwen (1996) identify important structural elements of image design, but may be overstating or overextending the implicitly linguistic formalism that underpins their conceptual framework.

CONCLUDING COMMENTS

Reflecting on the notion of a 'gendered' image presupposes that to display or present a 'version of your self' is at the same time to display your gender. On the one hand we all recognise that one of the first distinctions we make when meeting another human is with respect to sex (male or female). At the same time gender remains one of the most contested constructs within the social sciences, or to paraphrase Plummer (1996), something socially achieved, dramatically performed, a set of culturally produced practices of daily life which are open to much change and variability. In this brief summary and examination of gendered images it is clear that the predominant images of women focus on the body while those of men focus on identity and masculinity. The discourses of, and on, masculinity may highlight a number of difficult issues surrounding a man's experience, but this pales in comparison to a self-image predicated on being an 'object' of male desire. There is certainly a problematic question regarding whether it is possible to develop a discourse on this topic that is not, by definition, gendered. One is left with the passing observation, on thinking about forms of image analysis, that it may be no surprise that Kress and van Leeuwen are men and Williamson a woman. To paraphrase Roland Barthes, we can never step outside language into a domain of idealised objectivity, and notions of an idealised discourse of equality may remain forever a fantasy. Images of women and men can only be read within prevailing, and always ideologically saturated, contemporary discourses.

Theme III

External images and all that is 'out there'

PREFACE

We now reach the final theme of the text which concentrates on external images. Up to this point discussion and comment has focused either on images, ideas and associations of the 'private' and the internal, or on contexts where there is a particular kind of interdependence between the display or performance of an image and self-reflection on whatever that production might be. This book began with the observation that we experience a considerable range of diverse images from the external world while at the same time maintaining the idea that our 'private' self-reflections on that world remain separate and 'internal'. In part, then, the world is constituted by the images we find within it, along with all those processes of image production, reception and recognition understood either as sets of social practices or as internal cognitive mechanisms and procedures. In our investigations in the preceding theme it became clear that there are many instances where a sharp distinction between what is outside and what inside the mind cannot be made, or if it is made, rests on certain kinds of claims or positions which can no longer be taken for granted.

The final theme of the book considers topics, ideas and themes where the processes of image production and recognition appear quite distinct from internal image processes. The main areas we will look at are television and film, electronic image production (e.g. internet image production) and photography. Again, the choice is somewhat selective and always partial for that reason. However, there is an increasing interest in these areas from within social psychology, and throughout we will examine what particular contribution that part of psychology might make. Essentially, we will be looking at theories and research within three areas which have sought to understand the social-cultural processes of image production and/or how such images are understood and received.

8 The mass media of the moving image
Television and film

INTRODUCTION

For many people to talk of external images and their influence on us is to discuss mass-media communication as represented in television and film. Television and film are now such an important dimension of our cultural life that it is hard to envisage the effect early film had on early twentieth-century society. Stories of people rushing from the cinema when experiencing for the first time animals rushing towards them on the big screen have become part of the folklore which underpins contemporary fantasies about our present-day technical sophistication. Likewise, when television first became a mass-market commodity watching itself was a highly formalised activity, with pre-prescribed times of transmission, elaborate social codes and conventions for viewing – typically the father censoring what was permissible viewing material – and where presenters themselves envisaged the advent of TV in the home as a special and wholly new form of intrusion. This is evidenced in the observation that presenters on early BBC television would appear dressed in full formal evening wear. Having moving images of complete strangers in your front room was clearly perceived as potentially problematic, and codes and conventions for the successful introduction of the 'television intruder' built upon appropriate cultural practices of social interaction.

In this chapter the intention is to provide a summary selection of ideas and theories in television and film which touch upon issues for a psychology of the image. Despite the difficulties in demonstrating clear empirical evidence that film and television affect the ideas and images we have both of the world and of ourselves, undoubtedly these forms of media have considerable influence on our lives. The images we see, the stories told, the time spent viewing and the resources put into advertising hardly support the idea that these media are a subsidiary element in our daily lives. The question being addressed here is whether, after over thirty years of social science research into the media, we are any nearer understanding the relationship between perceiving and interpreting these external images.

Television and film have been considered separately within psychology, with television research focusing primarily on 'effects', rarely considering the nature of image production or audience engagement. In contrast film or cinema has theorised extensively on the relationship between image and the construction of the 'absent' viewing subject. If we need to understand why the images of television, film and what is more commonly termed 'mass media' have become a major focus for social science research, then we might note that the academy, along with certain elements of popular culture, conceptualises the phenomenon of mass communication often in negative terms. Kearney (1988), for example, argues:

> Seduced by the summary ideologies of the latest media cult or craze, we seem to have entered an age where reality is inseparable from the image, where the original has been replaced by imitation, where our understanding of the world is preconditioned by the electronically reproducible media of television, cinema, video and radio – media in which every 'live' event or performance is capable of being mechanically recorded and retransmitted ad infinitum . . . As printed matter was supplemented by, and eventually subordinated to, photography, radio and television, the representational images soon began to overshadow reality itself . . . The citizens of our post-industrial society . . . live in a world, where fantasy is more real than reality, where the image has more dignity than the original. We hardly dare face our bewilderment, because the solace of belief in contrived reality is so thoroughly real.
>
> (Kearney 1988: 252)

It is worth beginning by defining terms often employed in television and film research: mass communication, audience, medium, text and message. Mass communication is not really a concept that can be defined with precision, rather it is a common-sense category that is used to classify together a number of different phenomena in (generally) a non-analytic way. Typically this will include newspapers, magazines, cinema, television, radio, advertising and sometimes books and music (particularly the popular music industry). Added to this is the increasingly significant incorporation of computer based technologies, for example the bringing together of television facilities with computer media. One typical definition of mass communication is provided by O'Sullivan et al. (1983):

> Mass communication is the practice and product of providing leisure entertainment and information to an unknown audience by means of corporately financed, industrially produced, state-regulated, high technology, privately consumed commodities in the modern print, screen, audio and broadcast media.
>
> (p. 131)

In an earlier study of the relationship between images and mass-communication media, the historian Boorstein (1962) documented the ways in which

journalists produce non-existent news and film companies fabricate personalities or 'stars', distinguishing between what he called pseudo-events,
represented often by the 'big issues' that appear on the front pages of tabloid
newspapers, with images which are pseudo-ideals. Pseudo-events are in the
world of facts and pseudo-ideals in the world of values. According to Boorstein
(1962), images have to have certain distinct properties, they have to be believ-
able, simple and vivid, yet they remain ambiguous:

> Images are ambiguous: they float somewhere between the imagination and
> the senses, between expectation and reality . . . in another way, too, [the
> image] is ambiguous, for it must not offend. It must suit unpredictable
> future purposes and unpredicted changes in taste.
>
> (Boorstein 1962: 198)

As for the audience, this term is used to define the unknown individuals and
groups towards whom mass communication messages are addressed. As a definition it describes all members of society, whose consumption of and
interaction with media products constitutes 'at least a mark, and possibly
even a requirement of membership of modern society' (McQuail 1969: 94).
What is meant by the 'audience' has been one of the major concerns of mass-
communication research. Early research images of the mass-media audience
portrayed the audience as fragmented, passive and impersonal, thus under-
scoring the vulnerability of the individual exposed to powerful media stimuli.
This view has now been replaced by a more complex and productive set of
views on the socially structured nature of the audience, no longer seen as passive, instead involved in the co-construction of meanings and interpretations
during the act of viewing.

Another idea which has been central to the development of communication
research is the term media (or medium). This can be defined in a very broad
sense as an intermediate agency that enables communication to take place.
More specifically, the media is taken to include any technological development
that extends the channels, range or speed of communication. In a sense speech,
writing, gestures, facial expressions, dress, acting and dancing can all be seen
as media of communication capable of transmitting codes along a channel or
channels. This use of the term is decreasing, and it is increasingly being confined to the technical media, particularly the mass media. Sometimes it is used
to refer to the means of communication, for example, in 'print or broadcast
media', but often it refers to the technical forms by which these means are
actualised (for example, radio, television, newspapers, books, photographs,
films and records). McLuhan (1964) used the word in this sense in his famous
phrase 'the medium is the message', by which he meant that the personal and
social consequences of a new technological medium are more significant than
the uses to which it is actually put: the existence, use of, and response to television as a cultural artefact can be as significant as, if not more so than, the
actual content of programmes.

Commenting on the influence of McLuhan on communications research, McIlwraith (1994) notes that his ideas about the effects of television were often misunderstood by psychologists. In particular, he notes that McLuhan's analysis focused on the sensory and perceptual response of the viewer to a low-definition stimulus, while psychology focused, and still does, on the cognitive effort of the viewer trying to understand the content. Essentially McLuhan was talking about the effects of the hardware itself on the user and society; television was what he termed a 'cool' medium, McIlwraith (1994) commenting:

> McLuhan borrowed the terms 'hot' and 'cool' from jazz: hot jazz was more highly structured, while cool jazz was very unstructured and generated more listener involvement, he believed . . . McLuhan proposed that the low definition and poor quality of the television picture made it a highly-involving, highly-participating medium: a 'cool' medium. Psychologists have often mislabelled television a 'hot' medium when citing McLuhan's work (see for example, Williams 1986). The problem is more than just getting the labels reversed, however, since psychological theories are based on the view that TV is a medium of low involvement.
>
> (McIlwraith 1994: 333)

The idea of an active, constructive viewer having to work hard to realise an appropriate understanding of the moving images on television is not one we now typically think of when describing present-day viewing habits. The metaphor of the couch potato is probably a more common contemporary image we subscribe to.

Part of the reason why psychology has tended to focus on content (rather than the structure of television) can be traced to the assumption that somehow television content could be treated in the same way as printed media. This brings us on to another important idea, that of the text or message. Within communication research these two terms are often used interchangeably, and refer to any signifying structure composed of signs and codes which is essential to communication, encompassing a wide variety of forms, such as speech, writing, film, dress, car-design and gesture, to name a few.

Despite their frequent interchangeability, the terms text and message do have differences, and maintaining or even extending them is a worthwhile enterprise. Text usually refers to a message that has a physical existence of its own, independent of its sender or receiver, and thus is composed of representational codes. Books, records, letters, photographs are in this sense texts, and so is television. In contrast a gesture or facial expression, however, sends a message, but does not produce a text. The term message tends to be used by those working in the process school of communication, by sociologists and psychologists and engineers, and is used with the simple definition of 'that which is transmitted'. The image of the communication message can be traced back to the early work of Shannon (1948), whose mathematical theory of information was said to apply to any message, from any source, transmitted by any means to any receiver. Shannon's ideas played a significant part in the development of the information processing perspective in psychology.

Text, on the other hand, derives more from the semiotic or linguistic school, and thus implies the definition 'that which is central to the generation and exchange of meaning'. A text, then, consists of a network of codes working on a number of levels and is thus capable of producing a variety of meanings according to the social and cultural experience of the reader (Eco 1982). It is worth noting that more recent television research is now informed by post-structuralism, critical linguistics and cultural studies, incorporating and extending the more general term discourse.

TELEVISION

Arguably, mass-media research has come to mean, certainly for the non-academic, the study of television and the effect it has on people. Psychological research on television has been largely confined to the analysis of real or imagined effects (Martin and Smith 1997). There has been much less research or theorising in psychology about the process of actually watching television itself. In fact, there are few explanatory frameworks aimed at understanding exactly what it is that people are engaging with when watching television. Central to the development of such a framework would be some analysis of our emotional engagement with television, and in particular the characters, scripts and scenarios appropriated when viewing. We can ask, in what way is watching television 'interaction' in any communicative sense, even very loosely conceived. Certainly, on occasion, many people report a strong sense of affect when deeply involved in watching television and a certain sense of dialogic engagement in the narrative representations portrayed (Thomas, L. 1995). Arguably, however, psychology has not contributed a great deal to our understanding of what it means to be engaged with or involved in the narrative representations implicit to nearly all television programming (including news, documentaries and related 'fly-on-the-wall' observations). We turn then to what might lend support to such a proposal.

Whatever else, the generation which grew up without television are now in their late fifties and sixties and even for this group, the vast majority have been watching television for upwards of 20 hours a week for the last 25–30 years. The prevailing belief has been that people are passive recipients of television and need somehow to be protected from whatever interests are involved in television production (although recent ethnographic studies of television watching indicate that this view is incorrect – Gunter et al. 1997). Adopting a somewhat negative tone, Shapiro (1991) writes that the television screen becomes a psychological world where viewers are provoked to imagine life through the television story and in doing so are figured by what they imagine. Television, he suggests, intercedes in our everyday lives at an existential, psychological level by imaging us without seeing us and then inducing us to know ourselves through its images . . . The lifestyles presented on TV are prefabricated existences that we step into when we turn on the set . . . The luminous images of television seem to brighten our evenings and spice-up our home lives but their mirrors can sadly pervert the reality of lived reflection which is genuine human contact in a world of embodied feelings.

(Shapiro 1991: 162–164)

Not surprisingly, some researchers in mass-communication research view television watching much more positively, arguing that it enhances social affiliation and a sense of ontological security. In other words, we feel more secure about interacting with others through gaining knowledge of how they think and feel. For Cohen and Metzger (1998), in contrast to everyday interpersonal contact where we risk being rejected:

[television] allows more control over the terms of the social interaction in the sense that it is convenient and low risk, requiring no primping or emotional vulnerability on the part of the viewer. Stated otherwise, the mass media can provide a safe way of feeling included, but is 'intimacy at a distance'.

(Cohen and Metlzger 1998: 55)

Given psychology's emphasis on the effects of television, one or two points are worth noting. First, there is a long tradition of concern for the effects of television on children, which itself extends earlier fears and suspicions about the effects of radio (for a review, see Dennis 1998). The child is perceived as being particularly susceptible to images from the external world, a view which itself depends on images of development, and the essential passivity on the part of the viewer. For the most part it has been very difficult to 'prove', within the prevailing criteria of quantitative scientific methodology, that children are adversely affected by watching television (Durkin 1985; Martin and Smith 1997).

Second, many of the effects that have been found have tended to be rather short-lived and methodologically can be traced to the early research by social learning theorists concerned primarily with the effect of television on children's aggressive behaviour (Bandura and Walters 1964). For the most part research in this area has focused on the harm that television might have and only secondarily, potential positive effects.

Third, given the nature of the relationship between developmental psychology, education and social policy, whenever well publicised instances of child violence are reported in the media (particularly of very young children towards other children), public abhorrence at such extreme childhood aggression initiates a reappraisal of the potentially negative effects of television. In a sense, it is as if society has to believe that such acts must be caused by television, given the belief that children are essentially innocent and incapable of sophisticated moral reasoning.

Adopting a somewhat ironic tone, Livingstone (1990) comments on the contribution that effects studies have had on television research. She notes, you are likely to learn such facts as: children exposed to violent programmes are slower to seek adult help when they witness violence among other children (Drabman and Thomas 1975); being told that you are going to experience some pretty nasty things in a horror movie will increase the degree to which you will be frightened by the film (Cantor et al. 1984); men who viewed a series of films showing violence against women came to have fewer negative reactions to the films and to see them as less violent (Linz et al. 1984); and five- and six-year-old girls held less gender-stereotyped attitudes after watching a low-stereotyped cartoon, compared to those who saw neutral or high-stereotyped cartoons (Davidson et al. 1979).

Providing a useful review of the social-psychological work on television conducted between the 1950s and late 1980s, Livingstone (1990) considers contrasting themes within psychology and media studies (Table 8.1). She notes that social-psychological work emerged from attitude and persuasion research, through behaviourism and social learning theory, and then in line with the increasing dominance of information processing psychology moved towards a partial convergence reflected in social cognition research. In parallel with these themes, media studies focused initially on issues of mass media and institutional power, and was influenced during the 1950s and 1960s by information theory and behaviourism, before moving towards the contemporary focus on ideology, interpretation and issues surrounding a critical analysis of television content and structure.

Livingstone's (1990) own work on television seeks to bridge the gap between the social cognitive models of social psychology and critical theoretic

Table 8.1 Social psychology of television and mass media research

Approx. dates	Social psychology	Media studies
Late 1940s	Attitudes/persuasion research	Focus on power of mass media
1950s	Attitude formation	Information-flow models
Late 1950s, early 1960s	Behaviourism	Behaviourist/social-learning models
Late 1960s and 1970s	Critique and emergent cognitivism	Critical mass communication
Late 1970s to the present	Convergence; social cognition	Media and reproduction of ideology/Interpretation and decoding metaphors

Source: after Livingstone 1990.

perspectives in media studies. Her proposal is that television content should be viewed as a discourse constituted through a wide variety of narrative texts. Employing ideas and metaphors from critical theory and post-structural linguistics (e.g. Eco 1979), she argues that understanding audience reception is akin to understanding the role of the reader in text comprehension.

The appropriation of television texts, such as soap operas, is not a simple amorphous and passive process, rather

> the structure of the text, the experienced relation between the viewer and text, the interpretation made of the text, and the consequences of viewing are all complexly bound up together . . . [and] . . . The important questions concern the interrelation between the two (texts and viewer): how do people actively make sense of structured texts and events; how do texts guide and restrict interpretations. The creation of meaning through the interaction of texts and readers is a struggle, a site of negotiated meaning between two semi-powerful sources.
>
> (Livingstone 1990: 23)

Essentially, Livingstone (1990) supports a social-cognitive account of our response to television, one which attempts to do justice to both sides of the 'text–reader'/'text–viewer' equation. Again:

> To understand patterns in action, we must understand patterns in meaning or the social construction of reality. Thus, cognitive effects are the effects of interest. Cognition becomes involved with television in a circular fashion: not only is television interpreted through sociocognitive knowledge and processes but also television affects this knowledge and processes. Television does not only offer role models for action, which may be variously interpreted, but it also offers images and frameworks for everyday understanding, through which we subsequently interpret other social texts. It may not only tell us what to do but also what it means to do such and such, and what kind of a person you are to do this.
>
> (Livingstone 1990: 24)

We are constantly being presented then with images, frameworks and narratives which have a direct influence over other aspects of our lives. These external images have a direct effect in the sense that 'what we saw on television last night' becomes a topic in our everyday conversation with one another, but also indirectly in the sense that our views, opinions and interpretations of the world around us are informed by the discourses and implicit social texts of television programmes. And learning how to become a critically reflective television viewer is increasingly being viewed as an essential part of education (Brookfield 1986; Rhee and Cappella 1997).

One enduring image of television, however, is as something which can, if not take the place of social interaction, nevertheless simulate a sense of personal involvement. Kim and Rubin (1997) note that motivation to engage in day-time television watching predicts measures of 'parasocial interaction' and Pan and Koskicki (1997) argue that exposure to call-in talk shows has an important influence of opinion formation. Over the last twenty years or so, a particular genre of television has emerged, one that not only mimics certain aspects of social interaction but one that paints a picture of social involvement, participation as well as voyeurism and fantasy: the talk show. If we look at such shows in more detail we might see where the role of the external image finds a point of contact with more internal and interdependent image processes, such as self-disclosure, social identification, performance and display.

TALK SHOWS: IMAGES OF PARTICIPATION AND 15 MINUTES OF FAME

The rise of the influence of the talk show host has been documented by researchers in communication and media studies (Steenland 1990; Munson 1993). Testament to the popularity of these shows was the interest created when comments made by a well-known talk show host Oprah Winfrey, during a show transmitted in 1995, were reported in the world press. The US hamburger chain McDonald's instigated legal action over a negative remark, claiming that her comments had cost the company a considerable fortune in the resultant fall in share prices after her show was televised. Over and above such obvious examples of influence, it would seem that these shows offer a particular kind of interactive or dialogue engagement, one where the viewer is positioned within a distinct set of performance stagings. Consider the different roles involved in the show: the host, the studio audience, participants/guests, the experts invited to comment and the viewing audience. The format and procedures involved in the production of these television shows in some respects mirror participant role scenarios outlined by Goffman (1981), for example, ratified and unratified participants, overhearers, ratified and unratified observers, all subject to the same display and performance requirements discussed in Chapter 6 – the doctrine of natural expression.

The host represents the interests both of institutional media (e.g. the television station) and of the viewing public. He/she constructs his/her dialogue with respect to the viewing audience, asking questions of the experts and participants, in the main as if acting for them. However, it has been argued that talk show hosts channel participants' accounts in particular ways and undermine the control participants might have over giving an account of their life stories (White 1992; Alcoff and Gray 1993). Similarly, as ratified overhearers/onlookers, and only occasionally participants, the studio audience is selected so as to represent the producer's conception of the imaginary mass audience. In a sense the studio audience and the invited participants represent the implicit viewing audience, again occasionally asking the kinds of questions it is assumed viewers would wish answered.

The participants/guests themselves are positioned in a somewhat complex role which in part supports Baudrillard's (1988) claim that people now accord a higher status to a person's on-screen image compared to their everyday 'off-screen' selves. To have your image appear on television affords a particular kind of status and fame. In a study of the motivations and interests of participants Priest (1995) found that participants welcomed the opportunity to present themselves on television because:

> they passionately believed the public needed to hear their stories. Most of the panellists used self-disclosures during the show tapings as a stigma management tactic (Goffman 1963b) in their efforts to normalise images of their out-groups. They were fully aware of the freak show characteristics of the genre but agreed to step up to the forum nonetheless because of the potential to educate the public about topics generally neglected, bungled, or vilified by the press.
>
> (Priest 1995: 69)

One suggestion why panellists appear on such audience participation talk shows, is because of the therapeutic opportunities such programmes provide (Banks 1990). The main reason why participants were keen to take part, according to Priest (1995), is that they were given the opportunity to present a point of view generally positioned at the margins of cultural life, and after appearing, then experienced a considerable rise in their self-esteem, i.e. they 'felt empowered, chosen and worthy after years of languishing on society's periphery when producers provided them the chance to speak for themselves via the central medium of culture' (p. 82). As for the experts who are asked to contribute and comment on participants' accounts or behaviours, this is yet another role which occupies a position somewhere close to the concerns of the host or media producers but also often representing a relevant professional interest (e.g. clinical psychology).

Social psychology is taking an increasing interest in these programmes. Livingstone and Lunt (1994), for example, have looked in detail at the various participant roles in talk shows, noting in particular that the position of the expert does not fulfil Habermas's (1987) analytic predictions regarding the increasing status of 'technical rationality' in postmodern culture, that being, excessive and undue respect given to such experts because they appear on television. Analysing the discourse in talk shows, Livingstone et al. (1994) found that more often than not, the experts' views are not treated with exaggerated or excessive respect, rather the host acts as if representing the viewing audience demanding that the experts explain themselves. A somewhat different interpretation is suggested by Priest (1995) arguing that the disclosures on talk shows are resonant of the Protestant activity of testimony or witnessing before a group, yet paradoxically, 'participation is potentially empowering and transgressive – while the risks of containment and trivialisation are great' (Priest 1995: 70). Of course, this is probably the case as much for the experts as for the participants.

The remaining 'participant role' is, of course, the viewing audience, and the related question of why these talk shows are very popular. Undoubtedly a cross-cultural analysis of the participant 'topics' in such shows would highlight the different moral and ethical concerns of a given society as well as the distinct conventions for public display and performance (compare for example the US *Gerry Springer Show* with the UK's *Kilroy*). At the same time, it remains unclear what underlies the interest in such shows. In part there is probably a voyeuristic element not dissimilar to our interest when overhearing other people discussing intimate details of their private lives, particularly when knowing we remain unobserved by those we are listening to. There is also an element of social comparison between the viewer and the participants. One enduring image of 'viewer participation' and studio audience talk shows is television viewing as a distinct opportunity to project, reflect or fantasise about how we might, or might not, respond, feel or participate were we in the position of the invited participants. There seems something of a gap in our understanding of the processes whereby viewers experience this form of television. Before drawing together a number of summary points on the relationship between the images we perceive on television and the images of 'television' itself, we turn to the study of film.

FILM

One arena where there has been considerable theorising about the relationship between external image perception and internal reflection and imagery is film or cinema. For over a hundred years film has had a significant influence on the arts, culture and society and was certainly the first international communication medium (Balasz 1985). Film is both similar to and yet different from television. Each medium has a distinct history of development, particular contexts of production and reception, and is understood and theorised about in a particular way. In terms of engagement and participation, in contrast to the everyday embeddedness of television, within and contributing to our home lives, watching a film involves going out into the public domain and sitting with, and yet apart from, other people in the dark for a specified period of time. It is also a requirement that we suspend whatever we understand as the normal conventions, responses and perceptions regarding relations between reality and illusion. At the same time, like television, in film we are presented with series of moving images where the director has constructed a quite specific model of the viewing spectator, presupposed in whatever camera position we are presented with. Interestingly, while it is only relatively recently that we see the emergence of distinct analytic accounts of how we 'engage' with the images, narratives and discourses of television, in film theory we find a number of well-established conceptual frameworks influenced by semiotics, linguistics and psychoanalysis.

When semioticians first turned their attention to film and film criticism, their theorising was greeted with extreme scepticism and dismissed as pretentious and confused. Lapsley and Westlake (1988) trace out this early history noting 'semiotics was a procrustean enterprise comparable to painting by numbers, at once unwittingly absurd and insidiously political, practised by possessed sectarians, pod-people, and overdressed ladies bedecked in bangles and baubles, whose general demeanour had the poised vigilance of a lobotomised ferret' (p. 33). Clearly those engaged in film criticism at the time saw semiotics as a threat to their endeavours and livelihood.

Semiotics, as the scientific study of signs and signification processes was recognised as a significant challenge to the traditional aesthetic approach to film. Lapsley and Westlake (1988) note that ideas of art as organic unity were discarded and replaced by the supposition that all meanings and aesthetic effects were explicable in terms of determining structures and mechanisms. Art was open to scientific analysis and film images were signs whose signification was recognisable within the film as a system or structure. Although Piercean semiotics has had some influence in film theory – as in the work of Woollen (1969), who introduced critics to the tripartite distinctions of icon–index–symbol – Saussure's linguistic and Lacan's psychoanalytic version of semiotics have had the greatest influence. Metz (1974) introduced Saussure into film theory, noting however that film was not quite the same kind of arbitrary sign-system as found in written language. The signification of a film image cannot be derived solely from its position in a sign-system; instead to paraphrase Lapsley and Westlake (1988), the argument was that cinema duplicated rather than articulated reality, suggesting:

> Cinema transforms the world into discourse, and is not therefore simple duplication. But a semiotics of the cinema cannot work at the level of the image, since each image is unique, novel and analogous to reality, with its meaning produced not by its place within a system but by what it duplicates. There is no process of selection from a lexicon of images of cinema as there is from the verbal lexicon of a natural language.
>
> (Lapsley and Westlake 1988: 40)

One process which facilitates the transformation of film images into a form of discourse is the narrative. Narrativisation might be described as the production of a narrative version of unfolding experience and in cinema what generally holds together the unfolding sequence of film images is the narrative plot. Within film criticism narrative is one of the more dominant theoretical perspectives. Narrative has been defined as the devices, strategies and conventions governing the organisation of a story (fictional or factual) into sequence, and associated definitions have included a reference to what is not actually present, and the representation of an imaginary reality. Narrative depends on the metaphorical imagination and is produced through what Ricoeur (1976) calls the 'predicative assimilation', which grasps together and integrates into one whole and complete story multiple and scattered events, thereby schematizing the intelligible signification attached to the narrative taken as a whole.

(Ricoeur 1976: 185)

Extending remarks made in previous chapters, narrative has been described as a metacode, a human universal on the basis of which transcultural messages about the nature of a shared reality can be transmitted. Contemporary narratology can be subdivided into abstract narratology (e.g. the structural analysis of myth; the semiotics of narrative), and textual narratology (e.g. the discourse of stories). Pavel (1985) defines narratology itself as the integrated study of all levels of narrative phenomena, and recognises the problems associated with the rapid development of a field which has seen the proliferation of many competing schools. However, central to many conceptions of narrative is the distinction between plot, any arrangement of incidents, and story as the mere raw material awaiting the organising principles of an interpreter.

The work of narrative cinema is primarily directed to the effacement of all signs of its production (Lapsley and Westlake 1988). Production conventions in film-making focus primarily on the construction of a narrative space through the maintenance of a perspective. For example, there are well-established procedures for ensuring the spectator's identification with the camera, such as:

a   the provision of a master or establishing shot, enabling the spectator to orientate himself or herself with respect to each new shot in the sequence

b   the 180° rule, ensuring that the spectator always finds the same characters in the same part of the screen, i.e. matching 'screen space' and 'narrative space'

c   the 30° rule, which prevents the spectator experiencing a jump in space and permits a smooth continuity between shots

d   the orchestration of actors' movements so that reframing and camera movement do not draw attention to themselves . . .

(after Lapsley and Westlake 1988)

Building upon Propp's distinction between story and plot, Dick (1990) considers the relationship between temporal sequence and narrative event in film, distinguishing between plot, diegesis and discourse. Plot is simply the film's structure, i.e. the telling of the story represented in the ordered arrangement of incidents presented in the film. Diegesis, on the other hand, is the film's story world, the narrative presupposed by the recounting but always more than the presented account. Finally, discourse is taken to be the film's exchange of meanings with the audience, whatever interpretations are realised given the context, history and manner in which the text reaches the audience.

Within psychology one or two studies have taken up this essentially cognitive view of film narrative comprehension, proposing that the latter is a perceptual/cognitive activity based on narrative schemas. Such schemas are sets of culturally based expectations employed when segmenting, integrating and realising the film images/events as a causally ordered schema, where

> A spectator employs top-down and bottom-up cognitive processes to transform data on the screen into a diegesis – a world – that contains a particular story, or sequence of events.
>
> (Branigan 1993: 115)

However, the idea of a schema remains a potentially problematic idea, given that it represents a somewhat opaque formalism. In the early 1930s Bartlett, probably one of the first experimental social psychologists, developed the idea of the schema as a construct to help explain processes of selective remembering and forgetting. Rumelhart (1977) describes a schema as an abstract representation of a generalised concept of a situation and is said to account for a situation whenever the situation can be taken as an instance of the concept represented by the schema. Interestingly, Bartlett (1932) describes an image as a device for picking out bits of schemas, for 'increasing the chance of variability in the reconstruction of past stimuli' (p. 158). However, it is rather hard to see how this idea helps our understanding of audience response in film theory, that is, beyond making explanatory statements regarding processes of remembering. For the most part film theory has been deeply influenced by psychoanalytic thinking. As we noted in earlier chapters, in contrast to mainstream psychology which presupposes the position and status of the 'subject as identity' (Chapters 5 and 6), psychoanalysis has sought to formulate proposals regarding how subjecthood is possible at all, asking the question, How is it possible to establish that such a thing called identity can exist? In a now famous article written in *Cahiers du cinema*, Oudart (1969) considered how theorising about spectatorship in film could be understood within a psychoanalytic framework, particularly Lacan's concept of suture.

For Lacan, the child's realisation of identity through the experience of his/her positioning in the language of those he/she interacts with is interdependent with a growing sense of loss: identity of self in language as substitution for the loss of union (completeness) brought about by birth and separation in the first place. In Lacanian semio-psychoanalysis, suture names the relation of the individual, as subject, to the chain of its discourse, 'the subject is an effect of the signifier in which it is represented' (Heath 1981: 54). Lacan employs the metaphor of the suture (the stitching together of a wound) to describe the self as a thin discursive thread stitched over the essential lack or absence caused by the initial separation. And the suturing process is located within language and in particular the conversational context. Heath (1981) makes the point that while in art the static image binds the spectator in place (the suturing central position is the sense of the image – in place the spectator completes the image

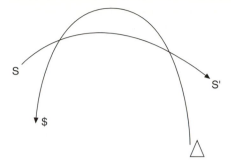

Figure 8.1 Lacan's development of the sign (after Lapsley and Westlake 1988)

as its subject), in film it flows with energies, moves in all directions, is 'potentially a veritable festival of affects' (pp. 53–54).

Film theorists also borrowed from Lacan another important idea: his modification of the linguistic sign (i.e. S/s, where S is the signifier and S' the signified). This implies that there is a continual sliding of signifieds under signifiers as these enter into new relationships. Meaning is not at all the stable relationship between signifier and signified presumed by Saussure. What stops the slide and momentarily fixes meaning is the punctuation of the signifying chain by the action of the subject, expressed by Lacan as in Figure 8.1.

Lapsley and Westlake (1988) make the point that meaning is produced by the subject in this process of punctuation, imposing on the series of film images a structure of meaning; but, equally the subject is produced by the meanings available in the signifying chain, for the subject this is such by virtue of a self-conception that is only available within discourse. The desire of the subject engenders varying interpretations of the unfolding text; the text offers in return the condition of subjectivity. For Lacan there is, therefore, an unceasing dialectic of the subject and meaning, an idea that would recur in various guises within film theory.

As one of the first film theorists to be influenced by Lacan, Oudart (1969) proposed that the process of reading a film began with an initial and joyous response to the image as image, immediately disavowed by the recognition of the frame or boundary of the film, in a sense a break in the experience of the perception of the image as 'immediate'. The film is now perceived as constrained by limits and is thus a representation 'for someone', i.e. designed and produced for a 'one who is absent', or as Heath (1981) puts it:

> Crucially what this realization of absence from the image at once achieves is the definition of the image as discontinuous, its production as signifier: the move from cinema into the order of discourse: 'The revelation of this absence is the key-moment in the fate of the image, since it introduces the image into the order of the signifier and cinema into the order of

discourse.' What then operates, classically, is the effacement (or filling in) of the absence, the suturing of the discourse – its movement as in a continuity of articulation – by the reappropriation of the absence within the film, a character in the film coming to take the place of the Absent One posed by the spectator; suture as 'the abolition of the Absent One and its resurrection in some one'.

(Heath 1981: 87)

This process or dialogic 'suturing' of the spectator's own position rests upon fantasy, speculation and imagination. Hillier (1999) comments that image and fantasy can have no meaning except through the symbolic, where the signifiers have value only in relation to other signifiers, 'fantasy involves desire for that which is unattainable, alienation because it is the desire of the Other, and perpetuated rather than satisfied because it is in place of the object of desire, representing what is absent and lacking' (p. 10). Employing a psychoanalytic interpretation of fantasy in film leads to a view of the unconscious which is seen as informing and determining the imagination, where each subject identifies and engages with the film according to their representation and constitution in the symbolic. The Lacanian proposal that each subject is uniquely constituted in the symbolic is one explanation for the variability of response to the same film by different spectators.

Consequently, film does not simply position the spectator 'as if determined' in the producer's own fantasy, but through the symbolic of language, the spectator is involved in a never-ending relationship with the signifying elements of language. The spectator's individual experience of the film is simultaneously a product of the film and a product of the spectator given that both rely on the signifier, that which structures, constrains and makes realisable all that is recognisable as communicative.

Psychoanalytically informed film theory also touches on the 'external–internal' relationship of engagement. The pleasure of the cinema revolves around denial: denial of the lack of the original objects shown in the film (their fictitious nature) and denial of the film's fundamental discontinuity. The film is a fictional construct, yet this knowledge, although recognised, is ignored, so that the spectator is disbelieving and believing simultaneously. In order to take pleasure in the fiction of the film, the spectator must transform it into a fetish, endowing the inanimate objects on the screen with a presence and significance which they do not have; believing them to be real while knowing that they are not, like the symbolism of dreams, the subject behaves and identifies with them as if they are potent realities. The signifiers of the symbolic function to make present what is absent, disguising the absence, but in doing so the absence must be acknowledged. As oppositions they are mutually interdependent and have no meaning except in relation to each other.

Again, within a psychoanalytic framework, as well as fetishism, film viewing is thought to rely on the sexual drives of scopophilia, the desire to see, and the invocatory drive, which Lacan calls the desire to hear. And in contrast to the oral drive which seeks unity with the lost object of desire, the desire to see and hear are based on the lack of the desired object that can never be overcome. Thus, the voyeurs, looking at and listening to others without being seen or heard themselves, must keep a distance. This again is similar to the look of the dependent infant, where the infant entertains the fantasy that they are in control of what they view, and yet are unaware of their own separateness from what they see and hear.

One model for identification in the cinema is therefore that of the screen resembling the mirror where the spectator psychologically assimilates the images and transforms them into a coherent whole. Primary identification which involves the formation of the personality in early childhood is a precondition for secondary identification with the objects and characters in the film. First, there is entry into the imaginary, and second, entry into the symbolic order (see Chapter 5). Laplanche and Pontalis (1988) comment that the process of identification is of major importance in both the appeal of cinema and the formation of personality during development. In the cinema, the spectator is placed in a privileged position of total perception, of seeing and hearing *everything* and being *everywhere* within the film, yet secure in the knowledge that the film, as a product for her/his perception, involves none of the demands and the responsibilities of life outside the cinema. The spectator is therefore free to imagine, fantasise and identify at will. Such a sense of engagement is said to be reminiscent of the secure and immobile infant whose only experience of agency is through that which is reflected back from the desire of the mother, looking at the self in the mirror looking back (and see Chapter 5).

CONCLUDING COMMENT

There is no question that film and television continue to be the principal domains where the significance and influence of the image is made manifest. To suggest that somehow the worlds portrayed are always kept at a distance is a little like saying we can use language but it does not really affect the way we think. In trying to understand precisely how these external images influence, affect and possibly construct our views of the world we need to note a number of things. Film and television occupy very different contexts in our daily lives: television is now very much a cultural artefact with correspondingly distinct and constantly changing social practices surrounding its use. Multiple ownership of television in homes and the proliferation of cable and satellite channels are as influential as the changing genres for programme presentation and participation. Film has also changed rapidly since the post-war era, now occupying a position of considered status as aesthetic culture – it could be argued that film has now supplanted the role literature once held regarding the 'textual' imagination.

Theoretical ideas about our response to film and television are markedly different, film focusing on issues of identification and spectator engagement, television on audience reception, text-construction and issues of narrative. Film theory is focused on how it is that the 'external' images of film become part and parcel of the 'internal' image identification processes central to the spectator constructing a meaning of the film. In contrast television at times concentrates on the interpersonal sense of engagement and appropriation with programme content, but also pervades our everyday life and activity to such an extent that the enduring image we are left with is of a mirror with potentially dubious intentions.

9   Virtual semiotics and electronic images

INTRODUCTION

In contemporary culture one context where we become particularly conscious of the significance of external images is with the computer, or more specifically the computer screen. For some critics to talk of images is to talk of computers (e.g. Robins 1996) and the associated development of imaging technologies making possible virtual realities, cyber-spaces and image-saturated sets of activities and social relations, from computer games to navigating the internet. The term post-photographic image technologies is used to describe the computer-based procedures involved in the creation of simulated virtual realities, computer-based graphics, and a whole range of associated digital image-based techniques. We talk of entering the information age where we will interact with our digital television/computer screen, go shopping on-line, have miniaturised computers attached to our bodies and read our email messages on the 'stick-on' screens attached to our fridge doors. Alongside the enthusiastic promotion of these technologies, interested parties spend considerable effort promoting new visions of our future lives, where many aspects of our daily experience will be transformed through the use of these digital technologies. This second chapter in the 'external images' theme considers the nature of a number of electronic images and ideas found in computer environments, such as the icon, window, hypermedia and world wide web, raising questions about how we understand and respond to them, as well as looking a little closer at the kinds of ideas which underpin their development and design. Where appropriate, questions are also asked about the relationship between post-photographic images and their associated technologies and images of the self, or the 'cyber-self'. Let us begin with the screen.

IMAGES ON THE SCREEN: WINDOWS AND ICONS

The everyday use of computers in contemporary society has familiarised working with, and taking for granted, numerous images, or icons, encountered on the screen. Such images are themselves metaphors for objects and actions associated with the workplace: the first, and now dominant, set of associated images represented on most PCs rested on an understanding of, and narratives about, the office – putting things into files, putting rubbish in a wastepaper basket and so on. Prior to the late 1970s imagery was not a part of everyday computer use. The main change arose from a development initiated by a photocopier company (Xerox), the 'desktop' metaphor. This was introduced into computing by Apple around 1979 and quickly changed the nature of computer use. The desktop metaphor provided an immediate sense of being able to manipulate data intuitively – in the sense that data could now be represented as icon-pages, folders, files, drop-down menus for selection and so on. It made using a computer much easier, or as one computing magazine commented:

> The people who developed the Macintosh made a very basic realisation about personal computing. The way a user interacts with a computer is as important as the computation itself: In other words, the human interface, as it has come to be called, is as fundamental to computing as any processor configuration, operating system, or programming environment. This philosophy further postulates that the ultimate goal of computer technology is, in a sense, to make the computer disappear, that the technology should be so transparent, so invisible to the user, that for practical purposes the computer does not exist. In its perfect form, the computer and its application stand outside data content so that the user may be completely absorbed in the subject matter – it allows a person to interact with the computer just as if the computer were itself human.
>
> (*MacUser*, March 1989: 89)

In line with such aims we have seen the gradual emergence of computer-mediated communication (CMC) research as a development from earlier human–computer interaction (HCI) research. Before we envisage the 'disappearance' of the computer, let us focus a little closer on the objects and images presented to us when using a PC. It seems more than mere coincidence that computer designers use the term 'icon' when referring to the 'image-objects' presented on computer screens, given the Byzantine historical association of the word: understood either as a picture that represents the divine or as the divine itself. For users of computers the 'magical' properties of these screen objects can promote an almost superstitious attitude – certainly in the sense that the meanings projected onto them always exceed the conventionally understood meanings the object might normally have. The graphical user interface is a world of pictures which is meant to be transparent but is in effect almost magical, certainly in the sense that users quickly realise they know how to use something or what something means, but often they are never quite sure why they know.

The idea of the interface is presupposed on a metaphor of human–machine interaction, an image of instrumentality where people are dealing with that boundary of anxiety between mastery and competence. In practice the interface is really a heavily mediated intersubjective context of communication between user and computer [machine]. This is one aspect of computing which is rarely addressed within either computer science or HCI. For many everyday users of computers they are essentially machines which are saturated with human intentionality. Reason (1997) has commented on the metaphorisation of the interface, observing that the construction of visual images is dominated by models of collage, for an ensemble of still images, and of montage, for an assembly of moving images. Arguably the multimedia interface can be construed as combining something of both modes in its construction while achieving a novel, and as yet unexamined, visual domain. Robins (1996), commenting on the nature of the images presented to us on computers, notes:

> The relation between the photographic image and the 'real world' is subverted, leaving the entire problematic concept of representation pulverised . . . and destabilising the bond the image has with time, memory or history. What this represents can, indeed, be justifiably described as 'a fundamental transformation in the epistemological structure of our visual culture' (Druckrey 1989). This is all the more so when the images are computer generated rather than simply computer-manipulated. If the computer image appears 'realistic' – if it "positively enshrines photographic realism as the standard, unquestioned model of vision' – it is the case that the referent is not, in fact, 'in the real world', but is itself an image, a mathematical-informational representation" (Slater 1996). Reality is no longer represented, but is simultaneously modelled and mimicked. Through this process of simulation, the whole question of accuracy and of authenticity becomes not simply problematical, but apparently, at least, anachronistic and redundant.
>
> (Robins 1996: 41)

In one sense such comments pre-empt the 'image to reality' question in photography addressed in the next chapter, by explicitly recognising that the figurative meanings of such images always bring into place an interpretative 'reading'. In the long-established tradition within computing of using acronyms whenever possible, the earlier screen interfaces were sometimes described as 'WIMP' environments. This stood for a environment which contained (w)indows, having (i)cons within it, alongside a (m)ouse device attached to the computer, which allowed the user to 'interact' with the objects in the screen through the use of a (p)ointing tool, i.e. a moving icon which could be used to 'act on' the iconic objects on the screen (and of course in the macho world of late 1970s computer system design, windows were for 'wimps'). What exactly is this iconic object the 'window', and how are we to understand it?

The first thing to notice is that windows have many moving parts and menus do not. For example you can close a window box, size it, use scroll bars, activate the 'drag' bar, change the sizing handle and so on, but nobody has told

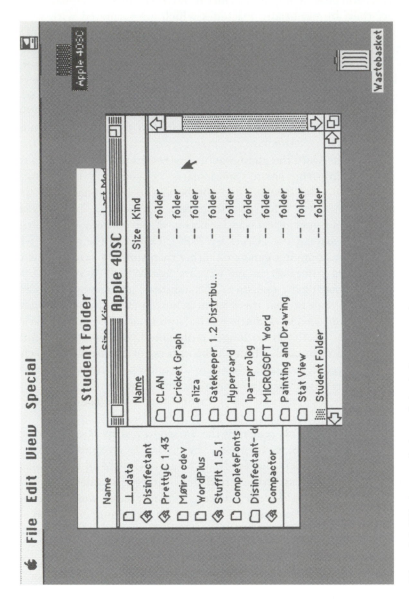

Figure 9.1 Window semiotics and the desktop metaphor

you about what it means to have a white space on a screen. And so, while you can change the box frame and reveal more paper, the question remains 'Where is the information which is not yet shown?' When the window comes to the front, where does the information come from? Similarly, where is the information occluded by the menu which drops down? And even is it on top? In fact it has to be asked what is IT and can it be said to be ON TOP? The screen invokes what you might call a 'virtual metaphysics' of a kind familiar from the crazy – yet semio-logical – physics of the children's cartoon. In such a world, it seems legitimate to ask questions such as: where is the flame when the candle is blown out?

For example, consider how a new user might interpret a 'window' and what he/she might think can be done with it. The window divides the screen into regions which have an inside and an outside, and usually a boundary frame divides these parts. (The frame itself may be further visually differentiated into scroll bars, title bar, sizing gadgets and so on.) The semiotic field invoked by the metaphor tempts us to think of the frame bounding a view onto something beyond the frame. The 'screen' apparently has a phenomenological depth, there are two 'levels' – the 'surface' and the 'beyond'. The window allows us to see what lies beyond it: a list of files and applications, perhaps, 'on' a 'sheet' which can be seen 'through' the window. It is this scenario which makes sense of the action of scroll bars, of course, and thereby incidentally contributes to the ambiguity of the 'direction arrows' on the bars: do they point in the direction in which we wish to look next, or in the direction in which we wish to move the sheet beyond the window?

The phenomenological depth expressed in the window's name, which orients the user to a set of expectations of possibility, is partially confirmed by its operation. There are important – if superficially minor – dislocations with respect to the prior behaviour of 'ordinary' windows, however. How do you influence the amount of the scene 'beyond' revealed by the window? Not – as the habits of perspective would suggest – by the viewer going nearer to or further away from the window, but by altering the size of the window itself. Although the window metaphor invites a carry-over of relevant experiences of window-related attitudes and understandings from the mundane world to that of the interface, it does so in a way which requires a progressive 'de-materialisation', as it were, of the actual ground which seems to support the initial usefulness and intelligibility of the metaphor. The concept 'window' must undergo a very rapid metamorphosis of signification if it is to grasp the nature of the developing interface. Computer designers seem intent on reinventing the wheel; or more particularly acting as if they are inventing a completely new set of problems and then having to 'bootstrap' realisable solutions to these wherever answers can be found, but always within a discourse which foregrounds the new, innovative and previously unimaginable. We might note that the cartoonist has already had to solve similar problems – how to create relevant objects within a world he is trying to convince us about, and often a non-Newtonian world!

Another question to ask of the cartoon world, when considering the screen interface, is whether our interactions within it, were this possible, would help us to understand it or not, which leads onto distinctions between the cartoon and the screen interface. Consider first the screen interface, which amounts to a visual picture akin to a set of screen shots or stills. What are the objects that a user is presented with? A cursor that moves, changes when interacting with other objects in the screen (e.g. into an I-beam when over text, yet into an arrow when over a menu, or into a rotating watch or egg-timer when too busy to permit user activity). In effect it provides information about properties of space and changes in form to show potential actions or possibilities within that space. Why then do users (particularly new or relatively inexperienced ones) find the screen confusing if not threatening?

In order to answer that, consider next the cartoon world. Here properties of objects are not the same as in the real world. It's not as if objects don't have properties, but rather consider how they behave. People can be flattened out and yet jump back up. If you are not conscious that you are in mid-air with no ground below you, then the chances are you will not fall down. When swallowing an object, the shape maintains its characteristics as it goes down. If this world has properties which we are not used to, why are we not confused? Most importantly we are provided with indications about properties through the narratives within which they are set, or unfold. The properties become visible in the context of characters trying to do things. The operations of characters reveal the properties of objects in the cartoon world. We are happy to appropriate the cartoon world in terms of narrative.

Returning to the screen world, here narratives are simply meaningless if you don't know what it is you want to do. Particularly for new users, if you have little knowledge of the task, purposes, procedures and possibilities available to you (as a set of embedded social practices germane to your everyday world), then there is no available background for the construction or unfolding of comprehensible narratives. Without such it is simply impossible to recognise the objects, signs and characteristics of properties within the screen domain. Furthermore the computer industry, being what it is, involves an ever increasing set of new possibilities being made available (somebody is always trying to sell a computer user new possibilities), however unless the icons, objects and structures are grounded or embedded within narratives about tasks, actions and procedures then it is quite possible they will remain unrecognised. We will return again to narrative when we consider hypermedia domains. For now let us consider in a little more detail one or two icons found on computer screens.

ICON(S) AND IMAGES

Recognising icons as objects within the screen environment is not necessarily obvious. Rogers (1989) provides one classification of the function and form of icons and proposes to develop a 'grammar' of icon forms: one which maps onto the underlying system structure. She points out that a great deal of effort is being expended in what she calls 'iconic interfacing', yet this development is taking place in something of a theoretical vacuum:

> Unlike verbal language, in which there are a set of syntactic and semantic rules which provide us with a means of disambiguating the meaning of verbal language, pictorial language has, as yet, no equivalent set of rules underlying its comprehension.
>
> (Rogers 1989: 106)

Rogers lists a number of the advantages and disadvantages of using icons; among the former are that they provide an impression of easiness, tap into the preference of facilitative nature for our living in a 'visual-spatial' culture, are universally meaningful, and overcome potential 'confusion' problems concerning implicit associations they may have. However, consideration of even an apparently simple sign calls into question the idea that they are universally meaningful. Consider a common 'sign' encountered when using a computer, as in Figure 9.2. Although the actions implicit in the recognition of this sign might appear obvious, there are a number of noteworthy aspects to the 'reading' of the sign. First, there are at least three things the hand might be doing, welcoming, saying 'hello' or saying 'stop'. Second, the little mark on the bottom of the hand indicates American design. In contrast to European hands found in road or information signs, American hands tend to be larger or chubbier (maybe indexing the economic superiority of the better-fed culture!). Third, the foreground/background of the hand indicates that the sign is transmuted from the American road traffic sign for STOP. Leaving aside the other signification processes presupposed by the language in the sign itself, it is clear that even a simple supposedly unambiguous sign requires some understanding of its production in order to give it an appropriate reading.

It is difficult then to defend the view that icons are universally understood. In a similar fashion, Horton (1995) argues that objects clearly do not have the same symbolic meanings around the world, and examples he asks computer designers to avoid include those shown in Figure 9.3.

Leaving aside the debate over icon design in computing and psychology, the relationship between icons and iconic languages remains relatively formalistic and categorical (e.g. Meunier 1998). What is important, however, is that the categorical structures implicit in iconic representation on the computer screen

Figure 9.2 Warning images at the screen interface

Type symbol	Example	Intended meaning	Why it fails
Pun		Post entries in an accounting program	In English the word post means both to write entries into a ledger and to mail an object. In other languages each meaning requires a different word.
Hand gesture		Precisely, yes	In France, this means zero or worthless. In Japan it is a reference to money. In South America it refers to the anus.
Mythological or religious symbol		Minor glitch	Is this a gremlin, a bat with a long tail, or a satanic emblem?
Totem animal as symbol		Copy, reproduce rapidly	Rabbits can symbolize rapid reproduction or sexual promiscuity. In much of Europe, rabbit is a dinner entree. In Australia, rabbits are vermin.

Figure 9.3 Some reasons why icons are not letters in a universal language

are seen as relatively successful because, 'a single icon by itself may be limited, but in a coherent set of other icons the rules are easily discovered by the user and hence each icon more easily decoded' (p. 822). Such a view side-steps the role of user interpretation. The initial value of icons on computer screens was that they alleviated the need for extensive text on screen, making valuable use of limited screen space and at the same time facilitating realisable metaphors of interactivity (alongside the use of a mouse/pointer). However, the attempt to make icons universal by somehow increasing their generic qualities may increase the likelihood that they appear ambiguous. As Peterrson (1994) notes,

> pictorial language must be adapted to the viewer's capacity for interpret-ing it. Communication can be said to function successfully . . . if the viewer understands, to the fullest extent, what the picture maker wants the picture to say, and if the message conveyed is unambiguous.
>
> (Peterrson 1994: 10)

Of course the icon/picture computer screen designer is no longer addressing the localised concerns of the 'stand-alone' personal computer. Increasingly the primary function of the domestic PC is to connect into the internet and the world wide web and so we turn to the hyper-images of the internet.

HYPERMEDIA: IMAGES OF INTERCONNECTEDNESS
AND A WEB OF POSSIBILITY

Within the contemporary educational world there has been considerable focus on hypermedia, defined in a shorthand form as general interactive media integrating text, graphics, audio and video in a computer-based or television-based environment. The definitions 'hypertext' and 'hypermedia' are sometimes used interchangeably, but essentially people reading hypermedia documents are often provided with links or interconnections which permit novel methods of 'navigating' information. The world wide web (WWW) is one example of a hypermedia environment, which emerged when electronic mail and hypermedia technology were brought together (note: the 'http' prefix to internet addresses stands for hypertext transfer protocol). The corresponding image of the hypermedia learner we sometimes come across is of:

> an information seeker not the end point of a communicative act . . . on the World Wide Web we are driven by genuine doubt, curiosity and playfulness to surf the net, to explore the many communities of discourse and practice found there . . . The dominant metaphor of education as efficient communication or knowledge consumption must change to that of the hunter-gatherer.
>
> (Cunningham 1998: 835)

Navigating hypermedia is commonly thought to be a problem (Conklin 1987; Bruza 1990). The internet user is said to suffer from cognitive overload and a tendency to get lost and disoriented. It is not clear why this view arose. The hypermedia environment seems often to have been pictured as an inherently disordered heap of items, some few of which would be of interest to a user. The problem of finding those items of interest evoked a metaphorical migration that led from rural haystacks and their needles to urban cities and their labyrinthine streets, their alphabetically indexed street-plans. The dominant imagery in thinking about the revolution in electronic communications drew conspicuously upon archetypes from an urban imagination formed in nineteenth-century Europe (addresses, paths, highways, the performed self of the stranger, the aimlessly strolling – surfing? – *flâneur*), from an earlier revolution in literacy (anarchic individualism, bookmarking, browsers) and a post-Enlightenment cultural ambivalence about technology that grants elemental potency to figures cognate with the hybridity of the 'cyborg' – net, web, search engine, spider. Lost in the city, lost in a book, a mere ghosting in the machine.

The navigational problem on the WWW was answered not by a change in representation of the Web itself, but in a shift in social orientation to its use: the introduction of Yahoo! (a search application) depended upon the sociality of the Web to build up its indexing databases, and surely brackets the users' (and the maker's) sense of any special problem in the representation of hyperspace. To all intents and purposes, the Web is Borges' 'Library of Babel', a library of unbounded extent, but one for which no catalogue (no book of all books so complete that it includes itself, and so inevitably spawns its own fatal incompletion) need ever exist.

Navigation is assisted by the provision of a conventional, metaphorical or allegorical framework which serves to organise (the user's orientation towards) its material constituents. The alphabet may serve, a scaffolding which transforms the hypermedia experience into a variant of that obtained when consulting a dictionary or encyclopaedia. A city map will do, providing for an experience of use, which shuffles from screens to roads to journeys to travellers' tales. (A 'Canterbury Tour' [see URL: http://www.hillside.co.uk/] employs (and enjoys!) this figuration, for obvious reasons, but so also did the Apple Electronic World interface.) We notice, however, that even though both encyclopaedia (alphabet) and city (map) provide an idiom for developing narrativised histories of use and activity, neither is itself a narrative. Indexes and images are not narratives, although they do furnish resources for organising narrative because they offer (shared and intelligible) resources for organising activity.

With reference to the authoring of hypermedia documents (and hypermedia environments generally) we might start by considering the differences between what we can call originating material and subsequent and successive (re-)authorings of that material. Originating or, even better, the establishing of hypermedia material is akin to relations of substance and form for the potter. Initial authoring is of course an interpretative act, but one of a distinct kind. Selecting a slab of clay and 'slapping the clay on the wheel' is a skilled activity and yet particular in that before the very act of throwing, the material could have been used for a square pot, a round pot or whatever. The initial impetus allows certain kinds of forms and constrains others. The 'throwing' itself provides an initial impetus which then 'in flight' determines, constrains, permits, encourages particularity. It is not so much the making available of structure which affords certain possibilities, more a sense of compliance. For hypermedia environments, the compliance of the hypermedia is the mode of the text in that initial environment. At this point we are unclear as to how such initial establishing conditions of the hyper-authored document play upon the perception and comprehension of that text/media for the reader, or how it bears on the subsequent evolving multiple reader-authored hypermedia. Whatever else, narrativisation is likely to be an essential element in comprehending and appropriating any such material (e.g. Landow 1992).

Notions (for there are many) of 'narrative' are employed in a variety of ways in the developing discourses of 'hypermedia'. We can distinguish two broad strategies in thinking about their relationships. The first takes the point of view of the maker of hypermedia artefacts. The second adopts that of the user of hypermedia products. From the point of view of the maker, narrativity – in both senses: the property of being a narrative, and the potential of being rendered or represented as a narrative in a process of narrativisation – tends to become associated with questions of control, structure and intelligibility. By investing hypermedia presentations with designed 'narrative pathways' through the use of tools for the design and recognition of narrative structure, it is usually hoped that the user will feel 'at home' in the hypermedia space, will recognise the achievement of goals, will develop tactics of use that are experienced as advancing the purposes of the user's use of the product (such a disposition is implicit in, for example, Plowman 1996; Landow 1992). (See URL: http://www.nationalgeographic.com/modules/pirates/maina.html for a typical narrative example.) It is striking that, as with film and television, the relationship between narrative and engagement with the images and representations in hypermedia domains is becoming a central focus for research. There is quite another sense of story-telling, however, in virtual environments, the narratives which surround the images and 'versions of the self' produced by those who find the internet an ideal arena for fantasy, projection, expression and performance.

ELECTRONIC PRESENCE: THE SELF IN THE SOMEWHERE/NOWHERE SPACE

Alongside the introduction and uptake of the mobile phone, the everyday use of electronic mail is testament to the significant impact that information technology has had on social-cultural life. Electronic mail is akin to letter writing yet different, but at the same time a form of discourse which subsumes both the private and the public in a hitherto unrealised fashion. As with other forms of communication, though, interdependent with our sending of an electronic mail message is an image or impression of the kind of person we are or wish to be seen as. At least four factors have a bearing on the communicative relations of electronic communication: the function of the message, the context within which it is made, the codes and conventions which bear upon how the message is written and received, and the history or sequence within which the message is positioned. In other words, as with other forms of communication, much will depend on the reason why the email is being sent (to a friend, colleague, boss or employee), the context (on a bulletin board, as a private message, in response to a 'cc:' of a previous email or whatever), the codes or conventions (which might range from formal address, through the use of signatures and the practice of 'flaming'), and the history or sequence of use (Schmitz and Fulk 1991).

More than any other factor, though, it is the very immediacy and 'time-dependent' nature of electronic communication which marks it out as a somewhat novel communication domain. Frequent users of email communication testify to the observation that there is an ongoing yet short period of time (approximately a few days and/or the last 5–10 emails on a given topic) which constitutes the active discourse realm (particularly on discussion groups and bulletin boards). There is also considerable concern and interest in preserving and maintaining certain types of images or 'versions of the self' pre-supposed in the messages people write. The production and maintenance of particular 'cyber-selves' is even more pronounced within 'chat-rooms' – on-line environments where participants are actively encouraged to take on and pro-mote fantasy versions of who they are (for example, one convention of such environments is to use a fictitious name).

While there is little doubt that email is becoming an increasingly important form of communication one could hardly argue that this is a form of 'interac-tion' as such. Notwithstanding the fact that there can be a sense of 'interactivity', particularly where participants are sending and receiving emails so quickly that it is 'as if' they are having a conversation, the messages remain texts and thus subject to the conventions of the written word (syntactic, gram-matical, semantic). In fact rather than insisting that one of the advantages of electronic communication is that it comes closer to interaction in the dynamic conversational sense, is the fact that it contains elements of interactivity yet avoids the potentially threatening or troubling demands of social interaction and talk. This is borne out by the observation that those who are particularly attracted to 'chat-rooms' (i.e. very frequent or 'addicted' users) are people who find everyday interaction rather problematic or challenging (Bays 1998). One cultural image we now have of the 'internet aficionado' is of somebody (often male) hidden away in an upstairs bedroom busily communicating with every-body and anybody through the internet, yet in a safe and unthreatening environment, where as a last resort, the PC can always be switched off.

Quite another image of the self/social identity found in contemporary writ-ing on electronic image technology surrounds the notion of cyberspace. In this essentially 'absent yet present, somewhere but nowhere' domain there are at least two identifiable discourses about virtual reality, as Robins (1996) notes. On the one hand there are the visionaries and prophets, including the late Timothy Leary, who outline utopian spaces in very much the tradition of the Kantian transcendental imagination, and on the other commentators such as Sadie Plant, who espouse a critical post-structuralist perspective where ques-tions of identity and the self are bracketed (Plant 1997). To paraphrase Robins, in this accommodating reality, the self is reconstituted as a fluid and poly-morphous entity. Identities can be selected or discarded at will, as in a game of fiction:

> Weaving together a blend of post-structuralist theory and cyberpunk fic-tion, this other discourse charts the emergence of cyborg identities. In the new world order, old and trusted boundaries – between human and machine, self and other, body and mind, hallucination and reality – are dissolved and deconstructed. With the erosion of clear distinctions, the emphasis is on interfaces, combinations and altered states . . . But, more than this, through the configurations of electronic and virtual space, it presents an all-encompassing censorial ecology that presents opportunities for alternative dematerialised identity compositions. In its most sustained

form – a kind of cyborg schizoanalysis – the collapse of boundary and order is linked to the deconstruction of ego and identity and the praise of bodily disorganisation, primary processes and libidinal sensation.

(Robins 1996: 91)

Over and above recognising the psychoanalytic parallels with film we noted in Chapter 8, the suggestion is that the new virtual technologies now provide a space in which to resist or embrace postmodernity. For Robins (1996), cyberspace is a bit like Oz – when we get there it has no location. The utopian space, the Net, the Web, the virtual community, is that nowhere–somewhere in which we shall be able to recover the meaning and the experience of community. Interestingly, however, he suggests:

it is time to re-locate virtual culture in the real world (the real world that virtual culturalists, seduced by their own metaphors, pronounce dead or dying). Through the development of new technologies, we are, indeed, more and more open to experiences of de-realisation and de-localisation. But we continue to have physical and localised existences. We must consider our state of suspension between these conditions. We must de-mythologise virtual culture if we are to assess the serious implications it has for our personal and collective lives. Far from being some kind of solution for the world's problems – could there ever be a 'solution'? – virtual inversion simply adds to its complexities.

(Robins 1996: 103)

The computer and associated post-photographic technologies certainly extend the domain of the image and we might note with interest the discourse of fear and suspicion in Robins's work and parallels with earlier responses to other image technologies, including radio, film and television. We forget that as far as 'internal images' are concerned we may already be embedded in 'virtual worlds', an observation supported by our night-time adventures in the dream world.

CONCLUDING COMMENT

There is little doubt that post-photographic technologies pose new issues for a psychology of the image. The icons and images we are presented with, and the metaphors, ideas and concepts designed so as to support a 'reading' of such signs, interpenetrate the host of projections, fears, fantasies and anxieties we bring to the computer. More than any other domain the experience of interactivity brings to the foreground relations between external and internal images. As yet the forms of analysis of these signs in psychology have been dominated by the formalism endemic to HCI. The most significant challenge ahead is to develop sufficiently rich theoretical frameworks to aid our attempts at understanding virtual images and our relations with them.

10 Photography and the photographic image

INTRODUCTION

Open up any photography guide and you will quickly find a popular reading of what constitutes photography, perception, seeing with a good eye, and all that is said to surround the construction of a good photo-image. For example, one of the companies which produce an easy to use and relatively low cost camera for the general population, advise their readers:

> Good photographs come from developing an eye for the picture . . . Success requires no more than the ability to make the essential creative leap from what you see to what will work as a photographic image . . . The secret of doing this is to train the eye to see images that will give pleasure when they are taken out of the complex confused and constantly shifting world and made into photographs isolated by their frames.
>
> (Kodak 1993: 17)

Here we have an implicit model of visual perception – develop a good eye to cope with the confusing, complex world; and an indication of the conditions within which an image can be called a photograph – for example the boundary frame; and advice about how one is only required to 'train the eye' to succeed. An introductory psychology student might expect that photography is the kind of area in which the discipline would have made a significant contribution, but sadly, this is not so. One popular idea of psychology is that, amongst other things, it investigates visual perception where the knowledge gained subsequently influences the development of applied related fields. While this may be the case for certain research areas such as neuropsychology, there remain relatively few studies into how we perceive photographs and an absence of theorising on photography. Canter (1988) notes that there has been a reluctance in psychology to consider directly the actual photographic material used in psychological research, resulting in there being very little psychological study of this medium. Why, we might ask, is there little theory and a relative absence of empirical work?

For the most part within psychology the photograph is treated either as an object of interest only in so far as it serves as stimulus material, e.g. in the numerous studies undertaken in face recognition (McKelvie 1991), or as an object of somewhat minor interest in social psychology (Beloff 1985), in as much as it provides an avenue into examining issues of identity and self-presentation (Ziller and Lewis 1981). In contrast, within cultural studies and critical theory, and increasingly social anthropology and sociology, there is considerable interest in photography and a number of theoretically rich analytic frameworks. Wells (1997) notes that theorising photography relies upon the development of complex models of analysis which take account of at least three distinct starting points: semiotic, socio-historical and psychoanalytic. She argues:

> Within this conceptual approach it is not the objective presence of the image which is at stake, but rather the force field within which it generates meaning. This contrasts with semiological stress on systems of signification. In effect we are invited to consider, not only the text, its production and its reading, but also to take account of the social relations within which meaning is produced and operates. Here, the semblance of the real underpins processes of interpretation. Photography is reassuringly familiar, not least because it seems to reproduce that which we see, or might see. In so far as visual representations contribute to constructing and reaffirming our sense of identity, this familiarity, and the apparent realism of the photographic image, render it a particularly powerful discursive force.
>
> (Wells 1997: 51)

This chapter will provide an overview of contemporary theories and ideas on photography, incorporating relevant studies from psychology, critical theory, social anthropology and sociology. The aim is to provide a context for considering different views on how these 'external' images influence, inform and interpenetrate our everyday lives. It will consider in addition the relationship between photographs and personal ideas of identity and the self-image, alongside some consideration of the social practices which surround this technology of image production.

There are essentially two views informing current debates in photography. One asserts the primary 'realism' of the photographic image, implicitly or explicitly pointing to the relationship between external reality and the image; the other focuses on the discourses, interpretations and codes which inform recognising and 'reading' a photographic image. Consideration will be given to realist and coding perspectives, drawing upon work within and beyond psychology, as well as approaches which have focused on relationships between photography and identity. Concluding comments touch on the nature of photography as social practice.

REALITY AND CODIFICATION IN THE
PHOTOGRAPHIC IMAGE

In her critical discussion of the status and nature of photography in contemporary culture, Wells (1997) suggests that there are two theoretical orientations in photography: the first focuses on the relationship of the image to reality, the second, on interpretative discourses, which form the basis for the reading of a photographic representation. Emphasising realism, John Berger (1972) proposed that 'photographs are records of things seen' and 'photography has no language of its own: there is no transformation, the only decision is the choice of moment to record and isolate'. In contrast, it has been argued that the meaning of the photographic image is determined in part through associated discourses, and through the context in which the photograph is used, and:

> By contrast with Sontag's emphasis on the relation between the image and its source in the actual historical world, Price (1994) starts from questions of viewing and the context of reception . . . in principle there is no single meaning for the photograph, but rather an emergent meaning, within which the subject matter of the image is but one element.
>
> (Wells 1997: 38)

In line with this view, Eco (1982) comments that if photography is to be likened to perception, this is not because the former is a 'natural' process but because the latter is also coded, echoing earlier comments in Chapter 2 regarding the nature of visual perception. However, the critical theorist Barthes (1982), while similarly emphasising the semiological nature of the photograph, comments that:

> Every photograph is a certificate of presence. This certificate is the new embarrassment which its invention has introduced into the family of images . . . [it is] . . . neither image nor reality, a new being, really: a reality one can no longer touch. Perhaps we have an invincible resistance to believing in the past, in History, except in the form of myth. The Photograph, for the first time, puts an end to this resistance: henceforth the past is as certain as the present, what we see on the paper is as certain as what we touch. It is the advent of the Photograph – and not as has been said the cinema – which divides the history of the world.
>
> (Barthes 1982: 87–88)

And echoing this idea that the photograph points to both the 'real' of the external world and the codifying nature of signifying practices, Sekula (1982) comments that all photographic communication takes place along the lines of binary folklore. He contrasts the 'symbolist' with the 'realist' folk-myth represented in the opposition 'art photography' vs. the 'documentary photography', where any particular photograph is positioned somewhere between these two realms of meaning:

> The oppositions between these two poles are as follows: photographer as seer vs. photographer as witness, photography as expression vs. photography as reportage, theories of imagination (and inner truth) vs. theories of empirical truth, affective value vs. informative value, and finally, metaphoric signification vs. metonymic signification.
>
> (Sekula 1982: 108)

There is certainly a sense in which the photographic image relates to 'that which really exists or existed'; however, simply asserting such a relation glosses over whatever implicit assumptions inform our understanding of visual perception. There is little doubt that one has to learn how to 'read' photographic images, evidenced in social anthropological commentary on the conditions under which people from 'non-visual' cultures display ambivalence towards or do not recognise the images of objects portrayed in photographs. This puts into relief the claim that the photograph 'captures' reality, in the sense that what is represented has some kind of one-to-one relationship to whatever was photographed. In what follows the aim is not to address the question of whether one or other perspective is more appropriate, rather to highlight the ideas and issues which inform either interpretation.

REALIST ORIENTATIONS TO THE PHOTOGRAPHIC IMAGE

In psychology there is a noteworthy silence on the question of the relationship between the photographic image and reality. This is something of a surprise given the debate within the discipline on whether perception is constructivist or direct (see Chapter 3). Even in instances where there is experimental evidence that perception of a photographic image appears subject to interpretative processes (Intraub et al. 1992), explanatory accounts bypass discussion of the image–reality question and favour a constructivist position predicated on cognitive rather than discursive processes. Unlike the question of representation in mental imagery, the photographic image is in no sense a theoretical object for contemporary perceptual psychology.

Within the ecological or realist approach to perception, however, the question of photography, or picture perception more generally, generates debate given the conception of vision as involving the detection of affordances available in the optical array (and see Chapter 2). To paraphrase Reed (1988), images are not copies of things or conventional constructions, but instead ways of manipulating optical information: visual realism is seen as a technique for providing information that is useful to an observer, 'and both the needs of the observer and the procedures of the displayer are historically developed cultural facts, as well as psychological and biological facts' (p. 259). Gibson (1979) argued that perspective on pictures (including photographs) could not be described as a kind of language, instead 'the essence of a picture is just that its information is not explicit. The invariants cannot be put into words or symbols. The depiction captures an awareness without describing it' (p. 285). For Gibson, understanding pictures is a matter of perceptually matching the information presented with corresponding information from the three-dimensional environment. Gibson (1979) proposed to call images in the photograph 'virtual objects', in that they are perceived and yet not perceived:

> the duality of the information in the array is what causes the dual experience. We need to understand the apprehension of virtual objects and . . . we do so in connection with the perceiving of real surfaces of the environment, including picture surfaces . . . a picture always requires two kinds of apprehension that go on at the same time, one direct and the other indirect. There is a direct perceiving of the picture surface along with an indirect awareness of virtual surface – a perceiving, knowing or imagining as the case may be.
>
> (Gibson 1979: 284)

Semioticians of photographic images have long recognised the dual nature of photographs – somehow tied to visual experience (reality) and yet nevertheless signs within a culturally determined sign-system. Photography as semiosis does not lend itself to the kind of linguistic structuralism developed by Saussure and Chomsky or the post-structuralism found in the writings of Eco and Derrida. Images are not signs in the sense that letters or words in a written language are, and we noted earlier the difficulties encountered with attempts at developing visual grammars (Kress and van Leeuwen 1996). Iconic imagery or visual semiosis have rarely been treated as a formal grammar, and Roland Barthes, arguably the post-structuralist most readily associated with critical commentary on photography, has commented that differences between language and iconic imagery become particularly marked with photography, 'In every photograph there is the stupefying evidence of this-is-what-happened-and-how' (Barthes 1982: 39).

Certainly while the linguistic sign has a completely arbitrary relationship to its referent, this is not the case with the photograph. There is no natural contingency which insists that the word 'cow' bears any direct association with the four-legged animal normally found in a field. However, with a photograph we implicitly understand that in some sense the image has been caused by whatever it is said to represent. For Gibson (1979) the information in the optic array (light) available to us when we see a table, for example, is the same information that is captured by the photo-sensitive chemicals involved in producing the image of the table on paper.

This relation of the image to the real is again emphasised by Barthes in his well-known essay on photography, 'Camera Lucida', where he comments:

In the photograph, the event is never transcended for the sake of something else: the Photograph always leads the corpus I need back to the body
I see; it is . . . in short, what Lacan calls the *Tuche*, the Occasion, the
Encounter, the Real, in its indefatigable expression . . . [but at the same
time] . . . The photograph is vaguely constituted as an object, and the persons who Figure there are certainly constituted as persons, but only
because of their resemblance to human beings, without any special intentionality. They drift between the shores of perception, between sign and
image, without ever approaching either.

(Barthes 1982: 4)

In semiotics we also find an empirical tradition of photographic analysis.
Giardetti and Oller (1995) argue that by definition, 'an undoctored photograph, unlike other "pictures" which may involve purely fictional or imaginary
objects, captures a moment that is real'. And emphasising this view, they
make the stronger claim that what is distinctive about photographs is that
they do correspond with an external reality:

Photographs . . . stand in a logical correspondence with whatever facts
they are photographic images of in much the manner of sensory-motor
representamens – though photographs, like written records, are relatively
more permanent than sensory-motor impressions. But, like all visual representations, and all other iconic signs, it turns out that photographs have
a more or less indeterminate meaning unless supplemented by appeal to
indexes (e.g. the actual pointing out of certain persons, places, times,
etc.) and more abstract linguistic or other symbols (e.g. names, captions,
texts) that are not subject to the same indeterminacy that icons are subject
to.

(Giardetti and Oller 1995: 138)

The proposal is that what is fundamentally distinct about photographs, in contrast to other iconic representamens, is that they are by definition images
which actually correspond to some real state of affairs in the external, material world, at some time and place in the past. In support of their position
Giardetti and Oller (1995) proposed, and then tested out, a Peircean theory of
photographic meaning by asking people to carry out a thematic categorisation
task, the results of which were then interpreted using factor analysis and correlation techniques. They argue that their findings indicate that there is a
'language' aspect to visual literacy, and 'conventional practices instilled by
socio-cultural experience enable us to devote cognitive resources to things
that surprise us while expected elements are handled routinely' (Giardetti and
Oller 1995: 142). One interpretation of their findings is that most of the
time people rarely find photographic images problematic, but when necessary
can learn to interpret ambiguous images in line with culturally appropriate
readings.

CODIFICATION AND INTERPRETATION: READING THE PHOTOGRAPHIC IMAGE

Within photographic theory one can identify implicit assumptions held regarding the nature of visual perception. The relationship between everyday perception and internal interpretations is often viewed as a somewhat amorphous and elusive mental process based on constructivist representational elements:

> The presence of photographs reveals how circumscribed we are in the throes of sensing. We perceive and interpret the outer world through a set of incredibly fine internal receptors. But we are incapable, by ourselves, of grasping or tweezing out any permanent, sharable figment of it. Practically speaking, we ritually verify what is there, and are disposed to call it reality. But, with photographs, we have concrete proof that we have not been hallucinating all our lives.
>
> (Wells 1997: 101)

The suggestion here is that the eye/brain's sensitive receptor cells are somehow constantly interpreting perceptual information in a dynamic fashion, and only with photography can we mimic the freezing of any one instance of perception. And thus within critical theoretic perspectives on the photograph it is not difficult to find underlying presuppositions about vision which originate from visual psychology.

It is no surprise to note that constructivist representational processes remain dominant within psychological research on photographic image processing, although as previously noted, there have been relatively few studies looking specifically at photographs. McKelvie and colleagues have examined face recognition in photographs and have noted such things as a tendency for people to find it easier to remember faces facing in a left-looking direction (McKelvie 1994); that people can recognise faces easier than cars (McKelvie et al. 1993); and that the orientation of a photographed face affects how easy it is to recognise (McKelvie 1983). A more general phenomenon reported by Intraub et al. (1992) and Intraub and Berkowits (1996) is what is termed 'boundary extension', a tendency for people to remember photographic close-ups as having shown more of a scene than was actually depicted. In these studies people are presented with photographs for very short periods of time, 500 milliseconds or so, and then asked to complete a task which involves recognising objects or scenes in the photographs. Discussing the boundary extension effect, Intraub et al. (1992) cite schema-representational explanations of visual perception. In particular they hold to Hochberg's (1978) argument that visual schemas are abstract representations which allow us to perceive an object through the integration of previous and present eye-fixations, alongside setting up expectations about what the next eye-fixation would be, noting that:

The expectation concerns what the next eye fixation would be likely to bring into view, were the boundary [the frame/edge of the photograph] not present . . . subjects remember seeing parts of the scene that are likely to have existed just outside the camera's field of view. In a sense, subjects are looking at pictures, but remembering scenes . . . scene perception and imagination activate the same schematic representation.

(Intraub et al. 1992: 191)

For semioticians a schema-representational view of photographic image perception is not a theoretically sufficient explanation of our response or reading of photographs. As noted earlier, Eco (1982) comments that it is often forgotten that perception itself involves codification procedures. Similarly, Tagg (1988) points out that when a photographer directs the camera it is focused on a world of objects already constructed as a domain infused with meanings and values, although the perceptual process seems to be simply normal, everyday and 'natural', i.e. non-interpretative. Photographs are material items

produced by a certain elaborate mode of production and distributed, circulated and consumed within a given set of social relations; images made meaningful and understood within the very relations of their production and sited within a wider ideological complex which must, in turn, be related to the practical and social problems which sustain and shape it.

(Tagg 1988: 189)

And further,

By more or less conscious adjustment of an infinite field of significant determinations ranging from the arrangement and lighting of this 'world of objects' to the mechanics and field of view of the camera and the sensitivity of the film, paper and chemical, the photographer abstracts from the distribution of reflected light from the objects to procure a pattern of light and dark on paper which can in no way be regarded as a replication of the 'given' subject. The pattern on paper is, in turn, the object of a perception – or reading – in which it is constituted as a meaningful image according to learned schemas.

(Tagg 1988: 189)

In a sense, Tagg's (1988) reference to learned schemas extends the constructivist interpretation within psychology, however emphasising the ideological conditions that inform the production of photographic images, that is, the social context within which the discourse which constitutes these 'learned schemas' is formulated and understood. This perspective brings to bear on the analysis of photography Foucault's theoretical outlook regarding knowledge and power. For Foucault, power and knowledge are interdependent in essential ways, with power producing knowledge: the exercise of power creates and causes conditions within which criteria for what constitutes knowledge are established. Furthermore, through the exercise of power new knowledge is created and diffused and, conversely, knowledge serves to induce effects of power. Tagg (1988) employs a Foucaultian critical-historical approach highlighting the significance of the photograph as a means of surveillance during the nineteenth century. The suggestion is that the photograph would not have had such an impact on society when first developed had it not been taken up by institutional interests which recognised its potential as a method of surveillance and control. Tagg cites the enthusiasm exhibited by Dr Diamond in 1856, the founder member of the Royal Photographic Society, and resident superintendent of the Female Department of the Surrey County Lunatic Asylum, who expounded his theories of the importance of photography for assisting medical truth:

> the Photographer secures with unerring accuracy the external phenomena of each passion, as the really certain indication of internal derangement, and exhibits to the eye the well-known sympathy which exists between the diseased brain and the organs and features of the body . . . The Photographer catches in a moment the permanent cloud, or the passing storm or sunshine of the soul, and thus enables the metaphysician to witness and trace out the connexion between the visible and the invisible in one important branch of his researches in the Philosophy of the human mind.
>
> (Tagg 1988: 78)

Such observations help remind us that the reading of a photographic image cannot be separated or abstracted out from the social and historical context within which it has come to be recognised, understood and used.

The development of the 'mug shot' genre of portraiture photography can be traced back to the power relations between sitter and photographer, reflecting the institutional interests of, for example, schools, mental hospitals, prisons, adoption authorities and so on. Tagg (1988) shows that there is a clear and repetitive pattern in these kinds of photographs, where the body is isolated with a narrow space around it, the sitter's pose reflects its subjection to an unreturnable gaze and there is close scrutiny of gestures, faces and features. These are all just as much evidence of power as is the clarity of illumination and sharpness of focus, and of course the names and number boards often used in such photographs. To paraphrase Tagg (1988), these photographs exemplify Foucault's arguments regarding state control, the coincidence of an ever more intimate observation and an ever more subtle control alongside an ever more refined institutional order, and an ever more encompassing discourse, 'an ever more passive subjection and an ever more dominant benevolent gaze' (p. 88).

Figure 10.1 Inmate of the Surrey County Asylum (Dr H.W. Diamond – Royal Society of Medicine 1852–1856). By kind permission of the Royal Society of Medicine

Adopting a similar ideological reading of the image, Burgin (1982) argues that the structure of representation in photography, the point of view and the frame, reflect and reproduce an ideological position that, because it is instantaneously and unselfconsciously 'mis-recognised', remains hidden. He points out,

> More than any other textual system, the photograph presents itself as 'an offer you can't refuse'. The characteristics of the photographic apparatus position the subject in such a way that the object photographed serves to conceal the textuality of the photograph itself – substituting passive receptivity for active (critical) reading. When confronted with puzzle photographs of the 'What is it?' variety we are made aware of having to select from sets of possible alternatives, of having to supply information the image does not itself contain. Once we have discovered what the depicted object is, however, the photograph is instantly transformed for us – no longer a confusing conglomerate of light and dark tones it now shows a 'thing' which we invest with a full identity, a being.
>
> (Burgin 1982: 146–147)

Burgin (1982) argues that the coherence, identity and wholeness of the scenes we see depicted in photographs involve similar imaginary projections on the part of the viewer – a refusal to recognise the nature of impoverished reality – similar to Lacanian conceptions of the developing self and the metaphor of the mirror (see Chapter 5).

THE PHOTOGRAPHIC IMAGE AND IDENTITY

As noted earlier in Chapter 6, notions of identity and the self are closely bound up with posture, display and performance. It is a little surprising then that photography has rarely been used in psychology either as the basis for analysing cultural conceptions of the self-display, or as a methodological tool in research exploring the relationship between self-concept and presentation. Photography has on occasion been employed as a therapeutic artefact in psychiatry and therapy. Anderson and Malloy (1976), for example, argue that the appeal of the photograph transcends the visual record and that photographs are akin to dreams, body language and handwriting in providing significant knowledge of what is 'beyond observation'. They give examples of how photographs can be used in therapy, suggesting that they 'capture complexities of individuals and their relationships . . . being lasting documents of personality and life, [they] are acknowledged as a valuable resource for therapists and patients' (p. 260). In such a context photographs are used by the analysand to map out a record of their history to aid in the telling of their life story: the photograph as a resource for the re-narrativisation of the analysand's life story.

In social psychology, personality theorists employ what they term the 'autophotographic essay', which involves asking people to take photographs of themselves and those close to them, and then analysing the content alongside assessment profiles of their personalities (Ziller and Lewis 1981; Dollinger and Clancy 1993). The suggestion is that when the people taking, selecting and directing the production of their photographic essays are themselves the subjects of the study, 'we are viewing the self in his or her own eyes as well as through their own' (Dollinger and Clancy 1993: 1064). Dollinger and Clancy argue that 'the variable' being more 'open to experience' predicts the richness of the photo essay, as does neuroticism and introversion in female photo essayists. Over and above these rather grandiose claims, we might note that the analytic criteria underpinning the rating scale for judging the content of the photographic essays in these studies provides us with one particular reading of what constitutes good photography in this scientific context. A low mark was deemed appropriate for 'booklets that could be characterised by the following qualities: concreteness, unimaginative or dull style, commonplace or prosaic selection of pictures and repetitive content'. Conversely, a high mark was given for 'abstractness, that is metaphoric or deeper meanings implied by a number of pictures, imaginative or creative interpretation of the photo task, evidence of an aesthetic or artistic sensibility, expressive or self-reflective themes and an interesting variety of themes' (p. 1068).

In another area of social psychological research, the work of Halla Beloff (1985, 1988), the photographic portrait provides the foundation for an analysis of self-presentation and identity. She suggests:

> A social psychology of any portrait would involve attention to the choice of pose, gesture, expression, costumes and props. The vision of the sitter and the ambience will provide information about the way in which the subject is to be understood and categorised as an individual who plays roles according to their own definition.
>
> (Beloff 1993: 115)

Analysing self-portraits of the early woman photographer Julia Cameron, Beloff (1993) argues that the spontaneous 'stances' portrayed leak out information regarding how the photographer saw herself, 'her idea of who and how she is' (p. 116). In this work, the photograph is considered as a frozen sample of a pattern of self-presentation. In a related study, and employing a form of discourse analysis, Beloff (1988) examines the self-portraits of eminent male and female photographers. She reasons that a group of professional photographers will be fully conversant with the 'tricks of the trade' regarding photo-image presentation and production, and that such sitters should be able either to present themselves in their ideal representation, or to highlight the procedures involved in making a picture that 'unmasks the process and their person' (p. 297).

Essentially, Beloff (1988) draws out marked differences between the male and female photographers, distinctions which highlight institutional elements bearing on the profession and on gender relations more generally. The men focus on communicating strong ideas about their vocation; employing elaborate stagings and genre play, 'they use portraits of themselves to persuade the audience of the validity and interest of their work' (p. 302), their personal selves drowned by these productions. In contrast, the women photographers employ signs, postures and props in line with the conventions of submissive

Figure 10.2 Margaret Bourke-White, aged 25 (from Beloff 1988)

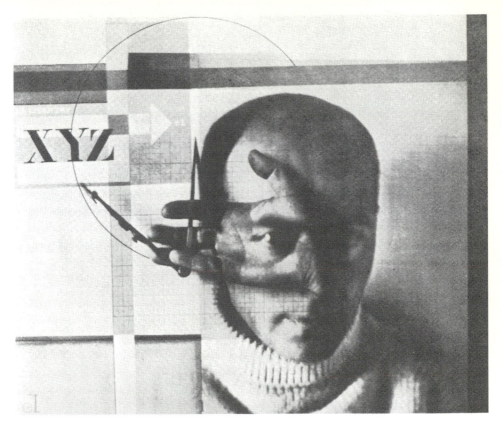

Figure 10.3 Self-portrait, El Lissitzky, 1929 (from Beloff 1988) © DACS 2000

feminine identity, 'the conventions followed in the women's images can be seen as dues paid to the membership of worthy womanhood, which denies their working position' (p. 310). Throughout, the vision or presentation of the self which comes out of this analysis derives more from 'the realm of communally available visual repertoires than in the clear communication of the individual I' (p. 310).

Further analysis on the role of identity and photography can be found in Beloff's (1994, 1997) analysis of Cindy Sherman's 'ultimate nemesis of identity in the post-modern world' – her archive of 230 self-photographic parodies (for a selection see Sherman 1991). Beloff (1994) comments:

> With our particular interest in the social construction of personhood we can further hope to use her beautiful pictures as a challenge to our technical advances in face processing and recognition . . . we would draw the conclusion that her exercises in existential creation of identities must demonstrate that we women could all be all of those women: the athlete,

the sex worker, the torch singer and even the 'ordinary' housewife. Even her cast of the damaged women in the midst of the metaphorical absolute of isolation, psychosis, physical abuse and indeed violently dead, we can identify with. It seems chance that we find ourselves with other tools for selfhood.

(Beloff 1994: 499)

Whatever else, these forms of analysis highlight the relationship between photographic images and identity and begin to articulate issues surrounding notions of what it might be to present an idealised self photo-image.

Within critical theory, photographic portraiture has been analysed as commodity production. Tagg (1988) asks how has it come about that photography is primarily a means of obtaining pictures of faces we know? We all possess school or passport photographs, holiday snapshots, the wedding album, the identity card and increasingly the photo on the web page. He comments that over and above noticing how repetitious such pictures are, these pictures seem to indicate that the 'truth' about a person is indicated by the head and shoulders. The pose of this image can be linked historically to the 'physionotrace', which involved tracing out the profile of the sitter so that it could be engraved onto a copper plate. Tagg (1988) states that photography was not initially limited by such a technique, however there already existed a complex historical iconography with

> elaborate codes of pose and posture readily understood within the societies in which such portrait images had currency . . . The portrait is a sign whose purpose is both the description of an individual and the inscription of social identity. But at the same time, it is also a commodity, a luxury, an adornment, ownership of which itself confers status.
>
> (Tagg 1988: 39)

Such comment reminds us that photography as an emerging technology rested upon existing social practices and conventions regarding identity representation. With that in mind we can turn to the relationship between photography and social context.

PHOTOGRAPHY AND SOCIAL CONTEXT

Considered from a perspective which emphasises social practice and the cultural/contextual basis for the sense we make of the objects and artefacts around us, photographs are considered as rather unique objects, and photography a highly conventional kind of activity. Susan Sontag (1977) has argued that photographs alter and enlarge our notion of what is worth looking at and the kinds of things we seem to have a right to observe. Photographs give people an imaginary possession of a past that is unreal but also help people to take possession of space in which they are insecure; however, 'To photograph people is to violate them, by seeing them as they never see themselves, by having knowledge of them they can never have; it turns people into objects that can be symbolically possessed' (Sontag 1977: 14).

The significance of photography as a set of social practices has been noted in the study in tourism. In line with Sontag's (1977) observation that to photograph is to appropriate the thing photographed, Dilley (1986) comments on the experiential cycle of tourist photography. He notes that first the tourist is attracted to a particular place, in part because of the images and pictures viewed in the travel advertisements. The tourist then goes in search of the experience of viewing whatever is imaged and somehow seeks to reproduce that experience through the taking of appropriate photographs 'capturing the event of viewing'. Subsequently, he/she returns home and now possesses a collection of images that are very similar to the original adverts produced by the travel agent.

Similarly, Ben Ari (1991) comments on the role of the tourist photographer in his analysis of a Japanese initiation rite, arguing that photographic techniques of documentation have transformed the manner in which traditional rites are remembered and interpreted. His ethnographic study highlights the ways in which the camera has had a significant effect not only on the cultural representations of such ceremonies, but also on the social roles and conventions within the event itself. In particular he documents the social consequences of the appropriation of such ceremonies by different groups (the performers, their families, the audience and the observing tourists and local media) through the medium of the camera. Photographs and the social conventions associated with their production and reception have become embedded within cultural practice; they have altered forever notions of what is worth looking at and changed the nature and conduct of traditional ceremonies.

We might also note that photographs, or more precisely photographic images, have a significant effect on how people understand charity. Employing a discursive approach Radley and Kennedy (1997) examined people's conceptions of need when responding or interpreting photo-images used by overseas aid agencies (e.g. to UNICEF). Their detailed analysis of the recorded discussions indicated that people did not simply categorise the images, but rather constructed extended narratives about the moral, ethical and economic aspects of giving money, which in large part depended on entering into an imaginary relationship between viewer and subject. When looking at such images, 'People are making and transforming the image in the course of explaining and justifying both the photographs presented and their standpoint to the subject and interviewer' (p. 454). Radley and Kennedy (1997) argue that this imaginary relationship is not personal, but cultural, in the sense that looking is both discursively and non-discursively ordered, and looking at photographs is always a situated activity.

The significance of the context within which the family photograph is discussed has been examined by Edwards and Middleton (1988) in their study of the ways in which children learn how to remember. They note that family photographs are both semiotically and culturally meaningful artefacts, 'semiotic in that they are depictions of past situations and events – signifiers and representations of something else – and cultural in that there are social and familial conventions involved in the set of pictures they are, who takes what sorts of pictures of what sorts of events, circumstances and subjects' (p. 6).

Edwards and Middleton (1988) looked in detail at the conversations which take place between mothers and their children when discussing family snapshots, noting that this gave rise to rich conversational content and facilitated elaborate inferential reasoning on the part of the child, when talking about events associated with the pictures. Mothers used the photographs as routes into non-depicted elaborations and in doing so, demonstrated important principles involved in learning how to remember. The children were particularly interested in seeing themselves and their siblings in different contexts and the photographs acted as mediators of the past, making it easier for the children to 'learn about remembering without actually having to remember' (p. 21). Such studies highlight the significance of the social and cultural practices which surround photography and serve as the basis for our reading of photographic images.

CONCLUDING COMMENTS

Theoretical interpretations, addressing the relationship between the photographic image and the object or event photographed, often reflect implicit assumptions about the nature of perception itself, whether one adopts a realist, constructivist or encoded/interpreted or semiotic perspective. Psychology has for the most part adopted a realist orientation, glossing over the possibility that the relationship between image and reality could be problematic. There is no doubt that we have to learn how to interpret such images and when doing so, appropriate culturally available discourses which make different readings possible (from the documentary realist through to the aesthetic or artistic, to paraphrase Sekula 1982). A psychology of the image recognises the fascination photographs have for us in our everyday lives and will need to develop richer theoretical frameworks for understanding the 'internal' affective responses we experience when interpreting these external images. Photographic images have a particular place in our personal lives in that they seem to capture something, or at least seduce us into thinking that 'something about us' has been captured. And we only have to reflect on the role of the family photo-album to recognise that photographs also play a significant role in the construction of our life stories.

11 Postscript to a psychology of the image

Some years ago, when I was involved in proposing a final-year or advanced undergraduate university course entitled 'psychology of the image' one or two colleagues voiced reservations about the nature of such a module, commenting, 'there doesn't seem to be much psychology in this course'. Part and parcel of the business of academic life involves defining and maintaining discipline boundaries and thus I was not particularly surprised by this response. Nevertheless, I felt it represented the somewhat contained view the discipline of psychology has regarding the nature of images. For many psychologists, the study of the image, or rather 'imagery', involves research into a particular kind of cognitive mental activity, a process as difficult to understand as the early stages of visual processing. Apart from a few social psychologists who recognise the significance of the image for personal and social identity, the term *image* is of such ambiguity and indeterminacy that whatever it might mean, its study probably belongs to the realm of communication and media studies.

Given the content and thrust of the previous chapters, my own view, unsurprisingly, is that this is a mistake, and in light of the significance images have in contemporary life, a psychological perspective on images and the processes which surround their selection, production and recognition is warranted and necessary. To reiterate an earlier comment, it seems particularly striking that we have one set of theories and ideas about our experience of external images, image technologies and image processes, yet quite another for understanding our internal image experiences, both conscious and unconscious. The study of mental rotation, cognitive maps and image processing informs cognitive neuropsychology, but results in findings which tell me nothing about my experience of dreams, the fantasies I have about myself or my responses to the myriad images I come across during the day. Psychology can make a significant contribution to the study of images and our relationship to them but needs to move away from an over-reliance on particular kinds of research methodologies and theoretical constructs. As a postscript or summary of the topics and issues covered in the book, this final chapter reflects on what has been achieved, not in the fashion of a critical deconstruction but more as a pointer to issues and topics which can further extend a psychological perspective on, and of, the image.

One aim of the book is to situate a psychology of the image within contemporary theories, perspectives and ideas which inform our understanding of images, within and beyond psychology. Presenting the study of the image as a dichotomy between and spanning the 'external' and the 'internal' serves to differentiate and locate the very different approaches one can find in the literature. Three different theoretical perspectives formed the basis for the framework used in the book and to a greater or lesser extent many of the topics and issues reviewed are derived from the theories of Peirce, Lacan and Goffman. It is important to emphasise, however, that this framework is not intended to constitute an integrated all-encompassing 'meta-theory': such an enterprise would fly in the face of the observation that image recognition and production processes are in many respects contradictory, ambiguous and ironic. We only have to remind ourselves that our daily experience of maintaining a 'self-image' is itself a contradictory exercise.

Beginning with Peirce, despite appearances to the contrary, what is important about the possibilities in this form of semiotics is the emphasis on learning, history and the social context within which the conditions for sign production and recognition are made manifest. In other words, in contrast to Saussure, whose semiotics engenders a formalism and abstraction centred on the linguistic sign, Peirce's essential conditions for sign recognition rested on his conception of a 'scientific social intelligence'. Being able to ask under what conditions sign recognition is possible at all relocates many individualistic accounts of image perception. In other words, raising the question of whether you would recognise a sign or image at all, if you hadn't already been trained in, or learned, the social conventions, presuppositions and practices which constitute human life, necessitates a social semiotic starting point for the study of the image. This is as true for advertising as it is for clouds meaning rain. Leaving aside the observation that Peirce may be best understood as a pre-Gibson Gibsonian, this approach also provides a helpful set of constructs for extending sign analysis in the tripartite distinction between icon, index and symbol. And throughout the book we find examples of this approach being used to study images (e.g. in interface design, advertising and photography).

The existence of an agent or a 'self' is at the core of the differences between Goffman and Lacan. We noted how Goffman's analysis of performance, masquerade and the folklore of sign recognition and display have been developed in innovative and fruitful ways within the study of gendered images and photography. In contrast, the psychoanalytic semiotics of Lacan underscores critical work in the study of self-identity, the role of the viewer in advertising and the positioning of the audience in film theory. For a psychology of the image we can find examples of Goffman's role-performance analysis providing the conceptual basis for understanding how people manage to 'present' themselves in everyday interaction, whether face-to-face or during mediated communication. The variety and accessibility of his writings provide a rich source of theories and ideas on images and our responses to them. And not least, Goffman's doctrine of natural expression, while being somewhat all-embracing at times, draws attention to those occasions in everyday interaction which highlight the chronically 'sign-based' nature of conventional behaviour. Only when the apparently fluid, orderly and natural business of everyday interaction breaks down does the social semiotic basis of appropriate behaviour become apparent. The 'natural' business of everyday life is indeed a doctrine and we rarely notice the degree to which we are compelled to display the appropriate signs and symbols of being human (in whatever membership category we find ourselves). And as agents we are indeed 'selves' who respond to the demands of the situation we are in and perform to whatever degree of appropriateness we feel compelled.

The question of agency for Lacan is, as we noted in Chapter 5, as much fantasy as reality. The whole issue of identity becomes problematic, and the relationship between the unconscious and language, and the entry into the symbolic order, the focus of analysis and critique. In many approaches to the study of the image we find the influence of Lacan (e.g. in film, photography and advertising), primarily because our responses to images, and our positioning by them, are so often ambiguous, uncertain and open to interpretation. We noted, for example, how Lacan employs the metaphor of the suture (the stitching together of a wound) to describe the self as a discursive process involving the appropriation of a subject positioning, a dynamic process stitching over the essential lack or absence caused by the initial separation. Likewise, we see how Lacanian perspectives can be realised in media and image studies: taking up the position made available by the film director, locating oneself as the object of the text in the advertisement, dialogically responding to the gaze of a self-portrait in photography, all theorised from within this psychoanalytic semiological project. Whatever else might be said of Lacan, his analysis situates the problematic nature of images of the self within the broader context of the cultural signs and systems of signification which inform our everyday experiences.

Over and above locating a psychology of the image within the theoretical contributions provided by Peirce, Goffman and Lacan, the correspondence between sign/discourse and image/representation requires further clarification. The relationship between any sign and the system of signification within which it forms an element (a discourse) has become one of the central features of critical analysis within post-structuralism and postmodernism. However, the relation between any image and its corresponding level of representation is not so clear-cut. In other words, while one can understand how a word only means what it does relative to all other words in a lexicon, an image does not have a delimited representational lexicon, which helps determine what it might mean. A psychology of the image should avoid falling into formalist limitations which work against the fruitful nature of more open-ended interpretation.

Clearly there are developments in image studies which consider image analysis along semiotic/grammatical lines (e.g. Kress and van Leeuwen 1996 with reference to advertising), and such formalisms remind us that images are often produced by someone for a specific purposes (we can always ask the question, who is the enunciator?) But there is a certain kind of seductive formalism in such enterprises, which may make it somewhat difficult to understand the unique nature of image analysis and interpretation, particularly with respect to contexts involving moving images. No semiotic grammar can ever do justice to the phenomenal experience of being deeply affected by a movie. One can understand why film criticism continues to be theorised from a predominantly psychoanalytic perspective, one of the few frameworks in psychology which places centre stage emotion or affect.

Turning to the 'internal–external' theme employed in the book, beyond acting as a convenient construct on which to place different issues and topics, this differentiation also serves to highlight the arbitrary nature of separateness within domains of image enquiry. Why the relationship between language and imagery, particularly internal mental imagery, dreams and self-identity, is rarely addressed in contemporary psychology becomes a little clearer. In particular one can see why the issue of the originating epistemic 'acting' subject is central to contemporary post-structuralist discussion on the self, and also the target of the emerging critique within critical psychology and social constructionism.

At the risk of oversimplification, and by way of moving towards a conclusion, there are two orientations or meta-theoretical perspectives bearing on the study of mental imagery, the self, social identity and the processes and phenomena involved in their interrelationships. One is predicated on the stability of the subject-self and a correspondingly unproblematic view of the nature of consciousness and the self. This is the view of cognitive psychology/cognitive science, social identity theory and also the view that figures comfortably with scientific discourses on the mind–body relationship. While still exhibiting a scientific scepticism regarding the nature of mental imagery as such, it is seen as very much a cognitive/representational activity, 'vision-like' and ultimately reducible to a 'mind–brain' analysis, including MRI scanning and related methodologies. Corresponding views of the self, identity and social cognition derive from this inherently individualistic 'mind-based' account of mental life.

In contrast, the other perspective on mental life, the subject-self and the problem of identity rests on an amalgamation of post-Freudian critical analysis, post-structuralism and associated ideas, theories and constructs which inform contemporary cultural thinking more generally. In this view cognitive life is a much more precarious business, always underpinned by unconscious motivations, where the subject-self is forever problematic and an object, state of mind, fantasy or narrative that has to be defended, produced in context, always contradictory, ambiguous and ultimately open to challenge.

The study of internal images has mirrored these very different orientations to the image-self. Mental imagery remains informed by an unproblematic view of visual perception and the associated various metaphors of information-processing consciousness. In contrast, in the study of dreams the essentially divided nature of the mind remains forever vulnerable to the motivations of the unconscious. Likewise, the study of gendered images in psychology has rested on constructs of the conceptual self, gender schema theory and related ideas, which for the most part produces a discourse of gender which emphasises difference. We noted how this is changing, in part as a response to the increasingly precarious relationship between identity and gender image projection. The psychology of self-esteem and social attribution has contributed to our knowledge of problems such as eating disorders, but does not provide us with a deeper understanding of how we appropriate or resist the lifestyles implicit in the images of women and men we see around us.

When we consider the nature of the photograph, again we have a specific kind of 'external' image, which influences our conceptions, fantasies and narratives of the self-image. And it does so within a specific social-cultural history that places a particular kind of significance on the seductively 'real' nature of what is captured by the camera. Psychology, particularly the social psychological branch of the discipline, is now bringing together the theoretical insights of critical theory and the methodological ingenuity of discourse analysis. We are only beginning to understand the unique nature of our responses to photographic images, and a psychology of the image provides us with a framework for further theoretical development.

Possibly more than any other domain of external images, the contemporary focus on computer mediated environments or what is becoming known as post-photographic technologies, has made the business of image production, recognition, response and enunciation more significant than could ever have been imagined. And imagination, fantasy and projection are key elements of everyday computer experience for internet users. Some people have always done this within fashion and the gendered images of beauty, 'if only I could attain those looks, clothes, attitude and lifestyle then I could transform myself into a different person, and inhabit a much nicer world', but the introduction of a technology which keeps a protective distance from the reality of the world opens up new possibilities. This 'nowhere but somewhere' cyber domain makes available to the computer user a unique space for fantasy and projection: who they might be, how they could be perceived, who they are communicating with, where and in what time all such interaction is occurring, and of course the images and narratives constructed, and deconstructed on their personal web pages. Here, the self is reconstituted as a fluid and polymorphous entity. Psychology, under the auspices of human–computer interaction, has not had the conceptual tools for theorising, and thus understanding, the significance of such developments for human communication or personal/social identity. Bringing together the insights of Goffman, the social semiosis of Peirce and psychoanalytic rereadings of Lacan can illuminate many aspects of this most recent image domain.

The image is an important construct in our daily experience. We talk of the images and impressions we have inside us, the desires we have to fashion ourselves in the images of idealised others, and sometimes we feel we have to protect ourselves and others from images that unsettle, disrupt or even rupture our current view of the world and our place within it. Psychology has much to contribute to our understanding of images and will benefit from moving beyond the traditional focus on mental imagery and further extending and developing a psychology of the image. Given the focus on images in contemporary life, a significant task for psychology in this new millennium will be to understand the relationship between external images and the ideas and feelings we hold about ourselves.

Bibliography

Abrams, D. and Hogg, M. A. (1988) *Social identity and social cognition*, Blackwell, Oxford.

Akhtar, S. and Samuel, S. (1996) The concept of identity: Developmental origins, phenomenology, clinical relevance, and measurement, *Harvard Review of Psychiatry* 3, 254–267.

Alanen, L. (1989) Of people large and small: An argument for a sociology of childhood, *Argument* 31, 79–89.

Albers, P. C. and James, W. R. (1988) Travel photography: A methodological approach, *Annals of Tourism Research* 15, 134–158.

Alcoff, L. and Gray, L. (1993) Survivor discourse: Transgression or recuperation, *Signs* 18, 260–290.

Allen, P. and Nelles, J. (1996) Development of auditory information integration abilities, *Journal of the Acoustical Society of America* 100, 1043–1051.

Ambrosi, E. and Schwarz, K. B. (1995) The professions image: Occupational therapy as represented in the media, *American Journal of Occupational Therapy* 49, 715–719.

Anderson, C. M. and Malloy, E. S. (1976) Family photographs: In treatment and training, *Family Process* 15, 258–267.

Antaki, C. and Widdicombe, S. (eds.) (1998) *Identities in talk*, Sage, London.

Archer, J. (1984) Gender roles as developmental pathways, *British Journal of Social Psychology* 23, 245–256.

Archer, J. and Lloyd, B. (1985) *Sex and gender*, Cambridge University Press, Cambridge.

Arias, C. (1996) Human echolocation by visually handicapped people, *Année Psychologique* 96, 703–721.

Armstrong, N. (1988) The gender bind: Women and the disciplines, *Gender* 3, 2–4.

Asamura, A. (1996) The transformation of children's cognitive maps: The development of map-like and sequential recognition of space, *Japanese Journal of Educational Psychology* 44, 204–213.

Atkinson, R., Atkinson, R. C., Smith, E. E., Bem, D. J. and Hilgard, E. R. (1990) *Introduction to psychology*, 10th edn, Harcourt Brace Jovanovich, San Diego, Calif., and London.

Baker, C. F., Garvin, B. J., Kennedy, C. W. and Polivka, B. J. (1993) The effect of environmental sound and communication on ccu patients heart-rate and blood-pressure, *Research in Nursing and Health* 16, 415–421.

Balasz, B. (1985) Theory of the film: Sound, in *Film sound: Theory and practice* (eds. Weis, E. and Belton, J.) Columbia University Press, New York.

Bandura, A. and Walters, R. H. (1964) *Social learning and personality development*, Holt, Rhinehart & Winston, New York.

Banks, J. (1990) Listening to Dr. Ruth: The new sexual primer, in *Talking to strangers: Mediated therapeutic communities* (eds. Gumpert, G. and Fish, S. L.) Ablex, Norwood, N.J.

Barlow, H., Blakemore, C. and Weston-Smith, M. (eds.) (1990) *Images and understanding*, Cambridge University Press, Cambridge.

Barnecutt, P. and Pfeffer, K. (1998) Auditory perception of relative distance of traffic sounds, *Current Psychology* 17, 93–101.

Baron-Cohen, S., Leslie, A. and Frith, U. (1985) Does the autistic child have a 'theory of mind'?, *Cognition*, 21, 37–46.

Barone, T. E. (1992) A narrative of enhanced professionalism, *Educational Researcher* 21, 15–24.

Barthes, R. (1982) *Camera Lucida*, Jonathan Cape, London.

Baruch, C. and Drake, C. (1997) Tempo discrimination in infants, *Infant Behavior and Development* 20, 573–577.

Bartlett, F.C. (1932) *Remembering: A study in experimental and social psychology*, Cambridge University Press, Cambridge.

Bateman, J. A. (1995) On the relationship between ontology construction and natural language: A socio-semiotic view, *International Journal of Human–Computer Studies* 43, 929–944.

Baudrillard, J. (1988) *The consumer society, myths and structures*, Sage, London.

Baumeister, R. F. (1986) *Public self and private self*, Springer, New York.

Bays, H. (1998) Framing and face in internet exchange: A socio-cognitive approach, http://viadrina.euv-frankfurt-o.de/~wjournal/bays.htm, Paris.

Beck, A. (1997) *Radio acting*, A. & C. Black, London.

Beck, A. (1998) Point-of-listening in radio plays, *Sound Journal* 1, 15–25.

Beck, C. T. (1994) Phenomenology: Its use in nursing research, *International Journal of Nursing Studies* 31, 499–510.

Beloff, H. (1984) The social psychology of the personal photograph, *Bulletin of the British Psychological Society*, 37, 47.

Beloff, H. (1985) *Camera Culture*, Basil Blackwell, New York.

Beloff, H. (1988) The eye and me: Self portraits of eminent photographers, *Philosophical Psychology* 1, 295–311.

Beloff, H. (1993) Facing Julia Margaret Cameron, *History of Photography* 17, 115–117.

Beloff, H. (1994) Reading visual rhetoric, *The Psychologist* 7, 495–499.

Beloff, H. (1997) Making and un-making identities: A psychologist looks at artwork, in *Doing qualitative analysis in psychology* (ed. Hayes, N.) Psychology Press, Hove.

Beltran, F. S. and Duque, Y. (1993) Processing typical objects in scenes: Effects of photographs versus line-drawings, *Perceptual and Motor Skills* 76, 307–312.

Bem, S. (1983) Gender schema theory and its implications for child development: Raising gender-aschematic children in a gender-schematic society, *Signs: Journal of Women in Culture and Society* 8, 598–616.

Bem, S. (1989) *The developing child*, Harper & Row, New York.

Ben Ari, E. (1991) Posing, posturing and photographic presences: A rite of passage in a Japanese commuter village, *Man* 26, 87–104.

Bennett, M. and Cormack, C. (1996) Others' actions can reflect on the self: A developmental study of extended identity, *Journal of Genetic Psychology* 157, 323–330.

Benyon, D. R. and Hook, K. (1997) Navigation in information spaces: Supporting the individual, in *Interact 1997*, Chapman & Hall, Southampton.

Berger, J. (1972) *Ways of seeing*, Penguin, Harmondsworth.

Biederman, I. (1987) Recognition by components: A theory of human image understanding, *Psychological Review* 64, 115–145.

Bishop, P. J. and Intraub, H. (1996) Visual dissociation of digitized photographs, *Behavior Research Methods Instruments and Computers* 28, 365–371.

Blagrove, M. (1992) Dreams as a reflection of our waking concerns and abilities: A critique of the problem-solving paradigm in dream research, *Dreaming* 2, 205–220.

Blaikie, A. (1994) Photographic memory, aging and the life-course, *Ageing and Society* 14, 479–497.

Blum-Kulka, S. (1993) 'You Gotta Know How to Tell a Story', *Language in Society* 22, 361–402.

Blum-Kulka, S. and Snow, C. (1992) Developing autonomy for tellers, tales and telling in family narrative events, *Journal of Narrative and Life History* 2, 187–217.

Bly, R. (1990) *Iron John: A book about men*, Addison-Wesley, New York.

Blyton, P. (1987) The image of work: Documentary photography and the production of reality, *International Social Science Journal* 39, 415–424.

Boltz, M. G. (1998) The processing of temporal and non-temporal information in the remembering of event durations and musical structure, *Journal of Experimental Psychology: Human Perception and Performance* 24, 1087–1104.

Boorstein, D. J. (1962) *The image*, Penguin, Harmondsworth.

Botstein, L. (1995) Hearing is seeing: Thoughts on the history of music and the imagination, *Musical Quarterly* 79, 581–589.

Bowey, J. A. (1990) On rhyme, language, and children's reading, *Applied Psycholinguistics* 11, 439–448.

Branigan, E. (1993) On the analysis of interpretive language, *Film Criticism* 17, 4–21.

Brannon, R. (1976) The male sex role: Our culture's blueprint of manhood, and what it's done for us lately, in *The forty-nine percent majority: The male sex role* (ed. David, D. and Brannon, R.) Addison-Wesley, Reading, Mass.

Brier, S. (1996a) Cybersemiotics: A new interdisciplinary development applied to the problems of knowledge organisation and document retrieval in information science, *Journal of Documentation* 52, 296–344.

Brier, S. (1996b) The usefulness of cybersemiotics in dealing with problems of knowledge organization and document mediating systems, *Cybernetica* 39, 273–299.

Bromley, D. B. (1993) *Reputation, image, and impression management*, Wiley, Chicester and New York.

Bronzaft, A. L., Ahern, K. D., McGinn, R., O'Connor, J. and Savino, B. (1998) Aircraft noise: A potential health hazard, *Environment and Behavior* 30, 101–113.

Brookfield, S. (1986) Media power and the development of media literacy: An adult educational interpretation, *Harvard Educational Review* 56, 151–170.

Brooks-Gunn, J. and Lewis, M. (1984) The development of early visual self-recognition, *Developmental Review* 4, 215–239.

Brown, P. and Levinson, S. (1978) *Universals in language use: Politeness phenomena*, Cambridge University Press, Cambridge.

Bruce, V. and Green, P. R. (1990) *Visual perception: Physiology, psychology and ecology*, Erlbaum, Hove.

Bruch, H. (1978) *The golden cage*, Harvard University Press, Cambridge, Mass.

Bruner, J. (1986) *Acts of meaning*, Basic Books, New York.

Bruza, P. D. (1990) Hyperindices: A novel aid for searching in hypermedia, in *First European Conference on Hypertext* INRIA, France.

Buellens, J. (1996) Nightmares in psychiatry, *Acta Neuropsychiatrica* 8, 12–16.

Burgin, V. (ed.) (1982) *Thinking photography*, Macmillan, London.

Burke, R. R. (1988) Subject emphasis in textbook photographs and journal reports in educational psychology, *Teaching of Psychology* 15, 164–165.

Burman, E. (1994) *Deconstructing Development Psychology*, Routledge, London.

Cameron, D. (1985) *Feminism and linguistic theory*, Macmillan, Basingstoke.

Camioni, L. (1994) *The development of intentional communication: A re-analysis*, Routledge, London.

Campion, A. and Fine, G. A. (1998) Main street on main street: Community identity and the reputation of Sinclair Lewis, *Sociological Quarterly* 39, 79–99.

Canter, D. (1988) Camera culture – Beloff, H., *Journal of Environmental Psychology* 8, 339–342.

Cantor, J., Ziemke, D. and Sparks, C. G. (1984) Effect of forewarning on emotional responses to a horror film, *Journal of Broadcasting* 28, 21–31.

Caplan, R. and Guthrie, D. (1996) Conversational repair in schizophrenic and normal children, *Journal of the American Academy of Child and Adolescent Psychiatry* 35, 950–958.

Carey, S. (1982) The development of face perception, in *Perceiving and remembering faces* (ed. Davies, G., Ellis, H. and Shephard, J.) Academic Press, London.

Carpenter, E. (1973) *Eskimo realities*, Holt, Rinehart & Wilson, New York.

Carr, D. (1986) *Time, narrative and history*, Indiana University Press, Bloomington.

Case, R. (1991) Stages in the development of the young child's first sense of self, *Developmental Review* 11, 210–230.

Cattell, R. B. (1964) *Personality and social psychology*, Knapp, San Deigo, Calif.

Chapman, M. (1986) The structure of exchange: Piaget's sociological theory, *Human Development* 29, 181–194.

Chase, M. H. and Morales, F. R. (1983) Subthreshold excitatory activity and motorneuron discharge during REM periods of active sleep, *Science* 221, 1195–1198.

Cheung, C. K., Leung, K. K., Chan, W. T. and Ma, K. (1998) Depression, loneliness, and health in an adverse living environment: A study of bedspace residents in Hong Kong, *Social Behavior and Personality* 26, 151–169.

Chion, M. (1994) *Audio-Vision: Sound on Screen*, Columbia University Press.

Chomsky, N. (1957) *Syntactic structures*, Mouton, Netherlands.

Clark, S. E. and Loftus, E. F. (1996) The construction of space alien abduction memories, *Psychological-Inquiry* 7, 140–143.

Cloud, D. L. (1996) Hegemony or concordance? The rhetoric of tokenism in Oprah Winfrey's rags-to-riches biography, *Critical Studies in Mass Communication* 13, 115–137.

Cohen, J. and Metzger, M. (1998) Social affiliation and the achievement of ontological security through interpersonal and mass communication, *Critical Studies in Mass Communication* 15, 41–60.

Cole, M. (1980) *Foundations of social thought*, Cambridge University Press, Cambridge.

Collins, R. (1988) *Theoretical continuities in Goffman's work*, Polity Press, Cambridge.

Conklin, J. (1987) Hypertext: An introduction and survey, *IEEE Computer* 20, 17–41.

Connell, R. W. (1987) *Gender and power*, Polity Press, London.

Cook, N. (1990) *Music, imagination and culture*, Clarendon Press, Oxford.

Costall, A. (1995) Socializing affordances, *Theory and Psychology* 5, 467–481.

Costall, A. and Leudar, I. (1998) On how we can act, *Theory & Psychology* 8, 165–173.

Crozier, W. R. (1998) Self-consciousness in shame: The role of the 'other', *Journal for the Theory of Social Behaviour* 28, 273–285.

Cruttenden, A. (1992) Clicks and syllables in the phonology of dama, *Lingua* 86, 101–117.

Cullingford, C. (1997) Parents from the point of view of their children, *Educational Review* 49, 47–56.

Cunningham, D. J. (1998) Cognition as semiosis, *Theory and Psychology* 8, 827–840.

Curtin, D. (1994) Dogen, deep ecology, and the ecological self, *Environmental Ethics* 16, 195–213.

Davidson, E. S., Yasuna, A. and Tower, A. (1979) The effects of television cartoons on sex role stereotyping in young girls, *Child Development* 50, 597–600.

Day, J. M. and Tappan, M. B. (1996) The narrative approach to moral development: From the epistemic subject to dialogical selves, *Human Development* 39/2, 67–82.

De Casper, A. J. and Fifer, W. (1980) Of human bonding: Newborns prefer their mothers' voices, *Science* 208, 1174–1176.

De Koninck, J., Christ, G., Hebert, G. and Rinfret, N. (1990) Language learning, dreams and REM sleep: converging findings, *Sleep Research* 19, 134–149.

Deaux, K., Reid, A., Mizrahi, K. and Ethier, K. A. (1995) Parameters of social identity, *Journal of Personality and Social Psychology* 68, 280–291.

DeBernardi, J. (1994) Social aspects of language use, in *Companion encyclopedia of anthropology* (ed. Ingold, T.) Routledge, London.

Delacour, J. (1995) An introduction to the biology of consciousness, *Neuropsychologia* 33, 1061–1074.

Demarest, J. and Garner, J. (1994) The representation of women's roles in women's magazines over the past 30 years, *Journal of Psychology* 126, 357–369.

Dennis, P. M. (1998) Chills and thrills: Does radio harm our children? The controversy over program violence during the age of radio, *Journal of the History of the Behavioral Sciences* 34, 33–50.

Descombes, A. (1980) *Modern French philosophy*, Blackwell, Oxford.

Dick, J. T. (1990) Film snobbery, *Library Journal* 115, 10–12.

Dilley, R. S. (1986) Tourist brochures and tourist images, *Canadian Geographer – Geographe Canadien* 30, 59–65.

Dollinger, S. J. and Clancy, S. M. (1993) Identity, self, and personality 2. Glimpses through the autophotographic eye, *Journal of Personality and Social Psychology* 64, 1064–1071.

Dore, J. (1983) Feeling, form and intention in the baby's transition to language, in *The transition from pre-linguistic to linguistic communication* (ed. Golinkoff, R. M.) Erlbaum, Hillsdale, N.J.

Doty, N. D. (1998) The influence of nationality on the accuracy of face and voice recognition, *American Journal of Psychology* 111, 191–214.

Drabman, R. S. and Thomas, M. H. (1975) Does TV violence breed indifference? *Journal of Communication* 25, 86–89.

Drakakis, J. (ed.) (1981) *British radio drama*, Cambridge University Press, Cambridge.

Drake, C. and Botte, M. C. (1993) Tempo sensitivity in auditory sequences: Evidence for a multiple-look model, *Perception and Psychophysics* 54, 277–286.

Drew, P. and Wootton, A. (eds.) (1988) *Ervin Goffman: Exploring the interaction order*, Polity Press, Cambridge.

Druckrey, T. (1989) L'amour faux, *Perspektief* 37, 37–41.

Durkin, K. (1985) *Television, sex roles and children*, Open University Press, Milton Keynes.

Durkin, K. (1995) *Developmental social psychology*, Blackwell, Oxford.

Eco, U. (1979) *The role of the reader: Explorations in the semiotics of texts*, Indiana University Press, Bloomington.

Eco, U. (1982) Critique of the image, in *Thinking photography* (ed. Burgin, V.) Macmillan, London.

Eco, U. (1996) How culture conditions the colours we see, in *The communication theory reader* (ed. Cobley, P.) Routledge, London.

Edelman, G. (1987) *Neural Darwinism*, Basic Books, New York.

Edley, N. and Wetherell, M. (1996) Masculinity, power and identity, in *Understanding masculinities* (ed. Mac an Ghail, M.) Open University Press, Buckingham.

Edwards, D. and Middleton, D. (1988) Conversational remembering and family relationships: How children learn how to remember, *Journal of Social and Personal Relationships* 5, 3–25.

Edwards, D., Potter, J. and Middleton, D. (1992) Toward a discursive psychology of remembering, *The Psychologist* 5, 441–447.

Eisenberg, N. (ed.) (1987) *Contemporary topics in developmental psychology*, Wiley, New York.

Eisenberg, N. (1992) The development of reasoning regarding pro-social behaviour, in *The development of pro-social behaviour* (ed. Eisenberg, N.) Erlbaum, Hillsdale, N.J.

Eisenberg, N., Murray, E. and Hite, T. (1982) Children's reasoning regarding sex-typed toy choices, *Child Development*, 53, 81–86.

Ekins, R. (1993) On male femaling: A grounded theory approach to cross-dressing and sex-changing, *Sociological Review* 41, 1–29.

Elliott, G. C., Zeigler, H. L., Altman, B. M. and Scott, D. R. (1982) Understanding stigma: Dimensions of deviance and coping, *Deviant Behaviour* 3, 275–300.

Elmstahl, S., Annerstedt, L. and Ahlund, O. (1997) How should a group living unit for demented elderly be designed to decrease psychiatric symptoms?, *Alzheimer Disease and Associated Disorders* 11, 47–52.

Elsbach, K. D. and Glynn, M. A. (1996) Believing your own 'PR': Embedding identification in strategic reputation, *Advances in Strategic Management* 13, 65–90.

Emde, R. N., Biringer, Z., Clyman, R. B. and Oppenheim, D. (1991) The moral self of infancy: Affective, core and procedural knowledge, *Developmental Review* 11, 251–271.

Emler, N. and Reicher, S. (1995) *Adolescence and delinquency, the collective management of reputation*, Blackwell, Oxford.

Engel, S. (1986) Learning to reminisce: a developmental study of how young children talk about the past, in *Graduate Centre*, City University of New York, New York.

Epstein, D. and Steinberg, D. L. (1998) American dreamin': Discoursing liberally on the Oprah Winfrey Show, *Women's Studies International Forum* 21, 77–94.

Epstein, J. and Straub, K. (eds.) (1991) *Body guards: The cultural politics of gender ambiguity*, Routledge, London.

Ervin-Tripp, S. and Mitchell-Kernan, C. (eds.) (1977) *Child Discourse*, Academic Press, New York.

Evans, G. W. and Maxwell, L. (1997) Chronic noise exposure and reading deficits: The mediating effects of language acquisition, *Environment and Behavior* 29, 638–656.

Evans, J. (1988) Camera culture – Beloff, H., *Media Culture and Society* 10, 119–121.

Eysenck, M. and Keane, M. T. (1995) *Cognitive psychology: A student's handbook*, Erlbaum, Hove.

Fagot, B. I. (1974) Sex differences in toddlers' behaviour and parental reaction, *Developmental Psychology* 4, 554–558.

Fairclough, N. (1992) *Discourse and social change*, Polity Press, Cambridge.

Farah, M. J. (1985) Psychophysical evidence for a shared representational medium for mental images and percepts, *Journal of Experimental Psychology: General* 114, 91–103.

Fayol, M., Largy, P. and Lemaire, P. (1994) Cognitive overload and orthographic errors: When cognitive overload enhances subject verb agreement errors – a study in french written language, *Quarterly Journal of Experimental Psychology Section A – Human Experimental Psychology* 47, 437–464.

Ferrington, G. (1993) Audio design: Creating multi-sensory images for the mind, *Journal of Visual Literacy. Published on the Internet at 'http://interact.uoregon.edu/ MediaLit/WFAEResearch/sndesign' in the World Forum for Acoustic Ecology (WFAE) Articles and Research Documents section.*

Ferrington, G. (1995) Soundscape experiences, 'Soundscape Experiences Questionnaire' Internet: WFAE Discussion Group, http://interact.uoregon.edu/MediaLit/WFAE HomePage.

Fine, S., Haley, G., Gilbert, M. and Forth, A. (1993) Self-image as a predictor of outcome in adolescent major depressive disorder, *Journal of Child Psychology and Psychiatry and Allied Disciplines* 34, 1399–1407.

Fivush, R. and Hammond, N. R. (1990) *Autobiographical memory across the preschool years: Toward reconceptualizing childhood amnesia*, Cambridge University Press, Cambridge.

Fodor, J. (1997) Do we have it in us? The failure of new attempts to explain how the cognitive brain works. Book review (J. L. Elman et al. *Rethinking Innateness*), *Times Literary Supplement*.

Forrester, M. (1998) Significant sound experience remembered. An unpublished report, University of Kent at Canterbury, UK, Canterbury.

Forrester, M. A. (1992) *The development of young children's social-cognitive skills*, Erlbaum, Hove.

Forster, J. (1998) The influence of motor perceptions on likeability judgments of attractive and unattractive portraits, *Zeitschrift Für Experimentelle Psychologie* 45, 167–182.

Foucault, M. (1972) *The archaeology of knowledge*, Tavistock Press, London.

Foucault, M. (1977) *Discipline and punish*, Allen Lane, London.

Foucault, M. (1988) The ethic of the care of the self as a practice of freedom, in *The Final Foucault* (eds. Bernauer, J. and Rasmussen, D.) MIT Press, Cambridge, Mass.

Foulkes, D. (1985) *Dreaming: A cognitive-psychological analysis*, Erlbaum, Hillsdale, N.J.

Fox, D. and Prilleltensky, I. (1997) *Critical psychology: An introduction*, Sage, London.

Fraedrich, J. P. and King, M. F. (1998) Marketing implications of nonmusical sounds, *Journal of Business and Psychology* 13, 127–139.

Frawley, W. (1992) *Linguistic semantics*, Erlbaum, Hove.

Freud, S. (1924) *The dissolution of the Oedipus complex: In the Standard Edition of the complete psychological works of Sigmund Freud (24 volumes)*, London.

Freud, S. (1925) *Some psychical consequences of the anatomical distinction between the sexes: In the Standard Edition of the complete psychological works of Sigmund Freud (24 volumes)*, London.

Freud, S. (1976) *The interpretation of dreams*, Pelican, London.

Friedan, B. (1963) *The feminine mystique*, Dell, New York.

Friedman, S. (1993) *The new language of change*, Guildford Press, London.

Frosh, S. (1993) The seeds of male sexuality, in *Psychological perspectives on sexual problems* (ed. Ussher, J. and Baker, C.) Routledge, London.

Futterweit, L. R. and Beilin, H. (1994) Recognition memory for movement in photographs: A developmental study, *Journal of Experimental Child Psychology* 57, 163–179.

Gallagher, S. and Meltzoff, A. N. (1996) The earliest sense of self and others: Merleau-Ponty and recent developmental studies, *Philosophical Psychology* 9, 211–233.

Gallup, G. G. (1998) Self-awareness and the evolution of social intelligence, *Behavioural-Processes* 42, 239–247.

Garfinkel, P. E. and Garner, D. M. (1982) *Anorexia nervosa: A multidimensional perspective*, Brunner/Mazel, New York.

Gaver, W. W. (1993a) How do we hear in the world: Explorations in ecological acoustics, *Ecological Psychology* 5, 285–313.

Gaver, W. W. (1993b) What in the world do we hear: An ecological approach to auditory event perception, *Ecological Psychology* 5, 1–29.

Gavey, N. (1989) Feminist Poststructuralism and discourse analysis, *Psychology of Women Quarterly* 13, 459–475.

Geerhardt, J. (1990) Monologue as a speech genre, in *Narratives from the crib* (ed. Nelson, K.) Erlbaum, Hillsdale, N.J.

Gell, A. (1995) The language of the forest: Landscape and phonological iconism in Umeda, in *The anthropology of landscape: Perspectives on place and space* (ed. Hirsch, E. and O'Hanlon, M.) Clarendon Press, Oxford.

Gergen, K. J. (1991) *The saturated self*, Basic Books, New York.

Giardetti, J. R. and Oller, J. W. (1995) Testing a theory of photographic meaning, *Semiotica* 106, 99–152.

Gibson, J. J. (1966) *The sense considered as perceptual systems*, Houghton-Mifflin, Boston.

Gibson, J. J. (1979) *The ecological approach to visual perception*, MIT Press, Cambridge, Mass.

Gibson, J. J. (1982) Discussion, in *Cognition and the symbolic processes*, vol. 2 (ed. Weimer, W. B. and Palermo, D. S.) Hillsdale, NJ.

Giddens, T. (1988) Goffman as a systematic social theorist, in *Ervin Goffman: Exploring the interaction order* (ed. Wooton, I. P. D. a. A.) Polity Press, Cambridge.

Giddens, T. (1991) *Modernity and identity: Self and society in the late modern age*, Stanford University Press, Stanford, Calif.

Gilbert, K. and Schleuder, J. (1990) Effects of color and complexity in still photographs on mental effort and memory, *Journalism Quarterly* 67, 749–756.

Gilbert, P., Pehl, J. and Allan, S. (1994) The phenomenology of shame and guilt: An empirical investigation, *British Journal of Medical Psychology* 67, 23–36.

Giles, H. and Johnson, P. (1981) Language in ethnic group relations, in *Intergroup Behaviour* (ed. Turner, J. C. and Giles, H.) Blackwell, Oxford.

Gilligan, C. and Wiggins, G. (1987) The origins of morality in early childhood relationships, in *The emergence of morality in young children* (ed. Kagan, J. and Lamb, S.) Chicago University Press, Chicago.

Goffman, E. (1959) *The presentation of self in everyday life*, Doubleday; Penguin (1971), Garden City, NY.

Goffman, E. (1963a) *Behaviour in public places: Notes on the social organization of gatherings*, Free Press, New York.

Goffman, E. (1963b) *Stigma: Notes on the management of a spoiled identity*, Prentice Hall, Englewood Cliffs, N.J.

Goffman, E. (1967) *Interaction ritual: Essays on face-to-face behaviour*, Doubleday Anchor, New York.

Goffman, E. (1976) Replies and responses, *Language in Society* 5, 257–313.

Goffman, E. (1979) *Gender advertisements*, Macmillan, London.

Goffman, E. (1981) *Forms of talk*, Blackwell, Oxford.

Golinkoff, R. M. (ed.) (1983) *The transition from pre-linguistic to linguistic communication*, Erlbaum, Hillsdale, N.J.

Gombrich, E. H. (1957) *Art and illusion: A study in the psychology of pictorial representation*, Phaidon, London.

Gray, P. (1991) *Psychology*, Worth, New York.

Grogan, S. (1998) *Body image*, Routledge, London.

Gunter, B., Furnham, A. and Beeson, C. (1997) Recall of television advertisements as a function of program evaluation, *Journal of Psychology* 131, 541–553.

Habermas, J. (1987) *Theory of communicative action*, Beacon Press, Boston.

Hacker, P. M. S. (1972) *Insight and illusion: Wittgenstein on philosophy and the metaphysics of experience*, Open University Press, London.

Halpern, A. (1988) Mental scanning in auditory imagery for songs, *Journal of Experimental Psychology: Learning, Memory and Cognition* 14, 434–443.

Hambleton, G., Russell, R. L. and Wandrrei, M. L. (1996) Narrative performance predicts psychology: A preliminary demonstration, *Journal of Narrative and Life History* 6, 87–105.

Harada, S. I. (1976) Honorifics, in *Syntax and semantics, 5: Japanese generative grammar* (ed. Shibatani, M.) Academic Press, New York.

Harrison, B. (1974) On understanding a general name, in *The integration of the child into a social world* (ed. Richards, M. P. M.) Cambridge University Press, Cambridge.

Hars, B., Hennevin, E. and Pasques, P. (1985) Improvement of learning by cueing during postlearning paradoxical sleep, *Behaviour Brain Research* 18, 241–250.

Hassett, J. (1978) *A primer of psychophysiology*, Freeman, San Fransisco.

Hawkins, R. and Pingree, S. (1990) Divergent psychological processes in constructing social reality from mass media content, in *Cultivation analysis: New directions in media effects research* (ed. Signorielli, N. and Morgan, M.) Sage, Newbury Park, Calif.

Hearn, J. (1996) Is masculinity dead? A critique of the concept of masculinity/masculinities, in *Understanding masculinities* (ed. Mac an Ghail, M.) Open University Press, Buckingham.

Heath, C. (1988) Embarrassment and interactional organization, in *Ervin Goffman: Exploring the interaction order* (ed. Wooton, I. P. D. a. A.) Polity Press, Cambridge.

Heath, S. (1981) *Questions of cinema*, Manchester University Press, Manchester.

Heatherton, T. F. and Nichols, P. A. (1994) Personal accounts of successful versus failed attempts at life change, *Personality and Social Psychology Bulletin* 20, 664–675.

Hebb, D. O. (1949) *The organization of behaviour*, Wiley, New York.

Henriques, J., Holloway, W., Urwin, C., Venn, C. and Walkerdine, W. (eds.) (1984) *Changing the subject*, Methuen, London.

Higgins, E. T. (1987) Self-discrepancy: A theory relating self and affect, *Psychological Review* 94, 319–340.

Higonnet, A. (1998) *Pictures of innocence: The history and crisis of ideal childhood*, Thames & Hudson, London.

Hildebrandt, F. W. (1875) *Der Traum und seine Verwerthung für's Leben*, Koninsberg, Leipzig.

Hillier, L. (1999) How has psychoanalysis influenced film theory?, Department of Psychology, University of Kent, Canterbury.

Hobson, J. A. (1988) *The dreaming brain*, Basic Books, New York.

Hochberg, J. E. (1978) *Perception*, Prentice Hall, New York.

Hochschild, A. and Young, T. R. (1995) *Building image: Managing individual and institutional identities*, Sage, Thousand Oaks, Calif.

Hodge, R. and Kress, G. R. (1988) *Social semiotics*, Polity, Cambridge.

Hogben, M. and Waterman, C. K. (1997) Are all of your students represented in their textbooks? A content analysis of coverage of diversity issues in introductory psychology textbooks, *Teaching of Psychology* 24, 95–100.

Hogg, M. A., Terry, D. J. and White, K. M. (1995) A tale of 2 theories: A critical comparison of identity theory with social identity theory, *Social Psychology Quarterly* 58, 255–269.

Hollos, M. (1977) The comprehension and use of social rules in pronoun selection, in *Child Discourse* (ed. Ervin-Tripp, S. and Mitchell-Kernan, C.) Academic Press, New York.

Hollway, W. (1984) Gender differences and the production of subjectivity, in *Changing the subject* (eds. Henriques, J., Holloway, W., Urwin, C., Venn, C. and Walkerdine, W.) Methuen, London.

Hollway, W. (1989) *Subjectivity and method in psychology: Gender, meaning and science*, Sage, London.

Hookway, C. (1985) *Peirce*, Routledge, London.

Horne, J. A. (1988) *Why we sleep: The functions of sleep in humans and other mammals*, Oxford University Press, Oxford.

Horton, W. (1995) Top ten blunders by visual designers, *Computer Graphics* 29, 20–24.

Howard, A. (1985) Ethnopsychology and the prospects for a cultural psychology, in *Person, self and experience* (ed. White, G. M. and Kirkpartick, J.) University of California Press, Berkeley.

Howe, C. (1993) *Language learning: a special case for developmental psychology?*, Erlbaum, Hillsdale, N.J.

Hron, A. (1998) Metaphors as didactic means for multimedia learning environments, *Innovations in Education and Training International* 35, 21–28.

Hubel, D. H. and Weisel, T. N. (1979) Brain mechanisms of vision, *Scientific American* 114, 150–162.

Hudson, J. A. (1990) Constructive processing in children's events memory, *Developmental Psychology* 26, 180–187.

Huebner, A. and Garrod, A. (1991) Moral reasoning in a karmic world, *Human Development*, 34, 341–352.

Hughes, J. N. and Hasbrouck, J. E. (1996) Television violence: Implications for violence prevention, *School Psychology Review* 25, 134–151.

Hyden, L. C. (1995) In search of an ending: Narrative reconstruction as a moral quest, *Journal of Narrative and Life History* 5, 1, 67–84.

Hyman, J. (1989) *The imitation of nature*, Blackwell, Oxford.

Imada, T. (1994) The Japanese sound culture, *The Soundscape Newsletter* 5, 12–50.

Ingram, D. (1985) On children's homonyms, *Journal of Child Language* 12, 671–680.

Intraub, H., Bender, R. S. and Mangels, J. A. (1992) Looking at pictures but remembering scenes, *Journal of Experimental Psychology–Learning Memory and Cognition* 18, 180–191.

Intraub, H. and Berkowits, D. (1996) Beyond the edges of a picture, *American Journal of Psychology* 109, 581–598.

Intraub, H., Gottesman, C. V. and Bills, A. J. (1998) Effects of perceiving and imagining scenes on memory for pictures, *Journal of Experimental Psychology–Learning Memory and Cognition* 24, 186–201.

Intraub, H., Gottesman, C. V., Willey, E. V. and Zuk, I. J. (1996) Boundary extension for briefly glimpsed photographs: Do common perceptual processes result in unexpected memory distortions?, *Journal of Memory and Language* 35, 118–134.

Irigaray, L. (1991) *The Irigaray reader*, edited and with an introduction by Margaret Whitford, Blackwell, Cambridge, Mass.

Jefferson, T. (1994) Theorising masculine subjectivity, in *Just boys doing business? Men, masculinity and crime* (ed. Newburn, T. and Stanko, E.) Routledge, London.

Jefferson, T. (1996) Mike Tyson: Subjectivity and transformation, in *Understanding masculinities* (ed. Mac an Ghail, M.) Open University Press, Buckingham.

Johannson, G. (1973) Visual perception of biological motion and a model for its analysis, *Perception and Psychophysics* 14, 201–211.

Johnson-Laird, P. N. (1983) *Mental models: Towards a cognitive science of language, inference and consciousness*, Harvard University Press, Cambridge, Mass.

Joiner, T. E., Wonderlich, S. A., Metalsky, G. I. and Schmidt, N. B. (1995) Body dissatisfaction: A feature of bulimia, depression, or both?, *Journal of Social and Clinical Psychology* 14, 339–355.

Jordan, R. (1991) *The nature of the linguistic and communication difficulties of children with autism*, Macmillan, London.

Junqua, J. C. (1996) The influence of acoustics on speech production: A noise-induced stress phenomenon known as the Lombard reflex, *Speech Communication* 20, 13–22.

Karmiloff-Smith, A. (1979) *A functional approach to child language*, Cambridge University Press, Cambridge.

Karon, B. P. (1996) On being abducted by aliens, *Psychoanalytic Psychology* 13, 417–418.

Kearney, R. (1988) *The parodic imagination*, Hutchinson, London.

Keltner, D. and Buswell, B. N. (1997) Embarrassment: Its distinct form and appeasement functions, *Psychological Bulletin* 122, 250–270.

Kerby, A. P. (1991) *Narrative and the self*, Indiana University Press, Bloomington.

Kim, J. K. and Rubin, A. M. (1997) The variable influence of audience activity on media effects, *Communication Research* 24, 107–135.

Klein, M. (1948) *On the theory of anxiety and guilt*, Hogarth, London.

Klingner, J. K., Vaughn, S. and Schumm, J. S. (1998) Collaborative strategic reading during social studies in heterogeneous fourth-grade classrooms, *Elementary School Journal* 99, 3–22.

Kodak (1993) *Creative photography: A practical guide to taking better pictures*, Chancellor Press, London.

Kohlberg, L. (1976) Moral stages and moralization: The cognitive-developmental perspective, in *Moral development and behaviour: Theory, research and social issues* (ed. Lickona, T.) Holt, Rinehart & Winston, New York.

Kohlberg, L. (1980) *The meaning and measurement of moral development*, Clark University Press, Worcester, Mass.

Koolstra, C. M., vanderVoort, T. H. A. and vanderKamp, L. J. T. (1997) Television's impact on children's reading comprehension and decoding skills: A 3–year panel study, *Reading Research Quarterly* 32, 128–152.

Kosslyn, S. M., and Ochsner, K. N. (1994) In search of occipita activation during visual mental imagery, *Trends in Neuroscience* 17, 290–292.

Koutstaal, W., Schacter, D. L., Johnson, M. K., Angell, K. E. and Gross, M. S. (1998) Post-event review in older and younger adults: Improving memory accessibility of complex everyday events, *Psychology and Aging* 13, 277–296.

Kress, G. and van Leeuwen, T. (1996) *Reading images: The grammar of visual design*, Routledge, London.

Kristeva, J. (1986) *The Kristeva reader*, Blackwell, Oxford.

Krueger, L. E. (1992) The word-superiority effect and phonological recoding, *Memory and Cognition* 20, 685–694.

Krumhansl, C. L. (1991) Tonal structures in perception and memory, *Annual Review of Psychology* 42, 277–303.

Kuhl, P. K. and Meltzoff, A. N. (1996) Infant vocalizations in response to speech: Vocal imitation and developmental change, *Journal of the Acoustical Society of America* 100, 2425–2438.

Kvale, S. (1992) *Psychology and postmodernism*, Sage, London.

Lacan, J. (1977) *Ecrits. A Selection*, Tavistock, London.

Lachman, R., Lachman, J. L. and Butterfield, E. C. (1979) *Cognitive psychology and information processing*, Erlbaum, Hove.

Landon, S. and Smith, C. E. (1998) Quality expectations, reputation, and price, *Southern Economic Journal* 64, 628–647.

Landow, G. P. (1992) *Hypertext*, Ablex, New Jersey.

Landwehr, K. (1988) Environmental perception: An ecological perspective, in *New directions in environmental research* (ed. Canter, D., Stea, D. and Krampen, M.) Gower, London.

Langer, M. M. (1988) *Merleau-Ponty's phenomenology of perception: A guide and commentary*, Macmillan, Basingstoke.

Laplanche, J. and Pontalis, J. B. (1988) *The language of psychoanalysis*, Karnac, London.

Lapsley, R. and Westlake, M. (1988) *Film theory: An introduction*, Manchester University Press, Manchester.

Lee, D. (1992) *Competing discourses: perspective and ideology in language*, Longman, London.

Legault, E. and Standing, L. (1992) Memory for size of drawings and of photographs, *Perceptual and Motor Skills* 75, 121.

Leslie, A. M. (1987) Pretence and representation: The origins of 'theory of mind', *Psychological Review* 94, 412–426.

Levinson, S. (1983) *Pragmatics*, Cambridge University Press, Cambridge.

Linz, D., Donnerstein, E. and Penrod, S. (1984) The effects of multiple exposures to filmed violence against women, *Journal of Communication* 34, 130–147.

Lippman, P. (1998) On the private and social nature of dreams, *Contemporary Psychoanalysis* 34, 195–221.

Lipscomb, S. D. (1989) *Film Music Paradigm*, UCLA, Los Angeles.

Lipscomb, S. D. (1997) How music can fit film, in *Internet discussion group: Analysis of film music and sound*, izzy2of@mv.oac.ucla.edu, .

Lipscomb, S. D. and Kendall, R. A. (1994) Perceptual judgement of the relationship between musical and visual components in film, *Psychomusicology* 13, 60–98.

Liu, K. C., Crum, G. and Dines, K. (1998) Design issues in a semiotic description of user responses to three interfaces, *Behaviour and Information Technology* 17, 175–184.

Livingstone, S. (1990) *Making sense of television*, Academic Press, London.

Livingstone, S. (1994) Watching talk: Gender and engagement in the viewing of audience discussion programs, *Media Culture and Society* 16, 429–447.

Livingstone, S. (1996a) Rethinking the oedipal complex: Why can't I have babies like mummy? *Feminism and Psychology* 6, 111–113.

Livingstone, S. (1996b) Television discussion and the public sphere: Conflicting discourses of the former Yugoslavia, *Political Communication* 13, 259–280.

Livingstone, S. and Lunt, P. (1994) *Talk on television: Audience participation and public debate*, Routledge, London.

Livingstone, S. and Liebes, T. (1995) Where have all the mothers gone?: Soap-opera replaying of the oedipal story, *Critical Studies in Mass Communication* 12, 155–175.

Livingstone, S., Wober, M. and Lunt, P. (1994) Studio audience discussion programs: An analysis of viewers' preferences and involvement, *European Journal of Communication* 9, 355–379.

Livingstone, S. M. (1993) The rise and fall of audience research: An old story with a new ending, *Journal of Communication* 43, 5–12.

Lloyd, D. (1995) Consciousness: A connectionist manifesto, *Minds and Machines* 5, 161–185.

Logie, R., Wright, R. and Decker, S. (1992) Recognition memory performance and residential burglary, *Applied Cognitive Psychology* 6, 109–123.

Lorenzicioldi, F. (1993) They all look alike, but so do we . . . sometimes: Perceptions of in-group and out-group homogeneity as a function of sex and context, *British Journal of Social Psychology* 32, 111–124.

Mac an Ghail, M. (ed.) (1996) *Understanding masculinities*, Open University Press, Buckingham.

Maestri, D., Laurence, J. R. and Day, D. (1996) Memory for a special event: Effects of repeated questioning on recall, suggestibility, photo lineup identification, *International Journal of Psychology* 31, 28–53.

Mancuso, J. C. (1996) Constructionism, personal construct psychology and narrative psychology, *Theory and Psychology* 6/1, 47–70.

Manning, J. T., Trivers, R. L., Thornhill, R., Singh, D., Denman, J., Eklo, M. H. and Anderton, R. H. (1997) Ear asymmetry and left-side cradling, *Evolution and Human Behavior* 18, 327–340.

Mans, L., Cicchetti, D. and Sroufe, L. A. (1978) Mirror reactions of Down's syndrome infants and toddlers: Cognitive underpinnings of self-recognition, *Child Development* 49, 1247–1250.

Manstead, A. S. R. (1996) Only connect? A sceptical view of the benefits of adopting a connectionist approach to studying human social behaviour, *Psychology and Health* 11, 619–622.

Marr, D. (1982) *Vision*, MIT, New York.

Martin, A. J. and Smith, I. D. (1997) Television violence: A review, suggested research design and statistical approach, *Australian Journal of Social Issues* 32, 407–430.

Maslow, A. (1962) *Towards a psychology of being*, Van Nostrand (Insight Books), Princeton, N.J.

Mauro, R. and Kubovy, M. (1992) Caricature and face recognition, *Memory and Cognition* 20, 433–440.

McArthur, L. Z. and Baron, R. M. (1983) Toward an ecological theory of social perception, *Psychological Review* 90, 215–238.

McHoul, A. (1978) The organisation of turns at formal talk in the classroom, *Language in Society*, 7, 183–213.

McIlwraith, R. D. (1994) Marshall McLuhan and the psychology of television, *Canadian Psychology* 35, 331–350.

McKelvie, S. J. (1983) Effects of lateral reversal on recognition memory for photographs of faces, *British Journal of Psychology* 74, 391–407.

McKelvie, S. J. (1985) Effect of depth of processing on recognition memory for normal and inverted photographs of faces, *Perceptual and Motor Skills* 60, 503–508.

McKelvie, S. J. (1987) Sex-differences, lateral reversal, and pose as factors in recognition memory for photographs of faces, *Journal of General Psychology* 114, 13–37.

McKelvie, S. J. (1991) Effects of processing strategy and transformation on recognition memory for photographs of faces, *Bulletin of the Psychonomic Society* 29, 98–100.

McKelvie, S. J. (1993) Effects of spectacles on recognition memory for faces: Evidence from a distractor-free test, *Bulletin of the Psychonomic Society* 31, 475–477.

McKelvie, S. J. (1994) Is memory for head orientation based on a left-looking schema?, *Journal of General Psychology* 121, 209–225.

McKelvie, S. J., Standing, L., Stjean, D. and Law, J. (1993) Gender differences in recognition memory for faces and cars: Evidence for the interest hypothesis, *Bulletin of the Psychonomic Society* 31, 447–448.

McLaren, N. (1971) Synchrony, Experimental animation film. Music Division: Paramount Studios.

McLuhan, M. (1964) *Understanding media*, Routledge & Kegan Paul, London.

McMahon, A. (1993) Male readings of feminist theory: The psychologisation of sexual politics in the masculinity literature, *Theory and Society* 22, 675–696.

McNay, L. (1994) *Foucault: A critical introduction*, Polity Press, Cambridge.

McQuail, D. (1969) *Towards a sociology of mass communication*, Macmillan, London.

Merleau-Ponty, M. (1962) *Phenomenology of perception*, Routledge, London.

Metz, C. (1974) *Film language. A semiotics of the cinema*, Oxford University Press, New York.

Meunier, J. G. (1998) The categorical structure of iconic languages, *Theory and Psychology* 8, 805–826.

Michaels, C. F. and Carello, C. (1981) *Direct perception*, Prentice Hall, Wiley, N.J.

Mickey, T. J. (1997) A postmodern view of public relations, *Public Relations Review* 23, 1130–1140.

Miller, D. W. and Marks, L. J. (1992) Mental imagery and sound effects in radio commercials, *Journal of Advertising* 21, 83–93.

Miller, J. (1994) *The passion of Michel Foucault*, Flamingo, London.

Minton, H. L. (1997) Queer theory: Historical roots and implications for psychology, *Theory and Psychology*, 7, 337–353.

Mishler, E. G. (1995) Models of narrative analysis: A typology, *Journal of Narrative and Life History* 5/2, 87–123.

Montangero, J. (1991) Dream production mechanisms and cognition, *New Ideas in Psychology* 9, 353–365.

Morris, C. (1971) *Writings on the general theory of signs*, Mouton, The Hague.

Morrow, V. (1996) Rethinking childhood dependency: Children's contributions to the domestic economy, *Sociological Review* 44, 58–77.

Morss, J. R. (1996) *Growing critical: Alternatives to developmental psychology*, Routledge, London.

Moscovitch, M. (1994) Do PETS have long or short ears? Mental imagery and neuroimaging, *Trends in Neuroscience* 17, 292–294.

Munson, W. (1993) *All talk: The talkshow in media culture*, Temple University Press, Philadelphia.

Myers, D. (1991) Computer game semiotics, *Play and Culture* 4, 334–345.

Myers, D. G. (1998) *Psychology*, Worth, New York.

Myers, P. N. and Biocca, F. A. (1992) The elastic body image: The effect of television advertising and programming on body image distortions in young women, *Journal of Communication* 42, 108–133.

Neisser, U. (1976) *Cognition and reality*, MIT Press, New York.

Neisser, U. (1988) Five kinds of self knowledge, *Philosophical Psychology* 1, 35–59.

Neisser, U. (1991) Two perceptually given aspects of the self and their development, *Development Review* 11, 197–209.

Neisser, U. (1993) *The perceived self*, Cambridge University Press, Cambridge.

Nelson, K. (1990) *Remembering, forgetting and childhood amnesia*, Cambridge University Press, Cambridge.

Nelson, K. (1996) *Language in cognitive development: The emergence of the mediated mind*, Cambridge University Press, Cambridge.

Neumeyer, D. (1997) Source music, background music, fantasy and reality in early sound film, *College Music Symposium* 37, 13–20.

Newman, R. S. and Jusczyk, P. W. (1996) The cocktail party effect in infants, *Perception and Psychophysics* 58, 1145–1156.

Noddings, N. (1989) *Women and evil*, University of California Press, Berkeley.

Ochs, E. (1988) Talking to children in Western Samoa, *Language in Society* 11, 77–105.

OED (1989) *Oxford English Dictionary*, Oxford University Press, Oxford.

Olcott, S. M. (1997) Photography after photography: Memory and representation in the digital age – Amelunxen, HV, *Library Journal* 122, 73.

Ong, W. J. (1971) World as view and world as event, in *Environ/mental: Essays on the planet as home* (ed. Shepard, P. and McKinley, D.) Houghton, New York.

Oshima-Takane, Y. (1988) Children learn from speech not addressed to them: the case of personal pronouns, *Journal of Child Language* 15, 95–108.

O'Sullivan, T., Hartley, J., Saunders, D. and Fiske, J. (1983) *Key concepts in communication*, Routledge, London.

Oudart, J. P. (1969) 'La Suture', *Cahiers du Cinema* 211, 36–39.

Paivio, A. (1991) *Imagery and verbal processes*, Holt, New York.

Palermo, G. B. (1995) Adolescent criminal behavior: TV violence one of the culprits, *International Journal of Offender Therapy and Comparative Criminology* 39, 11–22.

Palmer, C. V. (1997) Hearing and listening in a typical classroom, *Language Speech and Hearing Services in Schools* 28, 213–218.

Pan, Z. D. and Koskicki, G. M. (1997) Talk show exposure as an opinion activity, *Political Communication* 14, 371–388.

Pavel, T. G. (1985) Literary narratives, in *Discourse and literature* (ed. Van Dijk, T.) John Benjamins, Amsterdam.

Peck, J. (1995) TV talk shows as therapeutic discourse: The ideological labor of the televised talking cure, *Communication Theory* 5, 58–81.

Peirce, C. S. (1966) *Collected Papers*, Harvard University Press, Cambridge, Mass.

Penelope, J. (1990) *Speaking freely: Unlearning the lies of the fathers' tongues*, Pergamon, New York.

Perezrincon, H. (1994) Body and speech in psychiatry, *Salud Mental* 17, 1–6.

Perner, J. (1992) *Understanding the representational mind*, MIT Press, Cambridge, Mass.

Peterrson, R. (1994) Comprehensibility, in *3D meeting* (ed. Metalonois, N.) Montreal University, Research and Information Centre of Concordia University, Montreal.

Pick, H. L. (1987) Information and the effects of early perceptual experience, in *Contemporary topics in developmental psychology* (ed. Eisenberg, N.) Wiley, New York.

Pinker, S. (1996) *The language instinct: The new science of language and mind*, Cambridge University Press, Cambridge.

Plant, S. (1997) *Zeros + ones, digital women + the new technoculture*, Fourth Estate, London.

Plowman, L. (1996) Narrative, linearity and interactivity: Making sense of interactive multimedia, *British Journal of Educational Technology* 27, 13–45.

Plummer, K. (1996) Genders in question, in *Blending genders: Social aspects of cross-dressing and sex-changing* (ed. Ekins, R. and King, D.) Routledge, London.

Porter, M. (1992) *The environment of the oil company: A semiotic analysis of Chevron's 'People Do' commercials*, Erlbaum, Hillsdale, N.J.

Potter, W. J. and Warren, R. (1996) Considering policies to protect children from TV violence, *Journal of Communication* 46, 116–138.

Potts, R., Doppler, M. and Hernandez, M. (1994) Effects of television content on physical risk-taking in children, *Journal of Experimental Child Psychology* 58, 321–331.

Price, M. (1994) *The photograph: A strange confined space*, Stanford University Press, Stanford, CA.

Priest, P. J. (1995) *Public intimacies: Talk show participants and tell-all TV*, Hampton, Cresskill, N.J.

Psathas, G. (1995) *Conversational analysis*, Sage, London.

Pylyshyn, W. W. (1981) The imagery debate: Analog media versus tacit knowledge, *Psychological Review* 88, 16–45.

Quinn, P. C., Eimas, P. D. and Rosenkrantz, S. L. (1993) Evidence for representations of perceptually similar natural categories by 3-month-old and 4-month-old infants, *Perception* 22, 463–475.

Radley, A. and Kennedy, M. (1997) Picturing need: Images of overseas aid and interpretations of cultural difference, *Culture and Psychology* 3, 435–460.

Reason, D. (1997) Computers and fantasy, Unpublished paper given at a psychotherapy workshop, July 1997, University of Warwick, Warwick.

Redfoot, D. L. (1987) Camera Culture – Beloff, H., *Contemporary Sociology – A Journal of Reviews* 16, 555.

Reed, E. S. (1988) *James J. Gibson and the psychology of perception*, Yale University Press, New Haven and London.

Reichling, M. J. (1997) Music, imagination, and play, *Journal of Aesthetic Education* 31, 41–55.

Rhee, J. W. and Cappella, J. N. (1997) The role of political sophistication in learning from news, *Communication Research* 24, 197–233.

Ricoeur, P. (1971) *What is a text? Explanation and interpretation*, Nijhoff, The Hague.

Ricoeur, P. (1974) *The conflict of interpretations*, Northwestern University Press, Evanston.

Ricoeur, P. (1976) *Interpretation theory: Discourse and the surplus of meaning*, Texas Christian University Press, Fort Worth.

Ricoeur, P. (1984) *Time and narrative*, University of Chicago Press, Chicago and London.

Ricoeur, P. (1992) *Oneself as another*, University of Chicago Press, Chicago.

Robins, K. (1996) *Into the image*, Routledge, London.

Rodaway, P. (1995) *Sensuous geography: Body sense and place*, Routledge, London.

Rodger, I. (1982) *Radio drama*, Macmillan, London.

Rogers, C. R. (1968) To be that self that one truly is: A therapist's view of personal goals, in *Human dynamics in psychology and education* (ed. Hamachek, D. E.) Allyn & Bacon, Boston.

Rogers, Y. (1989) Icons at the interface, *Interacting with computers* 1, 105–117.

Rogoff, B. and Mistry, J. (1990) *Knowing and remembering in young children*, Cambridge University Press, Cambridge.

Roland, P. E., and Gulyas, B. (1994) Visual imagery and visual representation, *Trends in Neuroscience* 17, 281–283.

Romeflanders, T. and Cronk, C. (1995) A longitudinal-study of infant vocalizations during mother–infant games, *Journal of Child Language* 22, 259–274.

Ross, J. E. (1997) Music, the brain, and ecstasy: How music captures our imagination, *Library Journal* 122, 101.

Roth, I. and Frisby, J. P. (1986) *Perception and representation: A cognitive approach*, Open University Press, Milton Keynes.

Rumelhart, D. E. (1977) Toward an interactive model of reading, in *Attention and performance*, vol. 4 (ed. Dornic, S.) Academic Press, New York.

Russell, J. (1996) *Agency*, Erlbaum, Hillsdale, N.J.

Ryan, J. (1974) Early language development: Towards a communicational analysis, in *The integration of a child into a social world* (ed. Richards, M. P. M.) Cambridge University Press, Cambridge.

Sabbadini, A. (1998) On sounds, children, identity and a 'quite unmusical' man, *Sound Journal* 1, 1–10.

Sacks, H. (1992) *Lectures on conversation*, Blackwell, Oxford.

Sacks, H., Schegloff, E. and Jefferson, G. (1974) A simplest systematics for the organization of turn-taking in conversation, *Language* 50, 696–735.

Sampson, E. E. (1989) The deconstruction of the self, in *Texts of identity* (ed. Shotter, J. and Gergen, K.) Sage, London.

Sapir, E. (1921) *Language: An introduction to the study of speech*, Harcourt, Brace and World, New York.

Sarbin, T. R. (1985) *The narrative as a root metaphor for psychology*, Praeger, London.

Saussure, F. (1974) *A course in general linguistics*, Fontana, London.

Schacter, D. L., Koutstaal, W., Johnson, M. K., Gross, M. S. and Angell, K. E. (1997) False recollection induced by photographs: A comparison of older and younger adults, *Psychology and Aging* 12, 203–215.

Schafer, R. M. (1977) *The tuning of the world*, Alfred A. Knopf, New York.

Schegloff, E. (1988) Goffman and the analysis of conversation, in *Ervin Goffman: Exploring the interaction order* (ed. Wooton, I. P. D. a. A.) Polity Press, Cambridge.

Schegloff, E. A. and Sacks, H. (1973) Opening up closing, *Semiotica* 8, 289–327.

Schiefflein, B. and Ochs, E. (1981) *Language socialization across cultures*, Cambridge University Press, Cambridge.

Schmitz, J. and Fulk, J. (1991) Organizational colleagues, media richness and electronic mail: A test of the social influence model of technology use, *Communication Research* 18, 487–523.

Schultz, J. A. (1995) *The knowledge of childhood in the German Middle Ages, 1100–1350*, University of Pennsylvania Press, Philadelphia.

Schweitzer, R. (1996) A phenomenological study of dream interpretation among the Xhosa-speaking people in rural South Africa, *Journal of Phenomenological Psychology* 27, 72–96.

Sebeok, T. (1994) *An introduction to semiotics*, Pinter, London.

Seidler, V. J. (1989) *Rediscovering masculinity: Reason, language and sexuality*, Routledge, London.

Sekula, A. (1982) On the invention of photographic meaning, in *Thinking photography* (ed. Burgin, V.) Macmillan, London.

Sell, M. A., Ray, G. E. and Lovelace, L. (1995) Preschool children's comprehension of a Sesame Street video tape: The effects of repeated viewing and previewing instructions, *Educational Technology Research and Development* 43, 49–60.

Shannon, C. E. (1948) A mathematical theory of communication, *Bell System Technical Journal* 27, 379–423.

Shapiro, M. (1988) The influence of communication-source coded memory traces on world view. Paper given at the International Communication Association Conference, May, 1988, New Orleans, La.

Shapiro, M. P. (1991) Alienation, the self and television: Psychological life in mass culture, *The Humanistic Psychologist* 19, 158–169.

Sharrock, W. and Coulter, J. (1998) On what we can see, *Theory and Psychology* 8, 147–164.

Shepherd, R. (1990) On understanding mental images, in *Images and understanding* (ed. Barlow, H., Blakemore, C. and Weston-Smith, M.) Cambridge University Press, Cambridge.

Shepherd, R. N. and Metzler, J. (1971) Mental rotation of three-dimensional objects, *Science* 171, 701–703.

Sherman, C. (1991) *Cindy Sherman*, Kunsthalle Basel, Basel.

Singer, D. G. and Singer, J. L. (1998) Developing critical viewing skills and media literacy in children, *Annals of the American Academy of Political and Social Science* 557, 164–179.

Sinha, C. (1988) *Language and representation*, Harvester, London.

Sircar, S. (1997) An annotated 'Chhara-Punthi' + India, folklore, oral tradition, music – Nursery rhymes from Bengal, *Asian Folklore Studies* 56, 79–108.

Slater, A., Brown, E. and Badenoch, M. (1997) Intermodal perception at birth: Newborn infants' memory for arbitrary auditory-visual pairings, *Early Development and Parenting* 6, 99–104.

Slater, D. (1996) Image worlds, *Ten* 8, 35.

Smith, E. R. (1996) What do connectionism and social psychology offer each other?, *Journal of Personality and Social Psychology* 70, 893–912.

Smith, M. B. (1994) Selfhood at risk: Postmodern perils and the perils of postmodernism, *American Psychologist* 49, 405–411.

Smith, P., Cowie, H. and Blades, M. (1998) *Understanding children's development*, Blackwell, Oxford.

SmithBattle, L. (1995) A teenage mother's narratives of self – an examination of risking the future, *Advances in Nursing Science* 17, 22–36.

SmithBattle, L., Drake, M. A. and Diekemper, M. (1997) The responsive use of self in community health nursing practice, *Advances in Nursing Science* 20, 75–89.

SmithBattle, L. and Leonard, V. W. (1998) Adolescent mothers four years later: Narratives of the self and visions of the future, *Advances in Nursing Science* 21, 36–49.

Snow, C. and Ferguson, M. (eds.) (1977) *Talking to children: From input to acquisition*, Cambridge University Press, Cambridge.

Sobotkova, D., Dittrichova, J. and Mandys, F. (1996) Comparison of maternal perceptions of preterm and fullterm infants, *Early Development and Parenting* 5, 73–79.

Somers, M. R. (1994) The narrative constitution of identity: A relational and network approach, *Theory and Society* 23, 605–649.

Sontag, S. (1977) *On photography*, Allen Lane, London.

Spence, M. J. (1996) Young infants' long-term auditory memory: Evidence for changes in preference as a function of delay, *Developmental Psychobiology* 29, 685–695.

Stark, H. (1993) A theory of computer semiotics : Semiotic approaches to construction and assessment of computer-systems, *International Journal of Man–Machine Studies* 38, 543–545.

Steenland, S. (1990) Those daytime talk shows, *Television Quarterly* 24, 5–12.

Steinberg, M. P. (1997) Music, musicology and film, *Musical Quarterly* 81, 170–172.

Stokes, M. (1997) Voices and places: History, repetition and the musical imagination, *Journal of the Royal Anthropological Institute* 3, 673–691.

Sturrock, J. (1986) *Structuralism*, Paladin, London.

Sulloway, J. (1979) *Freud: Biologist of the mind*, Fontana, London.

Swan, S. and Wyer, R. S. (1997) Gender stereotypes and social identity: How being in the minority affects judgments of self and others, *Personality and Social Psychology Bulletin* 23, 1265–1276.

Synnott, A. (1983) Little angels, little devils: A sociology of children, *Canadian Review of Sociology and Anthropology – Revue Canadienne de Sociologie et d'Anthropologie* 20, 79–95.

Tagg, J. (1988) *Burden of representation: Essays of photographies and histories*, Macmillan, London.

Tajfel, H. (1972) Social identity, in *Introduction to Social Psychology*, vol.1 (ed. Moscovici, S.) Larousse, Paris.

Tangney, J. P., Niedenthal, P. M., Covert, M. V. and Barlow, D. H. (1998) Are shame and guilt related to distinct self-discrepancies? A test of Higgins's (1987) hypotheses, *Journal of Personality and Social Psychology* 75, 256–268.

Tarplee, C. (1996) *Working on children's utterances: Prosodic aspects of repetition during picture labelling*, Cambridge University Press, Cambridge.

Taylor, C. (1986) *Sources of the self: The making of modern identity*, Cambridge University Press, Cambridge.

Tessler, M. (1991) Making memories together: The influence of mother–child joint encoding on the development of autobiographical memory stories, in *Graduate Center* City University of New York, New York.

Thomas, J. (1995) Mothers and their children: A feminist sociology of child-rearing: Ribbens, J., *Sociological Review* 43, 865–867.

Thomas, L. (1995) in love with Inspector Morse: Feminist subculture and quality television, *Feminist Review* 5, 1–25.

Thomas, S., Smucker, C. and Droppleman, P. (1998) It hurts most around the heart: A phenomenological exploration of women's anger, *Journal of Advanced Nursing* 28, 311–322.

Thorn, R. (1998) Hearing is believing: The evidence, *Sound Journal* 1, 35–45.

Thornton, B., Kirchner, G. and Jacobs, J. (1991) Influence of a photograph on a charitable appeal: A picture may be worth 1000 words when it has to speak for itself, *Journal of Applied Social Psychology* 21, 433–445.

Todrank, J., Byrnes, D., Wrzesniewski, A. and Rozin, P. (1995) Odors can change preferences for people in photographs: A cross-modal evaluative conditioning study with olfactory uss and visual css, *Learning and Motivation* 26, 116–140.

Trabasso, T., van den Broek, P. W. and Suh, S. Y. (1989) Logical necessity and transitivity of casual relations in stories, *Discourse Processes* 12, 1–25.

Trainor, L. J. and Heinmiller, B. M. (1998) The development of evaluative responses to music: Infants prefer to listen to consonance over dissonance, *Infant Behavior and Development* 21, 77–88.

Trehub, S. E., Unyk, A. M., Kamenetsky, S. B., Hill, D. S., Trainor, L. J., Henderson, J. L. and Saraza, M. (1997) Mothers' and fathers' singing to infants, *Developmental Psychology* 33, 500–507.

Tseelon, E. (1995) *The masque of femininity*, Sage, London.

Turner, J. C. (1985) Social categorization and the self-concept: A social cognitive theory of group behaviour. In *Advances in Group Processes* (ed. Lowler, E. J.), Jai Press, Greenwich, Connecticut.

Tversky, B. and Baratz, D. (1985) Memory for faces: Are caricatures better than photographs?, *Memory and Cognition* 13, 45–49.

Ullman, S. (1980) Against direct perception, *Behaviour and Brain Sciences* 3, 373–415.

Underwood, M. K. (1997) Peer social status and children's understanding of the expression and control of positive and negative emotions, *Merrill-Palmer Quarterly – Journal of Developmental Psychology* 43, 610–634.

Viera, C. L. and Homa, D. L. (1991) Integration of nonthematic details in pictures and passages, *American Journal of Psychology* 104, 491–516.

vonBulow, G. (1996) Some aspects of the mental dimension of man in Ammon's humanstructurology, *Dynamische Psychiatrie* 29, 282–287.

Vygotsky, L. S. (1934) *Thought and Language*, MIT Press, Cambridge.

Walkerdine, V. (1993) Beyond developmentalism?, *Theory and Psychology* 3, 451–469.

Walton, K. (1994) Listening with imagination: Is music representational?, *Journal of Aesthetics and Art Criticism* 52, 47–61.

Warner, J. (1990) Semiotics, information-science, documents and computers, *Journal of Documentation* 46, 16–32.

Wells, G. (1981) *Learning through interaction*, Cambridge University Press, Cambridge.

Wells, G. L. and Bradfield, A. L. (1998) 'Good, you identified the suspect': Feedback to eyewitnesses distorts their reports of the witnessing experience, *Journal of Applied Psychology* 83, 360–376.

Wells, L. (ed.) (1997) *Photography: A critical introduction*, Routledge, London.

Wertsch, J. V. (1985) *The social formation of mind*, Routledge & Kegan Paul, New York and London.

Whalen, M. R. (1995) Working toward play: Complexity in children's fantasy activities, *Language in Society* 24, 315–348.

White, M. (1992) *Tele-advertising: Therapeutic discourse in American television*, University of North Carolina Press, Chapel Hill.

Whorf, B. (1956) *Language, thought and reality*, MIT Press, Cambridge, Mass.

Wiederman, M. W. (1993) Evolved gender differences in mate preferences: Evidence from personal advertisements, *Ethology and Sociobiology* 14, 331–351.

Williams, T. M. (ed.) (1986) *The impact of television: A natural experiment in three communities*, Academic Press, Toronto.

Williamson, J. (1978) *Decoding advertisements, ideology and meaning in advertising*, Boyars, London.

Willott, S. and Griffin, C. (1996) Men, masculinity and the challenge of long-term unemployment, in *Understanding masculinities* (ed. Mac an Ghail, M.) Open University Press, Buckingham.

Wittgenstein, L. (1953) *Philosophical investigations*, Blackwell, Oxford.

Woollen, P. (1969) *Signs meaning cinema*, Academic Press, London.

Wooton, A. (1997) *Interaction and the development of mind*, Cambridge University Press, Cambridge.

Wootton, A. (1994) Object transfer, intersubjectivity and 3rd position repair: Early developmental observations of one child, *Journal of Child Language* 21, 543–564.

Yu, C. J. and Geiselman, R. E. (1993) Effects of constructing identi-kit composites on photospread identification performance, *Criminal Justice and Behavior* 20, 280–292.

Ziller and Lewis (1981) Photographs and personality, *Personality and Social Psychology* 7, 338–394.

Zizek, S. (1989) *The sublime object of ideology*, Verso, London.

Zwaan, R. A. (1996) Processing narrative time shifts, *Journal of Experimental Psychology – Learning Memory and Cognition* 22, 1196–1207.

Zwick, E. and Horner, J. (1989) *Glory*, Tristar Pictures, USA.

Index